MANAGING IN UNCERTAINTY

The reality of everyday organizational life is that it is filled with uncertainty, contradictions and paradoxes. Yet leaders and managers are expected to act as though they can predict the future and bring about the impossible: that they can transform themselves and their colleagues, design different cultures, choose the values for their organization, be innovative, control conflict and have inspiring visions. Whilst managers will have had plenty of experience of being in charge, they probably realize that they are not always in control.

So how might we frame a much more realistic account of what is possible for managers to achieve?

Many managers are implicitly aware of their messy reality, but they rarely spend much time reflecting on what it is that they are actually doing. Drawing on insights from the complexity sciences, process sociology and pragmatic philosophy, Chris Mowles engages directly with some principal contradictions of organizational life concerning innovation, culture change, conflict and leadership. Mowles argues that if managers proceed from the expectation that organizational life is inherently uncertain, and interactions between people are complex and often paradoxical, they start noticing different things and create possibilities for acting in different ways.

Managing in Uncertainty will be of interest to practitioners, advanced students and researchers looking at management and organizational studies from a critical perspective.

Chris Mowles is Professor of Complexity and Management and Director of the internationally renowned Doctor of Management programme at the University of Hertfordshire, UK. Previously he worked as a senior manager in the public and voluntary sectors and was finance director of his own marketing company.

'This book provides a significant development of understanding organizational life from a complexity perspective. It takes the uncertainty of organizational life seriously; exploring reflexivity and making sense of one's experience in a manner that clarifies the paradoxes of organizational life. I am sure it will appeal to all thinking managers and to academic researchers.'

Ralph Stacey, Professor, Hertfordshire Business School,
University of Hertfordshire, UK

'For those tired of prescriptions and protocols as substitutes for thinking and practical judgement in the face of uncertainty, this book offers managers a refreshing and satisfying read full of thought provoking examples and discussion.'

Patricia Shaw, Fellow, Schumacher College, Devon and Visiting Professor,
Hertfordshire Business School, University of Hertfordshire, UK

MANAGING IN UNCERTAINTY

Complexity and the paradoxes of everyday organizational life

Chris Mowles

Routledge
Taylor & Francis Group

LONDON AND NEW YORK

First published 2015
by Routledge
2 Park Square, Milton Park, Abingdon, Oxon OX14 4RN

and by Routledge
711 Third Avenue, New York, NY 10017

Routledge is an imprint of the Taylor & Francis Group, an informa business

© 2015 Chris Mowles

British Library Cataloguing in Publication Data
A catalogue record for this book is available from the British Library

Library of Congress Cataloging in Publication Data
Mowles, Chris.
Managing in uncertainty: the complexity, ambiguity and paradox of everyday organizational life / Chris Mowles.
pages cm
Includes bibliographical references and index.
1. Management. 2. Uncertainty. 3. Problem solving. 4. Corporate culture.
5. Organizational change. I. Title.
HD31.M688 2015
658--dc23
2014036187

ISBN: 978-1-138-84373-8 (hbk)
ISBN: 978-1-138-84374-5 (pbk)
ISBN: 978-1-315-73089-9 (ebk)

Typeset in Bembo
by Integra Software Services Pvt. Ltd.

Printed and bound in Great Britain by
TJ International Ltd, Padstow, Cornwall

CONTENTS

ACKNOWLEDGEMENTS

I once bumped into my friend and colleague Doug Griffin in Toronto airport. He could not have been expecting to see me because I was due to arrive a good few hours ahead of him. On seeing me he expressed absolutely no surprise, but said this by way of greeting: 'Ah, Chris, I've been thinking about paradox.' I have absolutely no doubt that that is exactly what he was doing, as he took turn and turn about, waiting for his luggage. This provoked me to think about paradox, which eventually resulted in this book. In order to produce it I have drawn on the deep reservoir of Doug's knowledge and wisdom, and his consistent ability to reframe whatever I have been thinking.

I owe a deep debt of gratitude, too, to Ralph Stacey for his friendship, for his ideas, many of which I try to build on in this book, and for his support and patient reading of my work.

Thanks, too, to my colleagues Karen Norman, Nick Sarra and Emma Crewe, for their friendship, stimulating ideas and encouragement. Loyal colleagues all.

The research community of the Doctor of Management at Hertfordshire Business School, University of Hertfordshire, is a truly creative group, bubbling with ideas and insights which have helped to inform my thinking for this book.

Thanks to Michael Herzka for our long discussions and frequent collaborations, and to Nick Luxmoore, Dave Harding and Dave Waller for sustaining me through various dark nights of the soul. To Margaret Mowles, and to Tony Mowles, who would have been proud.

Lastly, and not least, thanks to Nikki, Rosa and George, who have been with me every step of the way.

INTRODUCTION

A book arising from uncertainty in everyday organizational life

This book aims to describe and better understand the constantly evolving, messy reality of day-to-day organizational life rather than producing the somewhat abstract concepts, tools and techniques which are found in much management literature. It takes as its starting point some of the discussions I have come across in organizations, or about organizations, and shows how they sometimes play out in practice. This is not to say that I will not use abstract concepts, but I intend to start with organizational experience and then try to understand it.

This is because when I am in organizations as an employee, as a manager or as a consultant I encounter a mismatch between the often rather grandiose and inflated claims of much management theory, reflected in the way that many managers talk about what they are doing, and what it is possible for them to achieve practically. I am not referring just to the more high profile disasters such as the mismanagement of banks which, amongst other factors, led to the recent financial collapse from 2008. Instead I notice that leaders and managers often articulate, or are invited to believe in, rather grand ambitions for 'transformational' change out of proportion to their quite ordinary circumstances. They are invited to assume that they can predict and control things which even a moment's reflection might lead them to realize are beyond their ability to do so.

Managers might be asked to believe six impossible things before breakfast: that they can 'transform' some aspect of organizational life, they can engineer 'culture change' programmes or 'align' their and others' values for the good of the organization, that they can engineer a 'world-leading' organization, meet 'stretch targets' or plan in advance to be innovative. There seems to be no limit to the ambitions of what leaders and managers are supposed to be able to achieve, no aspect of human experience which they cannot control.

This book attempts to explore some of the ideas behind this kind of managerial thinking, which I find so prevalent. What kind of intellectual assumptions are needed to proceed with this way of thinking? How robust are they, and what do they end up by excluding? Why are they so pervasive and what kind of activities do they lead to? How might we develop a more realistic account of what managers might be able to achieve and where might they focus instead?

As an example, I recently sat in on a meeting where a deputy CEO was taking a group of managers through his organization's next five year strategy. Absorbed in the logic and grandeur of his own presentation, what the deputy CEO appeared not to notice was the variety of reactions from the staff in the audience, in particular a pronounced restlessness among some. The five year vision involved being 'internationally renowned' for something or other but a number of staff were experienced managers themselves. Maybe they were unconvinced by the last strategy which had a vision quite similar to this one, or had worked in other organizations which had equally grandiose vision statements, but they seemed to be uncomfortable with this kind of fantastical thinking as I was myself.

Although this way of undertaking strategy based on Russell Ackoff's idealized design method (2006) is supposed to engender excitement and commitment in staff, it can also provoke the opposite, cynicism and boredom, particularly amongst change-weary employees. Some disgruntled staff expressed their disillusionment with quite aggressive questioning, which the deputy CEO swatted away by claiming that he knew what he was doing because he used to be a management consultant. The meeting ended finally with much muttering and shaking of heads amongst the staff as they headed off for coffee.

Where a senior manager had proceeded with the intention of uplifting his audience with an aspirational future he seemed instead to have confused many and demoralized some. This may have been partly to do with the method he had chosen which dealt in abstract, idealized terms very far removed from the daily experience of most of his audience. But it was also due to his inability to notice and respond to what was going on around him and in relation to what he was saying and doing. The greatest failure was an absence of mutual recognition: the senior manager failed to recognize the reaction and doubts of his audience, whilst many in the audience failed to recognize in the strategy and how it was being presented, with the ubiquitous PowerPoint slides, their everyday concerns. The deputy CEO cleaved to certainty, whilst some of his audience expressed their doubts; paradoxically, the greater the doubts the more emphatic his certainty.

As an outsider you might have cause to worry about this organization where some senior managers have a greater commitment to their slides and the systemic, inflated method underpinning them than the quality of participation between people. If you thought that the future health of an organization was not to be found in the logic of nested boxes, but in the spontaneous and skilful responsiveness of senior managers to what is going on around them you might conclude that there is still much strategy work to be done here, although not of the sort which relies on idealized design methodology.

This book, then, proceeds from my interest in ordinary confusions and disjunctures like these and the contradictions and paradoxes of getting things done together in organizations. It reveals my own assumption that uncertainty is an everyday occurrence, and that contradictions and paradoxes can be a helpful resource rather than a hindrance for attentive managers and leaders. I am not suggesting, however, that they can necessarily be harnessed for the good of the organization, a common assumption I engage with critically in this volume. Rather, I am pointing to the possibility that recognizing a paradox might be the first step to realizing the limitations of much conventional management thinking: that we are entering into complex territory which requires a more thoughtful and reflective response from managers. Working with paradoxical organizational experience requires a good deal more from managers than simply insisting that you are right or ignoring what you encounter.

The book is also inspired by the students and faculty of the Doctor of Management at Hertfordshire Business School, where I teach with my colleagues. The programme has been running since 2000 and has produced more than 60 graduates, 53 at doctoral level. It is a part-time programme often attracting senior leaders and managers from a variety of organizational backgrounds and from all over the world, who want to take something which is going on for them at work as the object of their study. For a minimum of three years students spend at least 16 days a year face-to-face when the research community comes together in quarterly residentials, discussing, writing, presenting their work, discussing further, revising what they are writing, then discussing some more. They draw on a body of ideas colleagues on faculty have termed complex responsive processes of relating, some of the main tenets of which I explore in Chapter 1 of this book.

Complex responsive processes of relating combines insights from the complexity sciences and processual theories of the social drawn from sociologists such as Norbert Elias and Pierre Bourdieu, as well as pragmatic philosophy and social theory informed by GH Mead, John Dewey, Richard Bernstein and Hans Joas. It focuses on everyday experience on the assumption that organizations, and society more generally, arise from this: there is no grand superstructure or system independent from what people do together. Complex responsive processes turns on the paradox that we form the social, just as the social forms us, both at the same time.

Many of the thinkers we draw on themselves develop paradoxes extensively in their work, and it has become a tradition on the programme to point them out and discuss them as they arise. The danger, however, is that we become so familiar with paradox as an idea that we begin to take it for granted, and to glide over it without thinking through the implications of what we are saying. This book is an attempt to pause on paradox, to defamiliarize it and to discuss it more extensively, to work through some of the implications for managers and leaders.

In this vein I hope the book is in keeping with the same spirit which motivated the original team of academics, Ralph Stacey, Doug Griffin and Patricia Shaw, to develop their ideas: their concern to help enquiring managers make sense of their everyday experience and thus to become more skilful managers.

Reference

Ackoff, R., Magidson, J. and Addison, H. (2006) *Idealized Design: How to Dissolve Tomorrow's Crisis ... Today*, London: Financial Times/Prentice Hall.

1

WHY ARE UNCERTAINTY, AMBIGUITY AND PARADOX IMPORTANT FOR MANAGERS?

In today's organizations leaders and managers are dealing with a great deal of uncertainty and ambiguity and must straddle a number of paradoxes. They are obliged to exercise a degree of control, and yet they must encourage their staff to be creative and independent thinkers. On the one hand, they may be very experienced but, on the other hand, their experience may blind them to novel opportunities which emerge in complex environments. Senior teams are often encouraged to change and to innovate, and at the same time they are expected to stand firm for the traditional values, and the 'brand' which their organization represents. Paradoxically, they are enjoined to change in order to stay the same: in other words they have to innovate to sustain organizational continuity.

And yet, despite the uncertain environment and contradictory injunctions, a lot of talk in organizations, and in management literature, is highly purposeful and deals in certainties. For example, the ideal for senior teams is that managers and leaders choose the future for their organizations, they set the 'right' conditions for their staff to be productive, and they can even change the culture. By implication senior managers and leaders get to their exalted place in their organizations from knowing what they are doing, and acting 'appropriately', decisively and authoritatively. Of course, this is no different from the dominant assumptions in a whole variety of different professions, where there is an equivalence drawn between being a professional and certainty. In this context uncertainty, ambiguity and paradox, profoundly disturbing and potentially paralyzing contradictions, might seem like very abstruse subjects to write about in a book about management and organizing. It might seem counterintuitive and unhelpful to deal in the ambiguous when I might instead be offering prescriptions to managers about how to act, which is the conventional tack to take in a book on organizing.

However, I do so because of my conviction that, ultimately, it is more helpful and more realistic to try to find ways of understanding organizational life in all its complexity, its blooming, buzzing confusion as William James once referred to experience, rather than relying on the thin simplifications which constitute the recommendations of much management literature. They are thin simplifications, a phrase I borrow from the political scientist James C Scott (1999), because they are abstractions from the rich and complex reality from which they are abstracted: in being general they are only generally useful. In my view it is just as important to treat what is, no matter how complex and messy, than what we think should be if it means that we have to reduce our ideas beyond recognition. It is my contention that managers both understand and do not understand at the same time what is going on in their organization, and this is a phenomenon worth thinking about and exploring.

First, though, I should deal with the terms I am using to explain briefly what I mean by them. As the book proceeds we will look at some of these ideas and how they manifest in organizational life in more depth. However, at this stage of the proceedings I understand uncertainty to arise from the interweaving of everyone's intentions. We may start out by forming intentions that are permeated by our world view, which we formalize in plans, but this is also what everyone else is doing at the same time. So uncertainty arises in social life because we act into a web of other people's actions and intentions: we can no more predict how we will respond when we encounter other people's actions than we can always anticipate what their actions will be, although we may have strong hunches. We often experience a great deal of ambiguity, that is to say, where we are alert to a variety of different meanings of what is going on, without there necessarily being a relationship between the meanings we make. Meanwhile, contradictions, for example the injunction to stay the same/innovate, may form part of this ambiguity and produce a relationship of negation between two different interpretations. Finally, paradox is a particular form of contradiction where to think one thing is automatically to call out its polar opposite, both at the same time. Paradox is a particular property of thinking which I explore as the book unfolds.

When contradictions present themselves in organizational life there is usually no obvious way to proceed, or perhaps there are a variety of ways which all have their upsides and downsides (or perhaps all choices are equally bad). Nonetheless and in my experience most managers and leaders are already coping relatively well with their own environment of uncertainty. They are able to sustain managing and not managing in their various contexts reasonably well. However, I experience a lack of facility in being able to talk about precisely what they are doing when managers are coping with uncertainty: although they know that organizational life is unpredictable, if you ask them directly, managers seem to have precious few opportunities to explore this consciously and publicly. So what I intend to do in this book is to focus a bit more on being in control and not being in control, on those interstices in organizations when it is not always clear what to do, and when there are contradictory pressures on managers. If we could dwell with the contradictions for a while and think about what might be going on this might be just as helpful as producing a generalized piece of advice which bears no relation to the contexts in which managers are obliged to operate.

The central premise of this book, then, is that exploration of ambiguous, contradictory and paradoxical experience, where sometimes mutually informing but contradictory ideas arise at the same time and potentially confound us may help us understand how to act into the unknown. This will involve enquiring into how we make our way with contradictions, and what we need to pay attention to and reflect upon as we do so. It requires paying attention to how we act when we are not sure what to do and a different way of thinking than using logic alone, or disaggregating parts/whole thinking.

Perhaps it would be best to illustrate why I think this area of enquiry is important by means of an incident that happened between a colleague and me when I served on a board of trustees. Using this as a practical example I can then go on to explore some of the themes at the heart of the matter for me.

Having values about not having values

A couple of years ago I was on the board of a not-for-profit organization along with a another academic with whom I had some quite large intellectual differences. For the most part we could cooperate fairly easily since the job of a board of trustees is to act as a critical friend to the director and her senior management team. In general it is not hard to develop a way of working together, within the board and between the board and the senior management team.

One day my academic colleague and I were both asked to talk to staff about our different views of social science to help them with the task they had of carrying out research to evaluate the work they were doing. My colleague was director of a unit which specialized in running randomized control trials (RCTs) of social development projects. RCTs are at the heart of contemporary medical research, and turn on the idea of measuring differences of response between groups of randomly selected patients to a particular medical intervention. Who receives the treatment is not known to the patients or to the researchers administering the trial, and therefore the intention is to remove researcher (and patient) prejudice as completely as possible from the experiment. The idea is that it does not matter what a particular expert, or patient, might believe will be effective: what counts is whether the experiment shows what is. In medical research a randomized control trial produces the highest form of evidence and is taken to be the 'gold standard' against which all other forms of evidence are measured.

So in what is known as a double blind randomized trial there would be a large group of patients chosen at random and with a particular medical condition who receive a trial drug or intervention, a similarly large randomly chosen group of patients with the same condition who receive a placebo, i.e. some kind of pill or intervention which is known to have no effect, and a randomly chosen group of patients with the same condition who receive nothing at all. After a given period measurements are taken to find out if there are any statistically significant improvements between the group which actually received the treatment and the two which did not. Other statistical tests are run to control for other possible confounding variables, such as age or social background, which might be affecting the results. The experiment would be written up in a systematic way so that it could be copied by any other group of researchers who would then run the experiment again and get the same results. If they do, and yet more experiments showed the same outcomes, then the results would over time be deemed to be robust. The experiment needs a statistically significant number of respondents involved in the study so that variable responses are averaged out.

When he took his turn to talk to members of staff about social research, my colleague on the board extolled the virtues of randomized control trials in social projects, arguing that they are the only method which produces scientific evidence. He claimed, rightly in the opinion of many natural scientists, they are equally applicable in a social setting; for example in projects which are designed to discourage underage young people living in the country in developing countries to migrate to the cities where they are easily exploited, the kind of project that this particular not-for-profit was designing and managing and was concerned to find out if they were effective.

My colleague was setting out the case for what is known as methods-driven research, which has a number of theoretical assumptions: in other words, a stepwise, logical, linear, controlled experimental approach, keeping the researcher as much out of the experiment as possible, is the only scientific way to design social research. This method treats a group of individuals as separate, discrete units, and looks to find out if a large enough number is affected to a large enough degree by a carefully defined social intervention: the central causal relationship is between the intervention, broken down to a number of variables, and the individual.

No account is taken of how individuals may interact with each other in response to the intervention. It produces results which count as evidence and which are assumed to be replicable in other settings because it expects the average human responses to be similar between groups. Once a researcher finds out 'what works', a specific intervention has a measurable effect on a significant number of individuals in a group, then a researcher can apply this knowledge to 'scale up' the intervention or do the same thing elsewhere. Scaling up, choosing a much larger group to receive the intervention, will be similarly successful because it is merely the same thing on a bigger scale. Implicitly he was also making a case that any other form of research, i.e. any argument I was about to make, might be interesting, but would be inferior to what he had just said, because it would be less scientific.

There are a variety of experimental methods used in research in the natural sciences, and many of them have migrated over to researching social phenomena as well, including in organizational research. RCTs are simply the purest example of a broader phenomenon. The overwhelming majority of research papers published in academic journals is of an experimental nature along the lines discussed above, where the researchers keep their 'objects' of research as much at a distance as possible in the quest for evidence. They put forward a hypothesis about the application of a particular and definable approach to management, and then they measure the results as to whether this proved effective or not.

However, and from my perspective, in social settings RCTs in particular have severe limitations and also lead to what I consider to be some very distorting behaviours, which call into question their usefulness. For example, it makes sense in a medical trial to standardize the dose of whatever treatment you are administering to patients. In social settings this attempt to standardize leads to the development of manuals and scripts so that social workers, for example, are encouraged to behave in exactly the same way and deliver as similar a social work intervention as possible so that there are not too many confounding variables in the project. In other words, and in my view, social development workers are encouraged to behave like robots so that they do not get in the way of the experiment.

It seems to me that in social development it is precisely the improvisational activities of development workers, negotiating a slightly different response with the people they are working with in every case, which can make the difference to success or otherwise, because of the uncertainty and ambiguity in any given situation, which I started out by defining at the beginning of this chapter. It seems to me that methods-driven approaches are trying to exclude the very factors which will cause the intervention to succeed. This is beside the point as to whether one adopts a theory of causation that it is the 'variables' which make a social project work, rather than how the people in the project are cooperating together to make it work. There are a number of other critiques that one could make about the use of RCTs in social development, for example the tendency to measure quite trivial and observable things and to have no views on broader phenomena such as culture, history and power relations, and whether a larger group is simply an aggregate of smaller groups, which I do not have the space to expand upon here.

When it came to my turn to speak I made an alternative case for what is known as problem-driven research, as opposed to methods-driven, where the first question arises from a particular practice context and focuses on what it is we are trying to find out, which then informs the question about which research method is most appropriate. In doing so I was pointing out what I saw as the weaknesses in my colleague's case, based on some of what I have set out above. Inevitably, when my colleague responded by reiterating his claim that his was the only scientific approach, the discussion became heated. This was particularly at the point when my colleague informed the staff that he operates according to three principles when designing an RCT: that he involves the client group he works with in the design, but only if they could offer suggestions which were logically consistent, and whatever they said had to be backed up with evidence (i.e. the sort which is provable by RCT), and that everyone, including him, left their values at the door.

As well as engaging with his argument more broadly, noting how he was silencing people who did not conform to his world view (just as I felt he was trying to silence me) I also pointed out to him that he had just demonstrated, paradoxically, that he had strong values about not having values and that logic alone was insufficient for stating or resolving practical problems. His stated values were of universalism and disinterestedness as a higher order of social engagement, but he was unaware of how he might be silencing people. Despite claiming that his position was logical and scientific, I told him I thought his argument also rested on rhetoric, paradox and power relations, as well as questions of method.

Engaging with uncertainty, contradiction and paradox as a way into ethics

Looking back on this incident now I am wondering what possessed us both to get so caught up with each other in front of staff whom we were supposed to be helping. I wonder what they thought of this back and forth between two academics who were members of their board, and who mostly were able to cooperate together to support their work, but here were clearly unable to do so on this occasion. And I suppose the short answer is that we could not help ourselves because what we were talking about mattered to us. This was not just a difference of opinion over technical considerations but a struggle over power and influence, which called into question who we were and what we thought was important: it raised questions of power, politics and ethics. Despite the fact that we were both experienced academics, neither of us could resist making our different cases as strongly as possible and to present our arguments to the good.

Although I want to explore further some of the different intellectual assumptions involved in our two positions, it's worth dwelling on this point, that my colleague and I were caught up in the moment despite ourselves, because I think it goes to the heart of my motivation to write this book. It might have been a memorable incident, perhaps for the two protagonists, and I suspect also for everyone present exposed to the warmth of the encounter, but in many ways it was also quite an ordinary, everyday experience in organizations. We found ourselves engaged in a conflict involving contradictory ways of understanding human interaction, which, rather than bringing about greater certainty, might have created greater uncertainty amongst those who were present. If they were looking for advice about how to proceed with their evaluation, they may well have left the meeting confused. The encounter also centred on different conceptions of the good, the role and function of the evaluation, as well as questions of method: there is no separating them. It was both an argument about the best method to use in a particular evaluation, but it was also a moral argument and a discussion about how we think about and resolve our problems.

One of the central contentions of this book is that daily life in organizations is far from ideal, and involves many such encounters where people try to persuade each other, more or less politely, more or less forcefully, of the strength of their position. They cooperate and compete to get things done together, they cajole and try to sway each other, frame their arguments using rhetoric, become impassioned about what they think is the right thing to do, and are generally·caught up in the game of organizational life. This is a political and an ethical game which involves many conceptions of the good in any particular situation and the constant unfolding of paradox. Players of the game are involved together in the task at hand, whilst trying to make sense of overall objectives, they try to control when in turn they are controlled and they strive to innovate whilst at the same time struggling to preserve the best of what makes their particular organization unique and successful. Sometimes they are lucid about how they are getting carried away with the task at hand as they find themselves responding to unpredictable contingencies which disrupt their projects and plans.

These are the contradictions and paradoxes, the situations which seem to confound 'common sense', that most interest me about working alongside other people in organizations which create the environment of uncertainty in organizations. I accept that, to a degree, organizational life has speeded up and is more complex because of technological innovation and globalization, but mostly my preoccupation is with the 'ordinary' complexity of getting things done with other people, which in my view has much more to do with being human than any special phase we may be going through. In every period of history people have thought of themselves as undergoing unprecedented change.

Of course, if organizational life was not so predictably unpredictable it would probably not be so absorbing, but you would be hard pressed to find this hurly-burly reflected in much of the management literature.[1] Instead, as my colleague above was describing, it aspires to being rational, scientific and to leave its values at the door. Contradiction, ambiguity and value judgments are assumed to get in the way of the work, and therefore must be eliminated or ignored. I am sure that my colleague on the board simply thought I was being difficult by drawing attention to the paradox in his thinking and that he had strong values about not having values. In most management theory leaders and managers are described as being detached, rational observers of the organizations in which they are working who choose the futures for them using reason and logic, shape the culture and even select the kinds of values that the staff working for them should have. This is assumed to be possible using rationality, which renders experience a matter of choices between different technical options.

Equally, in apparently more mystifying and contradictory areas of human experience, such as paradox, more of which below, leaders and managers are again assumed to be able to harness contradictions for the good of the organization and to generate creativity, harmony and sustainability. There is also a substantial minority literature on contradiction and paradox, which I treat in the next chapter but which does accept ambiguity as a given. In Chapter 2 I will set out the similarities and differences between scholars trying to work with uncertainty and paradox and my own position.

The evidence-based management movement and what it excludes

My colleague on the board was arguing in favour of what is generally accepted as the highest scientific methods for evaluating social development, namely RCTs. There is a similar school of thought in management and organization studies, the evidence-based management movement, which sets out the case for using more evidence in management decision-making as well as in the classroom in business schools. The intentions of those supporting evidence-based management are honourable in the sense that they seek to place the practice of management on a secure and scientific footing, but their arguments also have unintended consequences and exclude aspects of experience from consideration, such as judgments of value (unless they also consider value judgments to be subject to rational discussion). There are also questions as to the extent to which general theories of the social apply in particular cases, an argument I pursue further in Chapter 5.

For example, in an inaugural address, the then president of the Academy of Management (AoM), Denise Rousseau, set out the case for evidence-based management based on medical science almost exactly in the same way that my colleague on the board did (Rousseau, 2006). This movement is still very strong, but equally has run into a number of difficulties similar to the argument which developed in the organization where I was on the board. First, despite the call for practising management and teaching management on the basis of evidence, actually there is not very much evidence, particularly not of the most valued kind, from RCTs, as Reay et al. (2009) discovered in their article entitled 'What's the evidence on evidence-based management?' Secondly, it provoked a response from those scholars writing in a different social science tradition (Learmonth, 2006; Learmonth and Harding, 2006; Stacey, 2012) of which this book is an example, that what counts as evidence in the social is contested, and therefore is likely to produce a paradox: the more evidence is collected, the more contestation, so rather than creating greater certainty, the search for evidence may only create greater uncertainty and ambiguity, i.e. multiple meanings with no necessary connection between them.

Learmonth's second critique is to point to a second paradox, that the claim to being scientific rests on a number of exclusions which are taken as self-evident and are removed from scientific scrutiny: evidence-based management scholarship often takes its assumptions for granted, for example that it is a good thing to aspire to being a 'great manager in a great company' and that we all know and agree what that means. Stacey also points out that 'evidence' is used in a way which reinforces the dominant ideology of managerialism, that contemporary managers and management theory is an uncontestable good. In other words, what we take to be the good, questions of ethics and how we might live our lives, are considered secondary, if they are considered at all.

Learmonth and Stacey proceed to point out the contradictions in the president of the AoM's argument, and the evidence-based management movement in general, much as I did with my colleague on the board. Orthodox management research is often incapable of returning to itself and questioning its own assumptions and exclusions. And I am guessing that the president of the AoM might have found having this pointed out just as infuriating as did my colleague. I might argue, then, that much conventional management theory is incapable of paradoxical, reflexive thought, or bending back on itself and questioning its own assumptions, thus rendering questions of power, politics and ethics less visible.

It is still the case that scholarship which seeks to enlarge the evidence base for particular domains of management still proceeds from a taken-for-granted assumption that there is no problem with what we are seeking evidence about, or how we collect it, but merely whether it is implemented or taken up in the classroom. For example, a study by Charlier et al. (2011) tries to find out how much evidence-based management is taught on required MBA syllabi without setting out any of the arguments exploring what the term might mean, even in passing. However, and at the same time, it is clear that the argument which has developed about what we mean by evidence and how we might gather it has also shifted the ground of the debate.

For example, Briner and Rousseau (2011) now define evidence as: 'making decisions through conscientious, explicit, and judicious use of four sources of information: practitioner expertise and judgment, evidence from the local context, a critical evaluation of the best available research evidence, and the perspective of people who might be affected by the decision'. If this is now taken to be measure of good evidence, asking people what they think, taking account of the context, asking the people who will be affected and reading a bit, then it is hard to know what the evidence-based management movement is offering that is beyond what most managers and educators would probably be doing anyway.

Later on, in Chapter 5 on change and innovation in organizational life, I will extend the argument about some of the difficulties of making predictions in social life by bringing in the moral philosopher Alasdair MacIntyre (1981). What is interesting in MacIntyre's position is that he was always trying to reintroduce the notion of virtue and conceptions of the good, drawing on Aristotle, into our understanding of social practices. This is a philosophical rendering of some of the insights from the complexity sciences which I explore later on in this chapter. I am not making a claim that statistical approaches, logic and rationality are irrelevant to managing: they can afford helpful insights into large-scale phenomena and generate helpful ideas to pursue further. I am suggesting they are necessary but insufficient to understand the detail of how people make work work, and am pointing to the idea that they may not tell us all we need to know better to organize together. As Bourdieu observed (1990), the logic of practice is not the logic of logic.

Paradox and other forms of dualism

As an alternative to looking for evidence of 'what works', this book seeks to take uncertainty seriously to note how it produces contradictory and paradoxical conditions for managers. By exploring uncertainty and the political and ethical questions which it raises, the book tries to uncover insights about management and leadership to see how possible it is to generalize from them, but not in the sense of recommending 'best practice' or coming to a final view. Contradictions arise partly as a result of exploring one point of view, and then another, a process of dialectic which I will explain further below, but which I hope has been demonstrated both with my narrative at the beginning of the chapter and with the controversy surrounding what we might take evidence-based management to mean.

One point of view calls out an alternative, perhaps opposite point of view, which in turn calls out a modified version of the first. There is a back and forth dialectic which demonstrates a movement in thinking and generates more than one perspective: there is never just one best way. The kind of generalizability that I am looking for is not necessarily one which can be proved one way or another, but which triggers recognition in the reader, and perhaps rich resonances with the reader's own experience, and opens up other lines of enquiry and richer perspectives. Of course, this approach is not scientific in the strict sense of the word, but that does not prevent my approach from being systematic and from testing arguments as rigorously as possible. It is a way of arguing which seeks to establish whether an intellectual position is warranted, in John Dewey's terms (1941), and draws on a long Socratic tradition of arguing in public. But there is no requirement to come to a final resting place, with an agreement about what truth is.

First, however, I will set out more clearly what I understand paradox, a particular kind of contradiction, to be, since it figures so prominently in the writing of many of the writers I bring into this book. It is simply our ability to think the opposite of what we are currently thinking, for the mind to overreach itself in thinking, which produces an absurdity, something which is *para doxa*, or against common sense. There are two, mutually exclusive, self-referencing ideas which help define each other but negate each other both at the same time. To give an example, one of the earliest and most famous examples of semantic paradox is the so-called Cretan, or Liar's Paradox attributed to the Cretan poet Epimenides, who claimed that 'all Cretans are liars', a true/false paradox. Whichever conclusion we come to about this statement leaves us with a problem. If the statement is true, then Epimenides, a Cretan, is lying and the statement is false. If the statement is false, that not all Cretans are liars, then Epimenides must be lying, which makes the statement true. The statement is unresolvable because one conclusion immediately leads you to its opposite.

Each solution immediately produces a contradictory response, which is against common sense. This can be maddening, and it can also be helpful. In its maddening form it can produce thinking or behaviour, which loops back on itself and becomes stuck, endlessly repeating between the two poles: this is known as a vicious paradox, like this first example. Or it might be generative, allowing the exploration of a particular area of human experience in more than one dimension, and it is the second of these which I hope to further in this book.

Dualistic tension manifests itself in a variety of different forms in human thought. First of all there is the simple dilemma between two choices which present themselves, both of which have criteria for and against. Dilemmas appear frequently in organizational theory and are sometimes represented, unhelpfully in my view, as paradoxes. The most prominent example of this, which is repeated again and again in organizational literature, is March's distinction (1991) between the options for companies to explore further developments, or to exploit the developments they have already made, the so-called explore–exploit paradox. These two options are not mutually referential, nor do they necessarily negate each other: they simply describe an opportunity dilemma for managers.

Next, a double bind has many of the characteristics of a vicious paradox, and creates a negative spiral. As an example, take the U2 song '(I can't live) with or without you', or the famous joke about an overbearing mother who gives her son two ties and when he puts one on to show her, she asks him what is wrong with the other one. Here the tension produces two negative mutually exclusive alternatives, a rock and a hard place. Bateson (1970), who did a considerable amount of work on double binds in his exploration of schizophrenia, argues that there is a third negative condition of a double bind, which produces distress and anxiety in those experiencing it. There is no escape from it: a person is forced to choose between one negative alternative and another, neither of which resolves the situation (as in the U2 song) and the injunction to choose one or the other takes away all sense of freedom. Bateson was heavily influenced by cybernetic systems theory and made reference to Russell's 'Theory of Logical Types' (1908) to explain his idea of double bind. For him it was a confusion between logical levels of abstraction and a binding injunction to the person experiencing the double bind not to adopt a meta-position, to abstract further from their experience to yet a different level of logic.

In this book I am not assuming that paradox is a property of a system, or that it occurs at different levels of logic, although I will briefly explore in the next chapter the ideas of some scholars (Luhmann, 1995) who think it is. However, I am confident that many people working in organizations will have experienced double binds. These might arise in organizations undergoing 'culture change' programmes, for example, where staff are invited to believe in the organizational vision and align with company values on the one hand (and sometimes the extent to which they are following the company values will be measured), and on the other hand they will be invited to be their authentic selves, to speak out and be honest. So, first there is an injunction to staff to believe in a set of value statements and be judged whether they are conforming or not and thus give up their freedom; and at the same time they are told to be themselves and be authentic (but if they do they may contradict the company values). Staff are obliged to choose, but neither of the choices are good ones.

Additionally in terms of dualistic thought, there is irony, for which the English are supposed to be renowned. This arises as a result of the confounding of expectations, either verbally or in a particular situation. For example dramatic irony occurs where a theatre audience is given greater insight into the unfolding of a plot than the central characters. In *Romeo and Juliet* the poignancy of the plot is that we can see how their plans will cost their lives, although they are unaware of this. And in rhetoric there is chiasm, which is an arresting figure of speech such as President Kennedy's 'ask not what your country can do for you, but what you can do for your country', where the meaning is inverted in parallel clauses.

I hope to be relatively disciplined when talking about paradox in the strict sense in this book, differentiating it from double bind, dilemma, irony, chiasm and simple contradiction, although I do not intend to be pedantic. Cleaving to some sense of what a paradox is and why it is important may present opportunities for thinking about the complexity of organizational life. And when other scholars use the term it will afford the opportunity to think about what they mean by it, and therefore to make some distinctions bearing in mind the pragmatic *dictum* that differences make a difference.

Paradox in logic, literature and philosophy

Paradox has a rich history and has been explored over the centuries in the domains of logic, literature and philosophy. As I mentioned above, for natural scientists contradiction in logic is something to be avoided since it is evidence of weak thinking: so in Aristotle's *Metaphysics* (1998) he claimed that it is impossible for two opposing propositions to be true at the same time: 'The most certain of all basic principles is that contradictory propositions are not true simultaneously' (1011b13–14). However, this is far from saying that he was uninterested in oppositions, such as the one and the many, infinity and finitude, which pervades *The Metaphysics* and which he inherited from Plato via Parmenides.

In natural science and mathematics practitioners have clung to this basic standpoint, as did my colleague on the board of the not-for-profit, with spectacular results in predicting and controlling the natural world. However, mathematical logic has never quite done away with paradox as I will show in the penultimate chapter of this book, but demonstrably so following the work of the Austrian mathematician Gödel at the beginning of the twentieth century, who was intrigued by the attempt of Bertrand Russell and Alfred North Whitehead to develop a mathematical system which was devoid of contradiction in number theory. In order to prove this Russell and Whitehead's system would need to be both consistent and complete. With a series of elaborate proofs, and similar to the Liar's Paradox, Gödel produced two incompleteness theorems, demonstrating that no mathematical system could be either complete or consistent by reference to itself.

Gödel's theorems are extensively explored in Douglas Hofstadter's work (1979, 2008), where he argues that consciousness is an automatic property of sufficiently complex systems, which produce mechanical, recursive self-reference, the 'strange loop' in the title of his most recent book. In other words, he makes few distinctions between consciousness, mind and self, which I will unpick further below drawing on Mead (1934), and is satisfied instead with a material and mechanical explanation of consciousness, a reverberating loopiness of the brain as a complex system.

Paradox abounds in literature, too, and Linda Colie (1966) has written extensively about how paradox flourished in the Renaissance, particularly in the work of Shakespeare. Shakespeare brings together contradictions to confound expectations, just as his characters pretend to be other than they are and women leads play men, characters presumed dead are in fact alive, and nothing is quite what it seems. What this makes possible is a variety of surprising perspectives on love, truth, gender and power. However, in literature paradoxes are deployed to provoke, to complexify and to add aesthetic appeal but in no sense are they intended to develop an argument, as they are in philosophy, where they are deployed to explore an idea from different perspectives.

In this book I write about paradoxes in the natural sciences and mathematics in Chapter 7 and in the sciences of complexity below in this chapter, but for the most part I am concerned neither with logical nor literary paradoxes but with philosophical paradoxes. I will be sticking closely to what Kainz (1988: 43–44) argues are the properties of a philosophical paradox, which are four. First, we take paradox seriously, the unity-in-distinction which ordinary speech and logic would not allow. Secondly, we consider the paradoxes as far as possible which are non-vicious, unlike the double binds explained above or the semantic paradoxes like the Liar's Paradox, as a way of coming to understand a phenomenon in a richer and more dynamic way than just treating it as a case of static polar opposites. The third characteristic is that the setting in motion of opposites creates the potential for intellectual transcendence, the movement of thinking which parallels the dynamic of paradox. I discuss the paradox of consciousness below, and in Chapter 3, when exploring reflection and reflexivity which, I argue, is the root of the movement of thought. And lastly, a paradox needs to be able to sustain an argument and be demonstrated: that is to say that it is not dependent on belief or aesthetic intuition.

The link I am making to organizational research and management is that instead of excluding what might be of most use and perhaps greatest interest to practising managers and leaders, the often ambiguous, contradictory and paradoxical tensions in human and organizational life which call out political and ethical questions, this book will try to explore them more fully as a means of bringing about some kind of complex order. This exploration comes with a caveat though: I have no intention of moving towards any kind of final resolution of the contradictions I will be investigating because I am assuming that there is no meta-position to adopt in relation to them (although the process may fulfil Kainz's third criterion, that of provoking the reader into a dynamic movement of thinking), nor is there any final resting place. However, I will try to sum up what I think some of the important observations are for managers and leaders.

But this is a different method from that adopted by the majority literature on organization and management and I anticipate that it may be frustrating to some readers of this book more used to being given prescriptions for what to do. There will be no attempt at 'deparadoxification' in Luhmann's terms (1995), or to 'harness paradox' for greater organizational effectiveness, or to 'unleash' the creative forces of paradox, or even to take up paradox as a 'lens' if what is meant by this is that human beings can somehow choose to 'leverage' paradox as perspective. I am much less interested in tightly formulating 'what works' since, from my perspective, what works depends on who is involved, the context, the history and the relationships of power.

Just as Kainz recommends, I will set out an argument and it will proceed dialectically, which is to say exploring a position, then a counter position, then as a direct result of this, exploring the first position further. Whatever insight we gain from this way of theorizing is in the back and forth between one position and another, much as my board colleague and I engaged with each other in the narrative above. Setting out an argument brings out a counter argument, which in turn elicits another, which also points to different ethical claims. As Kainz (1988) explains, dialectical argument dates back to ancient Greek philosophy, and has itself developed and evolved from what he considers the original form of dialectic in Socrates, which takes place in living conversation in ordinary language, through Platonic and Aristotelian dialectic.

The method in this book bears close resemblance to the last of these, where there is an attempt to sift the arguments for and against some contentious topic, or my aim would be to make it more contentious than it currently is, as a way of investigating the theme more in the round and more systematically. The intention is not to resolve the topic, but to make it more complex: there is, then, something of a trade-off between trying to explore a theme in the round and consistent, conventionally logical argument leading to a conclusion. The other influence on my argument in this book is Hegel, who most consistently developed the idea of both dialectic and paradox, which I will explore in the next chapter, but first I want to explore paradox in the sciences of complexity and make a link between these and the social sciences as I develop my argument.

The link between the complexity sciences and paradox

For more than 20 years a group of academics at the University of Hertfordshire has been developing ideas derived from the complexity sciences (Stacey, Griffin and Shaw, 2000; Stacey, 2010; Mowles, 2011; Stacey, 2011; Stacey, 2012) using them as a source domain for thinking about life in organizations. From a perspective they call complex responsive processes of relating the Complexity and Management Group at Hertfordshire takes an interest in flux and change in organizational life, how it can demonstrate both stability and instability both at the same time. In doing so colleagues put people and what they are doing at work at the heart of their enquiry: how they talk to one another, how they are bound by relationships of power, how they make value judgments which express ideology. This perspective derives insights from the complexity sciences and makes arguments by analogy, linking them with similar ideas from the social sciences. It takes a particular interest in uncertainty, contradiction and paradox, for the reasons I will now explain.

Why turn to the complexity sciences for theories about organizational life? The complexity sciences have manifestations in biology, meteorology, neurology, zoology and computer science, usually in the form of computer-based mathematical models, to simulate, say, ant colonies, or the working of the human brain. These models are useful for looking at phenomena which are in constant flux and change and where there are complex interdependencies between different entities or actors. One of the things my colleagues at Hertfordshire have found interesting about complexity models is that they operate using non-linear equations which have no solution, but rather are useful for showing emerging patterns and calculating probability. Meteorologists, for example, will run a model of an evolving weather pattern, which has variables such as barometric pressure, wind speed, humidity, many thousands of times to calculate the probability of a particular weather pattern emerging.

That is to say, and in contrast to the way my colleague on the board was arguing in our heated discussion, in a non-linear model there is no necessary proportionality between a cause and an effect, nor is it possible amongst the interdependent variables which cause had which effect. A specified input may not bring about a predicted change in the way that is assumed in an RCT experiment, for example. A small intervention may bring about a big effect (popularly understood as the butterfly effect) and a large intervention may bring about no change at all. And in the large number of complex interrelationships it is not possible to isolate and identify exactly which cause led to which effect. So in an evolving weather pattern a slight change in wind speed or the jet stream may increase the likelihood of rain falling. An additional characteristic of non-linear mathematical models is that they do not move towards an equilibrium state, a solution in mathematical terms. Instead, the output from one iteration of an equation is entered as an input to the next. The models show qualitative changes in patterning over time, iterating then reiterating.

Here are two examples where non-linear mathematical models demonstrate paradoxical properties. In models of mathematical chaos, and at certain parameters, a graphed output will show a pattern of regular irregularity: that is to say, it is neither completely chaotic with no pattern at all, nor does it fluctuate in a pre-dictable way between one point and another. A pattern emerges which is neither completely stable, nor completely unstable, but stable and unstable both at the same time. Those readers of a particular age may remember computer screensavers, in the days when there were such things, which were based on fractals, or Mandelbrot sets. The screensaver patterns, named after the mathematician Benoit Mandelbrot, would develop of a highly complex kind, both regular and irregular at the same time and repeating similarly at any degree of scale. This is a phenomenon which can be observed very clearly in nature, in, say, the patterning of coastlines, or ferns, or every tree, which is symmetrically unsymmetrical.

A second example of a paradoxical property in the non-linear sciences of complexity can be found in complex adaptive systems models. The models are intended to simulate how order and disorder arise within a population of, say, ants or termites, or the synapses in a human brain; in each of these examples there is no obvious control centre, and the coherence of the whole population arises from the micro-activity of each of the individual agents interacting locally with other, similar agents. The analytical sociologist Peter Hedström (2005) has used complex adaptive systems models to simulate patterns of work-seeking and peer influence in unemployed young people in Stockholm.

So complex adaptive systems models contain populations of interacting agents, bit strings of code, which interact with neighbouring agents according to rules set by the programmer. If the interacting agents are the same, then a regularly irregular pattern will emerge such as flocking behaviour (Reynolds, 1987), exactly like the roosting behaviour of flocks of starlings, for example. If the agents are diverse, then diverse and changing patterns can emerge across the whole population of agents which are surprising and novel. The model demonstrates evolutionary development precisely and only because of the activity of the interacting agents. One paradox is that the local interaction of the agents produces the population-wide pattern, but at the same time the population-wide pattern imposes constraints on exactly how the agents can interact. Stacey (2012) has a much more extensive account of how these evolutionary models demonstrate the paradox of local agents forming a global pattern, yet being formed by it both at the same time.

Just to reiterate, then, to emphasize why the sciences of complexity might be of interest to anyone wanting to understand the complexity of organizational life: computer models developed by scientists working with non-linear equations and with multi-agent models are unpredictable over the long term and demonstrate paradoxical properties. They are paradoxically stable and unstable both at the same time (neither completely chaotic, nor completely symmetrically patterned), and are therefore predictably unpredictable. Complex adaptive systems models evolve through the local interactions of the population of agents to produce changing patterns, but at the same time it is those evolving patterns which constrain exactly how the local agents will interact with each other: the agents form the pattern and are formed by it both at the same time.

Complexity in the social

My colleagues at the University of Hertfordshire turn to the social sciences to try to understand what these insights from the non-linear sciences might mean in social terms. After all, it would be very reductive to think of ourselves as agents in a computer model, or as operating according to algorithms written by someone else. My colleagues feel that the sciences of complexity might have something very useful to say about what is known in sociology as the structure/agency debate, and about action, and stability and change in society. In other words, how we might account for the fact that social life appears to be ordered and structured, very much constraining how we can act and think, and yet at the same time we can act relatively autonomously, have aspirations, make decisions, dream dreams.

A number of social psychologists and sociologists have taken a view on what links the apparent 'structure' of society with individual activity, including George Herbert Mead (1934) (and other philosophers in the pragmatic tradition), who argued that society arises in the activity of highly social selves; Pierre Bourdieu (1977, 1982, 1990), who pointed to the *habitus*, an inherited bodily disposition to act in a particular way because the body is in the social world, but the social world is also in the body; and Norbert Elias (1978, 1991, 1939/2000), who argued that the individual and the social are two sides of the same coin – there is no I without we. We become a self only because there are other selves. The 'I in the we' always provokes all kinds of ethical dilemmas.

With these three scholars in particular one of the things to notice is the way they deploy paradox, mostly without drawing attention to the fact, to convey the complex recursivity of our thinking about experience and the stable instability of social life and its moral complexity. For these in particular, and for other philosophers, sociologists and organization scholars I adduce in the book, there is no one way of describing the complex flux of social interaction. It is best understood from a perspective which does as much justice as possible to the complexity of the phenomenon it is trying to describe. Where might we begin in our enquiry about social complexity?

The paradox of consciousness: reconciling dualisms

Perhaps the most complex question of all is how we become conscious and come to know the world, and the discussion has a long history in philosophy. During the Enlightenment there was an enormous flourishing of optimism that human beings could come to know themselves and the world through the use of reason and the development of the scientific method. The rational, calculating, objectifying methods of scientific enquiry involved producing a dualism between the thinking subject and the object of thought. The starkest expression of this split is Descartes's idea that the only thing we can be confident about is that we think: Descartes even doubted that he had a body. His assumption was that the thinking mind gives human beings their freest form as self-defining subjects. Nature, then, is to be doubted, and is no more than a mechanical apparatus to be dissected and studied at a distance by the thinking self.

Whilst dissatisfied with Descartes's and Newton's mechanical universe, discoverable from universal laws, Kant nonetheless perpetuated the same dualism, which he termed an antimony, by arguing that we can come to know phenomena, appearances, but we can never get to know 'things in themselves'. The search for truth is to try to get closer and closer to 'things in themselves', but which will always elude us. Reality was counterposed against the knowing subject: two poles of an antimony but which can never be reconciled.

Taylor (1975) notes how the rise of the Enlightenment also provoked a counter movement of thought in romanticism, which was a reaction against the perceived instrumentalization and objectification of nature. The rise of the Enlightenment was perceived to have stripped humankind of their spiritual home in nature. Taylor points out that Hegel felt impelled to work with these two counter movements of his age, to cleave to the promise of reason on the one hand, but to maintain human beings' place in an organic and purposive nature on the other. He developed an enormous body of work, which he referred to as a philosophical system, trying to work with dualisms which he considered unnecessarily separated out in Enlightenment thinking, such as for example, the split between the knowing subject and what can be known; the thinking mind and the body; the finite nature of man and an infinite god. To do so, Hegel deployed paradox extensively in an attempt to delineate and maintain countervailing forces.

In the *Phenomenology of Spirit* Hegel developed the insight from the work of Fichte that consciousness arises from our ability to be both the subject and object of our own thinking. We might think of this as the primary paradox from which all other paradoxes flow:

> I distinguish myself from myself, and in doing so I am directly aware that what is distinguished from myself is not different [from me]. I, the selfsame being, repel myself from myself; but what is posited as distinct from me, or as unlike me, is immediately, in being so distinguished, not a distinction for me. It is true that consciousness of an 'other', of an object in general, is itself necessarily *self-consciousness*, a reflectedness-into-self, consciousness of itself in its otherness.
>
> *(Hegel, 1807/1977, para 164: 102)*

We can both think, and think about ourselves thinking, that is, we can be both reflective and reflexive. Instead of separating the thinking self from what is thought about, Hegel includes the thinking self in the movement of thought, in the back and forth between subject and object. From this base of the paradox of consciousness Hegel's project was an attempt systematically to engage with the dualisms which develop in human thinking and to keep them in motion, in paradoxical relation, through dialectic. Who knows and what is known are part of the same movement of thought as we learn to reconcile the contradictions which are constantly presenting themselves in our thought.

But Hegel argued that the reconciliation occurs not through a cancelling out, but through the preservation of the contradiction in a higher order, a higher unity, which in turn provokes another contradiction. Hegel's term for this is *Aufhebung*, the unity in difference, and in my understanding this is an evolutionary theory which Hegel applies to all things, including the development of human society. The constant contradiction, reconciliation which preserves the contradiction, then a new contradiction develops higher and higher forms. I will explore these ideas again in a bit more depth in the next chapter, but it is exactly this back and forth of thought which I make the basis of this book and my explorations of organizational life.

It might be tempting to conclude that the theorizing of dead white philosophers has little to do with what managers have to do in the day-to-day. But Hegel's philosophy has been enormously influential on many of the thinkers brought into this book, such as Mead, Dewey Elias and Bourdieu and, more generally, on Marx and his inheritors. Both Elias and Marx, for example, draw heavily on Hegel's insight that societies progress from lower to higher orders of complexity through struggle, opposition and inner contradiction, although Marx mostly confined his analysis to struggle in the economic sphere. And to a large extent the argument Hegel is working through, what the relationship is between knower and known, is still relevant today and shows up in the dispute between my colleague on the board and me. My colleague is convinced that the highest form of knowledge is to choose one pole of the dualism between the researcher and the object of research, even to the extent of denying, after Descartes, that he has a human presence apart from his thinking. What is in question is the extent to which human relations can be objectified, what gets lost in the objectification process, and what alternative ways of knowing might be.

It is impossible to form theories about what happens in organizational life without coming down somewhere in the debate about how we can know what is going on there, and how we might form theories about it. In this book I am trying to work with a dialectical understanding of organizational life which puts paradox at the heart of the enquiry, and keeps the researcher and the researched together. I am trying to bring together theory and practice, certainty and uncertainty, stability and change.

The paradoxes of mind, self and society

Mead developed Hegel's insight about consciousness in psycho-anthropological terms. In Mead's work what distinguishes us from other animals is our ability to take the attitudes of other people, what he termed the 'generalized other', to ourselves. In other words, because we are capable of seeing ourselves as others see us, a peculiar property of our central nervous system, we are able to take ourselves as objects to ourselves.

This is what Mead termed the I/me dialectic: the mutually constitutive, mutually negating dynamic of individual and social. We might think of this as a double paradox: we are subjects to other people, who are our objects, but we are also objects to ourselves because we can take their perspective on us. Rooted in Hegel's insights, Mead argues that we become a self intersubjectively. I think what Hegel and Mead are pointing to here is the constant movement of the mind as social phenomenon, where we can hold onto ourselves as not-ourselves in relation to other minds, which turns on paradox.

Indeed, we can go further as the German sociologist Axel Honneth does (1995) to say that we would not become ourselves without the struggle of recognition with and through others: we recognize ourselves through the recognition of others. Consciousness is a social phenomenon which requires other conscious beings and involves a struggle over negation, and negation of that negation to establish evolving social norms.

If we were to draw on psychoanalytic theory, however, we would understand the subject/object split not as something that we are born with, however, but as something which develops over the first few months of our lives.[2] As infants we experience no separation between our mothers and us. But without the growing realization of separateness, that the mother is a distinct being, and that she who provides food and comfort can also withhold it, we would not be able to go on to make the other distinctions we do. The growing ability to make distinctions between what is us and not-us develops in the growing infant but has also evolved through the ages, according to both Norbert Elias (1939/2000) and the Canadian philosopher Charles Taylor (1992) and experienced a full and conscious flourishing during the Enlightenment.

In previous centuries we made much less of a distinction between natural phenomena and our feelings about them: our growing ability to separate ourselves from the phenomena we wanted to understand has led to a much greater degree of control. If we could not tell the difference between us and not-us, then science, which relies on this demand for separateness from the objects of study, would not be possible. But perhaps there is an argument that the evolution of, and aspiration for, objectivity about social phenomena has a tendency to exclude the very phenomena which may be illuminating for us about ourselves. This was Hegel's project, along with the pragmatist school of philosophy (Peirce, James, Mead, Dewey, Bernstein, Rorty). This book, by focusing on reflection and reflexivity, is a small attempt to bring managers and what they are thinking and feeling back into to the discussion about what happens in organizational life with an assumption that our understanding is enriched as a consequence.

The means of keeping subject and object in relation is the back and forth exchange of what Mead terms significant symbols. A symbol is significant if it has a similar meaning for someone communicating with it, as for the person being communicated with. When we converse with others, we gesture towards them with significant symbols which call out in ourselves the response we anticipate calling out in them: the paradox of gesturing to ourselves as an object, of recognizing the self in the recognition of others, enables mind, a sense of self and thus a society of conscious selves to arise. The gesture calls out a dual and mutual anticipation between ourselves and others. Mead argues that social life would be impossible without this mutually anticipatory gesture and response, which allows us constantly to adjust to each other in the contexts we find ourselves, and the particular people we are dealing with. So from the primary paradox of consciousness a number of other paradoxes arise, for example that the process of individualization is a social process. We become a self because there are other selves. Equally, thinking is the internalization of a social process of gesture and response directed by the body towards itself. The clear demarcation between what happens 'inside' and 'outside' ourselves as human beings breaks down because we are social even in our private thought processes.

The mutual and paradoxical formation of the individual and society was also a core theme for Elias (1991), who put forward the idea that changes in our psychological make-up are reflected in structural changes in society and vice-versa. The one brings out the other:

> One finds then – in adopting a wider, dynamic viewpoint instead of a static one – that the vision of an irreducible wall between one human being and all others, between inner and outer worlds, evaporates to be replaced by a vision of an incessant and irreducible intertwining of individual beings, in which everything that gives their animal substance the quality of a human being, primarily their psychical self-control, their individual character, takes on specific shape in and through relationships to others.
>
> *(Elias, 1991: 32)*

Previously I mentioned the complexity sciences where interacting agents in a complex adaptive system form and are formed by the population of which they are part: Elias offers us the sociological equivalent. We form, and are formed by, the social. The paradoxes of individual and social, inclusion in groups and exclusion from them are generated by our interdependencies with others, the fluctuating relationships of power, which enable and constrain how we behave. As I mentioned earlier, Elias never explicitly mentioned his use of paradox, but his writing is infused with them. I explore Elias's ideas more thoroughly in the rest of the book.

Summing up

Paradox arises from a contradictory tension of thinking and I have been arguing in this introductory chapter that organizational life is filled with such tensions which break out all the time, sometimes provoking conflict over different ideas of the good. I gave an example from my own experience. As human beings we have been aware of the contradictions in the way we think about the world for a very long time. But I have made the case that many contemporary researchers try to design them away when they study social phenomena, based on assumptions derived from the natural sciences that a contradiction, a flaw in logic, impedes good research, and that scientific methods have little to say about what we take to be the good.

Instead, they may argue that there are indeed contradictions in organizational life, but the controlling leader or manager can choose one pole of the contradiction over the other. I have been making an alternative case, drawing on the complexity sciences and sociologists and philosophers interested in complex, contradictory phenomena, that there are good reasons for exploring them, which I intend to do in the rest of this book. This will involve looking at what I have termed the primary paradox of consciousness and self-consciousness and everything that seems to me to flow from this, in terms of the social process of how our actions and intentions form our societies, which in turn form us at the same time.

Organizational uncertainty, ambiguity and paradox – outline of this book

In Chapter 2 I return to Hegel, whom I mentioned in the first chapter, to explain briefly how his philosophical system is a radical rendering of contradiction and paradox. I explain further how his insights have been developed by pragmatic philosophy in particular to justify the position that I take up in this book that there is no 'god's eye view' to take up on paradox: it can only be understood from within the paradox itself. I give a brief overview of two other perspectives on paradox, functionalist sociology and psychology and psychoanalysis. Both have a tendency to render paradox in abstract and systemic terms and to imply that it is possible to take a meta-level view.

I then look briefly at the way that other writers on organizations take up paradoxes and work with them. In general I conclude that most organizational researchers adopt the position that managers and leaders can harness paradox for the good of the organization or can somehow instrumentalize it. The reason for taking issue with their position is that it puts managers and leaders back in control and assumes uncertainty away. I argue that staying with the unsettling nature of uncertainty offers no guarantee of success, but may be more realistic than traditions of research which claim to be realist.

Chapter 3 explores the paradox of consciousness and self-consciousness which I described earlier on as being the primary paradox. I do this by way of reflecting on our ability to take the perspective of the airman and the swimmer, Norbert Elias's phrase from his book *The Society of Individuals*. Managers are obliged to think about longer-term trends but are also caught up in the moment of everyday contingencies: they are caught in the paradox of involvement and detachment. The chapter considers in detail some of the arguments developed in one thread of the leadership literature: so-called 'entrepreneurial leadership'. I discuss whether the term has any merit and try to locate it within the broader discourse about leadership.

The chapter then turns to a discussion of reflection and reflexivity and their importance for leading and managing, although it concludes that reflexivity is no panacea. Reflection and reflexivity are not tools or techniques to be taught, but can be cultivated and managers made more skilful in their use. Thinking about what is going on, and thinking about how we are thinking about what is going on are not recipes for success, however, and it involves exercising our moral judgment. For Hannah Arendt, whom I quote in this chapter, it is our moral judgments that most make us human.

The next step in my argument in Chapter 4 is to explore the idea of culture, which emerges through the interaction of conscious and self-conscious human beings, those social processes which we form, but which form us at the same time. In particular I write about organizational culture, if such a thing could be thought to exist separate from both particular and broader social processes. I raise the question about how much leaders and managers can manipulate culture in the way claimed by more orthodox management texts, and what it means for our freedom if they can. Control of culture is a big prize in organizational discourse, but what does it really mean for the practice of management and how possible is it to change how people think and feel, rather than just how they behave?

I discuss the perspectives of some prominent organizational theorists on culture, and then compare and contrast these with the work of process sociologist Norbert Elias, who argues that culture arises in shared collective and symbolic identification. I then go on to discuss culture from the perspective of practice, as habituated and context-specific action informed by tradition, drawing on Alasdair MacIntyre, Gadamer and contemporary Aristotelian philosopher Eikeland. All three philosophers are interested in the immanence of ethics in everyday conversational life.

Finally there is an extended discussion of the National Health Service in the UK which has been an organization at the heart of contestation and struggle over the perceived need to change culture to see what it can tell us about the practice of management and what we consider to be the good.

Chapter 5 develops the idea of organizational culture and argues that organizations are both stable and unstable at the same time and investigates what this might mean for the ubiquitous contemporary narrative about innovation. To what extent can we plan to be innovative? I discuss some of the difficulties of the innovation agenda. First, the idea that we can plan to be innovative contains an irony, and secondly the majority discourse contains a false binary, promoting the idea that innovation is always good and stability is inhibiting. Even cursory reflection on, say, the development of complex financial instruments at the start of the twenty-first century will demonstrate that innovations can be both creative and terribly destructive. I go on to argue in this chapter that organizations are always sites of paradox where both stability and change arise at the same time.

I discuss why social science is unlikely ever to have the predictive power of the natural sciences by drawing again on the moral philosopher Alasdair MacIntyre. Generalizations in the social sciences, like management, will always be phrased as holding 'in general, and for the most part'.

The chapter concludes by drawing on some organizational literature in the process school, which still leans towards suggesting that managers can design innovation processes.

Chapter 6 is a further exploration of what we might think of as culture and turns on an investigation into the paradox of conflict and cooperation and argues that they are two sides of the same coin. Despite much contemporary management literature assuming that conflict can be managed for the good, I explore whether this is really possible, and what the paradox of conflict and cooperation might mean for the emergence of the novel. There are clear links to the chapter on innovation, because the argument I set out here is that innovation is occurring every day in both small and large ways, and that this arises from the exploration of difference through conflict, large or small.

The chapter discusses the way that conflict is explored in organizational literature, then puts forward alternatives from sociological and psychoanalytic literature. The chapter concludes that there is no way of avoiding conflict in organizations and nowhere for managers to stand which is a neutral position. Managers can only engage with the necessary contestation.

Chapter 7 is a brief review of the way that paradox, ambiguity and contradiction are still vital to the methods employed in the natural sciences. In the introductory chapter I have mentioned that a more naïve view of the exact sciences is that they exclude contradiction. Here I try to demonstrate that even the natural sciences thrive on ambiguity and sometimes even on paradox. Examples are taken from the domains of mathematics, physics and neuroscience.

The point of the chapter is the social sciences, including management, do not need to suffer from physics-envy, since even natural scientists develop their work drawing on the mind's ability to veer round to its opposite.

Chapter 8 is a concluding chapter and tries to bring some of the threads of the book together setting out the implications for the management of organizations. These are that ambiguity, contradiction and paradox are pervasive in organizational life and cannot be wished or managed away. This is not to imply that there is nothing for managers to do, however. The chapter dwells on the importance of reflection, reflexivity and practical judgment, and the agonistic engagement with colleagues. It recommends that managers take everyday experience seriously and notice more carefully their own participation in the game of organizational life. To do so may make organizations richer and more complex, and perhaps even more human.

Notes

1 There are of course some notable exceptions, some of which I explore in this book.
2 For example, Melanie Klein (1975) drew on Freud to argue that the infant learns to cope with the world by 'splitting' good and bad objects.

References

Aristotle (1998) *The Metaphysics*, London: Penguin.
Bateson, G. (1970) *Steps to an Ecology of Mind*, Chicago: University of Chicago Press.
Bourdieu, P. (1977) *Outline of a Theory of Practice*, Cambridge: Cambridge University Press.
——(1982) *Leçon sur la Leçon*, Paris: Editions de Minuit.
——(1990) *The Logic of Practice*, Cambridge: Polity Press.
Briner, R. B. and Rousseau, D. M. (2011) Evidence-Based I-O Psychology: Not There Yet, *Industrial and Organizational Psychology: Perspectives on Science and Practice*, 4: 3–22.
Charlier, S., Brown, K. and Rynes, S. (2011) Teaching Evidence-Based Management in MBA Programs: What Evidence Is There?, *Academy of Management Learning & Education*, 10(2): 222–36.
Colie, R. (1966) *Paradoxia Epidemica: The Renaissance Tradition of Paradox*, Princeton, NJ, Princeton University Press.
Dewey, J. (1941) Propositions, Warranted Assertibility, and Truth, *The Journal of Philosophy*, 38(7): 169–86.
Elias, N. (1978) *What Is Sociology?*, New York: Columbia University Press.
——(1991) *The Society of Individuals*, Oxford: Blackwell.
——(1939/2000) *The Civilizing Process*, Oxford: Blackwell.
Hedström, P. (2005) *Dissecting the Social: On the Principles of Analytical Sociology*, Cambridge: Cambridge University Press.
Hegel, G. W. F. (1807/1977) *Hegel's Phenomenology of Spirit*, Oxford: Oxford University Press.
Hofstadter, D. (1979) *Gödel, Escher, Bach: An Eternal Golden Braid*, New York: Basic Books.
——(2008) *I Am a Strange Loop*, New York: Basic Books.
Honneth, A. (1995) *The Struggle for Recognition: The Moral Grammar of Social Conflicts*, Cambridge: Polity Press.
Kainz, H. (1988) *Paradox, Dialectic and System: A Contemporary Reconstruction of the Hegelian Problematic*, London: Pennsylvania State University Press.
Klein, M. (1975) *Love, Guilt and Reparation and Other Works: 1921–45*, New York: The Free Press.
Learmonth, M. (2006) Is There Such a Thing as 'Evidence-Based Management'? A Commentary on Rousseau's 2005 Presidential Address, *Academy of Management Review*, 31(4): 1089–91.
Learmonth, M. and Harding, N. (2006) Evidence-Based Management: The Very Idea, *Public Administration*, 84(2): 245–66.
Luhmann, N. (1995) *Social Systems*, Stanford: Stanford University Press.
MacIntyre, A. (1981) *After Virtue: A Study in Moral Theory*, Notre Dame: Notre Dame Press.
March, J. G. (1991) Exploration and Exploitation in Organizational Learning, *Organization Science*, 2(1): 71–87.

Mead, G. H. (1934) *Mind, Self and Society from the Standpoint of a Social Behaviourist*, Chicago: University of Chicago Press.

Mowles, C. (2011) *Rethinking Management: Radical Insights from the Complexity Sciences*, London: Gower.

Reay, T., Whitney, B. and Kohn, K. (2009) What's the Evidence on Evidence-Based Management?, *Academy of Management Perspectives*, 23(4): 5–18.

Reynolds, C. W. (1987) Flocks, Herds and Schools: A Distributed Behaviour Model, Proceedings of Siggraph '87, *Computer Graphics*, 21(4): 25–34.

Rousseau, D. (2006) Is There Such a Thing as 'Evidence Based Management'?, *Academy of Management Review*, 31(2): 256–69.

Russell, B. (1908) Mathematical Logic as Based on the Theory of Types, *American Journal of Mathematics*, 30(3): 222–62.

Scott, J. C. (1999) *Seeing Like a State: How Certain Schemes to Improve the Human Condition Have Failed*, Yale: Yale University Press.

Stacey, R. (2010) *Complexity and Organizational Reality: Uncertainty and the Need to Rethink Management after the Collapse of Investment Capitalism*, London: Routledge.

——(2011) *Strategic Management and Organisational Dynamics: The Challenge of Complexity to Ways of Thinking about Organisations*, London: Pearson Education, 6th Edition.

——(2012) *The Tools and Techniques of Leadership and Management: Meeting the Challenge of Complexity*, London: Routledge.

Stacey, R., Griffin, D. and Shaw, P. (2000) *Complexity and Management: Fad or Radical Challenge to Systems Thinking*, London: Routledge.

Taylor, C. (1975) *Hegel and Modern Society*, Cambridge: Cambridge University Press.

——(1992) *Sources of the Self*, Cambridge, MA: Harvard University Press.

2

TAKING PARADOX SERIOUSLY

One must not think ill of the paradox, for the paradox is the passion of thought, and the thinker without the paradox is like the lover without passion: a mediocre fellow. But the ultimate potentiation of every passion is always to will its own downfall, and so it is also the ultimate passion of the understanding to will the collision, although in one way or another the collision must become its downfall. This, then, is the ultimate paradox of thought: to want to discover something that thought itself cannot think.

Kierkegaard, Søren. *Philosophical Fragments* (1844) p. 37

In the introductory chapter I set out the case for taking contradictions and paradoxes seriously as a way to help us think about the difficulties, dilemmas and ambiguities that arise daily in organizational life. And of course I am by no means the first person to recommend this. In this chapter I explore how other thinkers and organizational scholars have written about ambiguity, contradiction and in particular paradox, to compare and contrast between my position and theirs. This is also a dialectical process, a back and forth between what I take other scholars' ideas to be and my own in order to provoke my own thinking, and hopefully that of the reader. Thinking moves in the making of distinctions. Of course, there is no intention on my part to reach a reconciliation of positions, or to claim I have truth on my side. This will not prevent me from setting out my critique strongly, however. I hope the process will better clarify their position as well as my own.

First it means engaging further with what I take paradox to be and to see how other sociologists and philosophers have dealt with it. The reason for doing so is that their ideas often show up in organizational literature. For example, those thinkers like Luhmann who consider a paradox to be a property of a system are taken up in work by organizational scholars who also make the same assumption. What this often leads to is that attention is focused on the more abstract areas of organizational life, on structure or strategy, which leads in my view to reification, turning organizations into things, which can be manipulated by managers to resolve the paradox. Instead, I would like to focus on how paradoxes manifest themselves practically, in everyday activity in organizations, as a way of provoking leaders and managers to think about what they are actually doing.

But first I attempt a brief philosophical interlude to reprise Hegel's idea of dialectic, the contradiction of opposites, which produces an ascending order of complexity because I think Hegel had the most comprehensive system for treating contradiction and this might be helpful for us. I believe it is worth exploring his work further in order that we might set his ideas alongside the work of other scholars. Thereafter I review how paradox is taken up in the organizational literature.

I appreciate that what follows in this chapter is quite theoretical, and it may be some readers would prefer to skip to the next chapter, which has more practical examples of paradoxes in organizational life.

Hegel again in brief

On speculative logic

Hegel developed a theory of 'speculative logic' as a complementary method to ordinary logic, not as a replacement for it. He regarded deductive logic, which is central to mathematics and which permits no contradiction, to be an important method of thinking. But, according to Hegel scholar Stephen Houlgate (2008: 124), Hegel argues that a fully self-critical logic should be presuppositionless. In other words, it should not assume that particular categories of thought are to be understood in a particular way, or even that there are categories of thought at all.

This is a direct response to and critique of Kant's idea that we come to understand the world because our thinking is already structured in a particular way in categories of thought with which we are born: they structure our understanding a priori. Kant argued that the structure of our understanding reflects quantity, quality, relation and modality; he deals with all four headings in the *Critique of Pure Reason*. As an alternative to Kant's categories, Hegel argues that it is not that thinking starts from nowhere, because we inherit categories of thought when we are socialized into language (although not because we are born with them). However, if we try to be mindful of the task we have in hand then thinking can call into question the categories we take for granted.

In this way Hegel's philosophical system is an anti-foundational approach to truth, similar to that pursued latterly by pragmatist philosophers Peirce, Mead, Dewey, Bernstein and Rorty, all of whom were influenced by Hegel. That is to say, none of these philosophers assumes that knowledge proceeds from a ground, a fixed and secure point like Descartes's thinking self, but emerges in the interaction of thinking subjects with the world and with other thinking subjects. Philosophers in the pragmatic tradition have a radically evolutionary understanding of selves and of knowledge, that neither the categories nor the content of knowledge is fixed, but it emerges and evolves in social relations. Nor do they assume a point of view outside of the development of knowledge, what Dewey (1929) referred to as a spectator theory of knowledge, where there is a separation between the knower and the known. Whatever one thinks about Hegel's philosophy, it is clear that his radically evolutionary position is carried further by the pragmatists and influences theory to this day.

In order to be presuppositionless and without ground, speculative logic additionally does not assume any rules in the same way that deductive logic does, the rule of the syllogism. That is, a syllogism posits a major premise, a minor premise and a conclusion, like this famous example: all men are mortal; Socrates is man, therefore Socrates is mortal. Hegel's idea was that the 'simplicity' of thought should reveal categories in the process of thinking and that any rules should demonstrate themselves in the same way, provided that one observation followed on from and was suggested by the last. 'When I think,' he argues, 'I give up my subjective particularity, sink myself in the matter, let thought follow its own course; and I think badly whenever I add something of my own' (from Hegel's *Encyclopaedia of Logic*, quoted in Houlgate, 2008: 126).

It is not that the speculative logician does nothing in the speculative process, but he or she thinks actively guided by what is immanent in thought. Hegel is not describing a kind of daydreaming, but a rigorous mental process where the thinker tries to make as explicit as possible the categories of thought that thinking suggests by making the content of thought as specific as possible, and leaving no vagueness. He is also trying to avoid the radical subjectivism of Descartes, who roots all of his thinking in the 'I': I think, therefore I am. This process may make the categories of thought change as one is thinking about them, which demands a great deal of mental dexterity. One has to be alive to the possibility of flux and change even as one is trying to make concepts clear and come into view.

The link I want to make here is with what I was saying about problem-driven as opposed to methods-driven research in the last chapter. What Hegel is suggesting, in my view, is that it may be possible to start out with few preconceptions about experience but to try and engage with it by allowing experience to experience itself. This perspective has been taken up extensively in what are known as phenomenological approaches to research, which try as far as possible not to impose preconceived assumptions on the subject/object of research. Rather, the phenomenological researcher tries to engage with the object of their research as they find it and as they find themselves, thus rendering more explicit the structures of their own thinking and experience.

This is very similar to the methods that we encourage students to experiment with on the Doctor of Management at the University of Hertfordshire when they are carrying out their research. This rather abstract and perhaps off-putting idea has practical relevance for researchers and managers coming to understand what might be puzzling them in organizations by recommending that there may be nothing to be 'applied' to the problem except systematic thinking and discussion.

Of course, this has to be combined with Hegel's insight that thinking has to be confirmed in experience: theory and practice are also an inseparable unity which suggest each other. Theory arises out of our experience in the world, but also informs our experience. The process of taking experience seriously, becoming more conscious about one's preconceptions through discussion and the back and forth of exchanging ideas, allows one to progress one's thinking about what one is trying to think about.

What I am calling problem-driven research, trying to engage with the matter at hand in all its complexity, is in contrast to methods-driven research, which often starts out with a preconceived and developed idea about how the research should proceed and applies a particular method to the 'problem'. Research students who embark upon a research degree are often sent off for some months to learn a variety of different methods, which they then apply to their research project in stepwise fashion as the method recommends. In Hegel's system, there is nothing to be applied to anything else as Kainz (1988) argues: this is not the movement of the mind imposed on external content but the idea that process and content are one and the same. This makes Hegel's logic and concept of dialectic very difficult to formalize, or to turn into a linear method.

Hegel and dialectic

Even dialectic, which we broached in the last chapter, is not something which is pre-given, but is created by the process of thinking. What Hegel claims to have noticed in contemplating the concept of being, for example, is that being can only exist with its opposite, nothing. When we contemplate the idea of being, Hegel argues, this immediately calls out, and is defined by nothing: the two concepts both suggest and define each other, each being logically unstable in relation to each other. The one vanishes into the other and then back again. In Houlgate's words:

> What we discover at the start of Hegel's logic is thus not only that being and nothing vanish into one another, but that each simply *is* its own *vanishing*. As such, each is immediately the coming-to-be of the other. With this insight we reach a new category neither being nor nothing is purely itself because each is nothing but the *becoming* of the other.
>
> *(Houlgate, 2008: 129)*

In this way Hegel claims to have proven that dialectic is a characteristic of the nature of thinking, rather than a method which is brought to bear on concepts. Thinking's inner dialectical form is made explicit when we are systematic and scientific about thinking. Nor does this come about because thinking is heading towards some end point, or to use the philosophical term, because it is teleological. Categories of thought turn into their opposite by trying to remain as they are – they are not trying to become parts of some greater whole – and when we try to fix them, so they turn into their opposite. And finally, what we referred to previously as *Aufhebung*, the process where a concept and its contradictory opposite are transcended in a unity of opposition, is a process which generates itself through thinking. In other words, there is no external position to take on dialectic: in the terms of philosophy, it is immanent. In contemporary parlance, dialectic is not a 'lens' to apply to ideas, or a perspective to adopt, but arises in the struggle of thinking.

Summary of Hegel's ideas and why they are important for thinking about organizations

Readers may remember I described my academic colleague on the board wanting to exclude things from the research project which he thought might contradict with the smooth functioning of reason, including his own values and any logical contradictions. He was demonstrating that ways of thinking based on conventional logic depend upon choosing between contradictions, opting for one side of a polarity of opposites which may arise at the same time. I then went on to argue that management literature which aspires to being scientific also rests on a number of exclusions.

What Hegel is offering is a different way of understanding contradiction in experience, which I have tried to argue is pervasive in social life. Knowledge arises in paradoxical contradictions which emerge from thinking, in the dialectical process between the thinking self and the object of thought. There is no way to resolve the paradox and nowhere to stand outside of it; it generates itself and is 'self-grounding': one concept calls out its opposite which is both defined and negated by it. Staying with the mutually negating ideas and noticing how it sends the mind moving, as uncomfortable as it may be, can provide further opportunities for reaching a more intense understanding of the paradox that one is experiencing.

It might be worth spelling out again why I am persisting with Hegel, and what it is that I find so helpful in his ideas about paradox and dialectic. In the last chapter I explained, drawing on Mead's development of Hegel's ideas, that we become ourselves because there are other selves. In a slightly clumsy phrase used by philosophers, we emerge inter- and intra-subjectively, in the paradoxical movement between the self and other. For Hegel, knowledge arises in the dialectical movement of thought in a populated world, and through human practices. Human beings and what they are doing, thinking and acting is what causes social evolution.

Although my reading of Hegel would lead me to conclude that he thinks that society evolves to a higher and higher order, and ultimately a progressive order, there is nothing which suggests to me that he thinks that this is necessarily always a positive process or that dialectic is just creative. This would be splitting apart the paradoxical poles of positive/negative, creative/destructive if it were to be the case. This is an important point to consider when we go on to discuss how paradox is taken up in organizational literature where there is often a suggestion that paradox can somehow be 'harnessed' for the good, or that developing a greater comfort with paradox enables managers to 'unleash creativity' in their organizations. Although on the one hand I take the view that noticing the mind's ability to move to its opposite can enable a richer understanding of what is happening in organizations, this is not the same as arguing that managers can in any way harness, encourage, tip, embrace or otherwise instrumentalize paradox for the good.

Nor do I read Hegel to suggest that there is some kind of equilibrium or optimum state for a paradox to be in, as one might be led to think, particularly with some organizational scholars who explore the idea of dynamic equilibrium (Smith and Lewis, 2011), which I discuss later on. I think the idea of optimizing or balancing is due partly to the tendency to accommodate paradox and dialectic within systems theory, and partly from a misunderstanding of the word *Aufhebung*, the idea of sublating or transcending contradictions, which is sometimes rendered in English translation by the word synthesis (thesis, antithesis, synthesis). In my understanding the movement of thought is always in a state of becoming and is always contradictory, one thing and its opposite both at the same time.

In my view taking Hegel's ideas seriously offers both researchers and managers a different way of engaging with organizational complexity. The first stage is to admit the contradictions as they arise and then to pursue them systematically in thinking and discussing with others. The social process of reflection and reflexivity, which I explore in the next chapter, is the manner in which we become more comfortable with apparently immovable contradictions, although this does not mean that it simplifies them. What is possible is greater insight, perhaps even greater comfort with some of the dilemmas that organizing produces, but there is no suggestion of resolution or even of control.

Of course, Hegel is not without his critics even amongst his admirers. The Hegel scholar Allen Wood (1990) regards Hegel's attempts at speculative logic as a failure, and claims that even Hegel abandoned it as too ambitious (1990: 4). However, what Wood retrieves from Hegel's experiment is his force as a speculative ethical philosopher engaged in a project to reconcile human beings to their moral and social world, still working with the paradoxes of the particular individual and the general world, subject and object, self and other. For Wood, Hegel understands ethics as constantly evolving and dynamic, situated in a particular time and a particular place, and arising from the struggle between individuals and the institutions they create to actualize justice and freedom. Similarly, the contemporary German philosopher Axel Honneth (1996, 2012) derives his evolutionary theory of social development from Hegel's thought, understanding social development as a 'struggle for recognition'.

Different ways of dealing with paradox

Now I am going to deal very briefly with two different approaches to dealing with paradox because these responses echo throughout contemporary organizational theory, which I will explore later in the chapter. The first of these is to consider paradox as a property of a system. In choosing an example of a thinker who does this, Niklas Luhmann, I am selecting someone more complex than most systems theorists. This is because he was very prolific, had a long career and drew on a variety of different disciplines for his work. Paradox figures prominently in his attempts to describe the complexity of social life. Although I think the tenor of this book as a whole is very far removed from Luhmann's thesis, his conviction that social life always defies our attempts to plan and control it is something I share with him. From a very different perspective, Luhmann is also writing about complexity, although his paradigm is complexity understood in systemic terms.

The second tradition of thought which frequently refers to paradox is the psychological and psychoanalytic literature. In both these disciplines paradox is thought to play itself out in the contradictions which arise between the conscious and the unconscious, and between the individual and the group. Both perspectives are helpful in the sense that they bring to our attention some of the attendant paradoxes of our social life with others. On the other hand, the literature tends to privilege the individual at the expense of the social, which is different from the perspective I am taking in this book where the individual and the social arise simultaneously. As I will try to demonstrate later in the chapter, organizational literature often plunders psychoanalytic and psychological insights selectively in order to promote the view that 'harnessing paradox' tends to the good and leads to creativity.

Luhmann

Niklas Luhmann (1927–98) was a sociologist in the tradition of Talcott Parsons, under whom he studied. Luhmann, like his mentor, took a functionalist view of social life. That is to say, he understood society in systemic terms, that it arises from the interaction of systems and sub-systems which tend towards equilibrium. Both thinkers drew on a wide variety of natural science disciplines and cybernetic systems theory in order to develop social science, in the tradition of Max Weber, as an analytic discipline. Their intention was to make sociology a rigorous and abstract science: the idea of a system was a necessary one for both theorists because it rendered less complex the infinite variety of the world to make it more comprehensible.

Conceiving of the social world in terms of a system obliges us to focus down on one part of the world and make it comprehensible, as Luhmann expressed it: 'in light of the unalterably meagre extent of the human attention span, increased efficiency is possible only through the formation of systems, which ensure that information is processed within a meaningful framework' (Luhmann, 1970). Luhmann went on to develop significant differences with Parsons: for example, he considered social systems to be auto-poietic, or self-referencing, after the work of Chilean biologists Maturana and Varela (1980) (although they themselves expressed scepticism that their findings could be applicable to the social sciences).

A system persists because of interactions with itself, rather than because of interaction with the environment, although it is open to the environment, and changes occur because of internal variation, which are internal responses to external conditions. A system can be perturbed, but not changed, by the environment in which it functions. Self-referencing systems are made of networks of components which recursively, through their interactions, generate and realize the network which produces them. It is the logic of the self-referencing system itself which is pre-eminent. This allowed Luhmann to escape from the strictures of Parson's systems theory, where each sub-system contributes to the overall whole: auto-poietic systems are largely autonomous.

Luhmann was trying to generalize beyond the kind of anthropocentric view of the social which I have sketched out in the preceding paragraphs, where human beings and their interdependencies are at the heart of social stability and change: he eschewed a micro-social view of social life. Human beings are stripped out of his theories altogether, which became a focus of critique from some of his contemporaries, such as Habermas. What maintains social systems as far as Luhmann is concerned is communication and meaning-making, which is something above and beyond the communications of individual human beings, but is a property of the system of which they are part. Social systems are defined by the constant production and reproduction of meaning, to which human beings contribute, but is not reducible to them. It is not actors acting which causes society to evolve, but communication communicating.

Luhmann was preoccupied with paradox ('There are paradoxes everywhere, wherever we look for foundations' (1988: 154)). They arise in particular when systems are involved in observing, but cannot observe themselves observing. Just as Gödel demonstrated in mathematics – a self-referencing system can only take account of itself. In making an observation the system can only observe itself and its own operations, taking itself to be reality, but not as reality really is. Each system exists in a blind spot where it mistakes the part of reality it can observe for the whole: it is trapped in a paradox.

For a system to make sense of its observation involves a further observation, a second order observation, which observes the observing system in the act of observation. What Luhmann terms 'deparadoxification' occurs because the system can never catch itself in the paradox in which it is enmeshed, so it invents new distinctions, which do not resolve the paradox but relieve it of its paralyzing power (Luhmann, 1995). Paradox for Luhmann is a source of great creativity in the social and a spur to invention as systems try to cover over their paradoxical nature and endow their communications with meaning.

So Luhmann too writes about the pervasiveness of paradoxes and realizes their creative potential, and their support for offering explanations about how the social continues to evolve. But he does so from a depopulated systems perspective: we gain little insight into what people are actually doing in social life. Similarly in organizational theory, many scholars automatically assume that paradox is a property of the organization understood as system, although often they will also assume that the leader or manager can take up a perspective from outside the system in order to adopt Luhmann's second order observational position. This way of abstracting from what people are doing is very common in organizational literature, as we shall discover later on, but it seems to me to cover over as much as it explains.

Psychoanalytic and psychological and perspectives

Psychoanalytic perspectives draw on Freud's original insights that the unconscious disrupts our conscious states of mind, and that the individual, in order to individuate, has to repair the disorganized sense of groupness, experienced originally in the family. The individual somehow has to reorganize their inner representation of disorganized, or unorganized previously experienced family relations.

A good example of this perspective in the literature is Manfred Kets de Vries's book *Organizational Paradoxes* (2001), which turns on a variety of paradoxes arising from neurotic behaviour of leaders and managers. For example, charismatic leaders may arise at a time of crisis in organizations, but they may equally be acting out their own paranoid tendencies which perpetuate the crisis in which they emerged as a leader. On the one hand, the charismatic leader calls out strong group cohesion, high organizational morale and goal directedness; on the other hand the leader may only do so by polarizing the organization into two groups, those who are with the leader and those against, and may demand constant positive reinforcement that what they are doing is both correct and necessary, leading to group think. Kets de Vries concludes that: 'the dividing line between pathological developments and corporate success is a thin one' (2001: 85). What Kets de Vries refers to as the paranoid potential of leadership, particularly charismatic leadership, is a double-edged sword and can lead to both organizational success and failure, depending on the circumstances.

In their book entitled *Paradoxes of Group Life* (1987) Smith and Berg rehearse the history of paradoxical concepts manifested in the evolution of psychoanalytic and group theory. They cite Newman (1974), for example, who reviews the paradoxes to be found in Bion's (1961) work. She notes how Bion argues that, although individuals agree to come together in order to undertake a particular task, they then spend a great deal of time discussing the task and can thus spend more time destroying it than completing it. Additionally, individuals might join a group to overcome loneliness, but then they struggle not to be swallowed up in the group and lose their identity, thus contributing even more to their sense of loneliness. Lastly, an individual may join a group to overcome a sense of inadequacy, but membership of the group also calls out its own sense of inadequacy as the individual is obliged to take up roles on behalf of the group.

One thing to notice about the psychoanalytic literature cited by Smith and Berg, including the review of Bion above, is that it causes a separation between the individual and the group: the experience of paradox within an individual is compounded or exacerbated by the experience of the individual in the group. The paradox is understood to be occurring at two separate but related levels of experience. This is a departure from the radically social view of the formation of self which I set out in the introductory chapter, drawing on Mead and Elias. In the latter there is no separation between the I and the we: they are two sides of the same coin.

Smith and Berg go on to confirm this separated understanding of paradox later on in the book in reference to Bateson (1970), whom we mentioned in the last chapter, and who thought of paradox occurring at different levels of abstraction (similar to Luhmann, above). Alternatively, Smith and Berg argue, consciousness has developed as a result of the emergence of digital communication, which allows for the possibility of describing something and its opposite. This option is not available in analogue communication. Smith and Berg consider 'not' a meta-communicative boundary between a self and a not-self, which is a precondition for consciousness and self-consciousness. This leads them to the idea of reframing, or redrawing the boundaries in order to adopt a meta-position on paradoxical experience.

Smith and Berg, and the thinkers they adduce, are struggling with the same problem when paradox is construed as the property of a system with a boundary. As both Gödel and Luhmann observed, self-referencing systems are incomplete: in Luhmann's terms they have blind-spots which cannot observe themselves observing. At bottom I think this is a problem for self-referencing systemic theories of paradox which can only resolve themselves by reframing, redrawing the boundary, or taking up a meta-position.

I think Mead approaches the problem differently with his double paradox of consciousness, that we gesture and call out in ourselves a similar response to the one we call out in other selves. In other words, there is no boundary separating us from others because becoming ourselves involves an internalization of the generalized other. As selves we are both individual and social at the same time: the group is already part of us.

Bourdieu expressed this in his own formulation (1982: 38), drawing on Merleau-Ponty, by saying that 'the body is in the social world, but the social world is in the body'. Perhaps another way of thinking about this, drawing on the complexity sciences, is to consider consciousness to be analogous to a fractal where the repeating pattern, regular irregularity, repeats at every degree of scale. There are not separate paradoxes, or even compounding paradoxes, but a singular and plural version of the same contradictions.

The psychological literature dealing with paradox also tends to proceed from the individual and move to the social, assuming a separation between one and the other, and also assumes that what is desirable is a dynamic balance of opposites. There is a strong thread of literature on positivity and creativity, which seems to draw in particular the positive psychology movement (Seligman and Csikszentmihalyi, 2000) and studies of artistic and scientific creativity (Rothenburg, 1979). In this second work Rothenburg identified the concept of Janussian thinking, based on the Roman god Janus, who was able to face both ways at once. Rothenburg's idea is that creativity involves being able to bring into play and sustain multiple contradictions. I discuss Rothenburg's ideas and how they relate to the development of science in Chapter 7.

This idea is also adopted by Csikszentmihalyi (1996), for example, to suggest that creative people are always balancing antithetical characteristics, such as humility and pride, playfulness and discipline, extroversion and introversion. To do justice to Csikszentmihalyi, he also thinks that the balancing of contradictions brings creative people pain and suffering as well as reward. However, this idea of the creativity and positivity of paradox has been widely taken up in the organizational literature, as we see later in this chapter.

I have some degree of sympathy with Csikszentmihalyi's argument that creative people demonstrate paradoxical abilities, partly because I am saying something similar in this book by adducing a number of thinkers who are able to sustain paradoxical opposites in their arguments. However, I disagree that the poles of a paradox can be brought into dynamic balance; nor do I think that one can necessarily choose to be creative by 'embracing paradox', as some of the organizational theorists suggest.

I am less convinced by the power of positive thinking than are proponents of the positive psychology movement. What seems to be missing for me is that, paradoxically understood, creativity also involves destruction, as the economist Schumpeter once observed of capitalism. In giving creativity pre-eminence those who stress only the positive nature of paradox lose the contradiction to which they are pointing. If it were possible to 'embrace' paradox there is always the possibility that to do so would bring about the opposite of what one intends.

Summary of the argument so far

At the beginning of this chapter I tried to develop my argument about contradiction as paradox, explaining how it emerges in thought and experience by drawing once more on Hegel. The reason for exploring Hegel further is that I am sympathetic to his perspective that paradox and contradiction arise in humans and between humans in the everyday activity of being conscious, thinking, doing and discussing. Hegel posits the idea that paradox emerges immanently through systematic thinking about who we are and what we find ourselves doing together. If we are to take this idea seriously then there is nowhere outside of paradoxical thought to take up a view on it, to choose one pole of the paradox or another, to split or manipulate it. It poses a profound problem for managerial intentions of harnessing paradox for the good or instrumentalizing it in any way. It also makes the idea of paradox very ordinary: it does not arise because we are living in extraordinary times of unprecedented social change, although this may also be true, but because we are human beings trying to achieve things with others.

I then explored two threads of discussion of paradox in the work of Luhmann and in the psychoanalytic and psychological literatures as a way of assessing the similarities and differences between my argument drawing on Hegel, and how others who take paradox seriously have tried to understand and work with the concept. The reason for doing so was to try and trace the origins of similar themes which crop up in organizational literature on paradox, which we are now going on to discuss. In both the disciplines I am using as comparators, scholars have tried to understand paradox in systemic terms, as caused by the operation of boundaries between one system and another, or arising from cognitive framing and levels of abstraction, or as a contradiction between the individual and the group.

In the next section I will explore the way that paradox is taken up in organizational theory. I have not done so exhaustively, but have referred instead to some prominent scholars and articles as a means to give some examples of the sort of argument that one can find about paradox in books on management.

Paradox in the organizational literature

Broadly speaking there are two types of organizational literature dealing with paradoxes. The majority literature is generally managerialist in character and assumes an instrumentalizing approach to paradox. In general the reader will find that these organizational scholars make three assumptions about contradictions and paradox in organizational life: that it is identifiable and manipulable by managers, and in particular leaders (or it arises as a consequence of choices which leaders make); that when it is embraced or 'harnessed' it brings about positive consequences for the good; and that it arises as a property of the organization understood as system because of contradictions between the individual and the group, or between different levels of the system. The pervading sense is that paradox can be optimized.

I have found one exception to this in a short, playful, almost gnomic volume by Richard Farson (1997), which became a *Business Week* bestseller. In this he too laments particularly American scholars' pursuit of the controllable:

> I find it disquieting to see the term paradox entering management literature in a way that indicates that it can be 'managed'. I suppose I should expect this because of the sense of omnipotence that plagues American management, the belief that no event or situation is too complex or too unpredictable to be brought under management control.
>
> *(Farson, 1997: 15)*

Although serious in his intentions in this short and interesting book, Farson fails to sustain his arguments for very long, taking an almost chiasmic approach to the paradoxes he investigates, arguing for a while in one direction, then promptly turning round and arguing the opposite. In this sense he fails Kainz's definition of a philosophical paradox which I set out in the introductory chapter, that a paradox needs an extended argument.

Alternatively, there is a minority literature in a more critical tradition, which assumes that paradox is unresolvable, and draws on the concept as a way of pointing to unfolding tensions and contradictions in organizational life. A good example of the second type is Rasche's treatise on *The Paradoxical Foundation of Strategic Management* (2008), where he draws in particular on Derrida and deconstruction to write in detail about the practices involved in strategizing. Some of his conclusions are similar to the ideas that I explore in this book. He calls, for example for a reuniting of theory and practice, for 'thick descriptions' of what strategy practitioners are actually doing in particular organizations at particular times; he argues in favour of single case qualitative methods which place the researcher as active participant in organizational research; he argues for different criteria for evaluating organizational research other than a narrow definition of scientific rigour; and, finally, he argues for engaged scholarship, being able to call accepted arguments into question as a result of reflection and reflexivity. There is much that I find to agree with in Rasche's book, although he comes at the problem from a different theoretical base.

Similarly, in an edited volume Koot et al. (1996) explore the paradoxes arising from cultural conflicts as a way of gaining greater insight for managers.

In what follows I engage mostly with the majority literature to understand the arguments better, as well as to further develop my own.

Paradox as competing values

Robert E Quinn has written a large number of management books and was one of the first scholars to address the idea of paradox (1988). In *Beyond Rational Management* Quinn notices exactly the same kinds of phenomena in organizations that we have been paying attention to in this book, that uncertainty and ambiguity is part and parcel of everyday organizational life, that there are not always obvious right answers about how to proceed, and that 'problem' situations are constantly evolving:

> What exists in reality are contradictory pressures, emanating from a variety of different domains. The fact is important because much of the time the choice is not between good and bad, but between one good and another, or between two unpleasant alternatives. In such cases the need is for complex, intuitive decisions, and many people fail to cope successfully with the resulting tension, stress and uncertainty.
>
> *(Quinn, 1988: 3)*

I think it is worth examining Quinn's argument and prescriptions more thoroughly in this chapter because what he calls the competing values framework, which he develops in the book, is the basis for much of his subsequent work and has stimulated a lot of other scholarship. Additionally, the way he deals with paradox is a very good example of the way in which other scholars have come to treat the idea. It is Quinn's view that paradoxes in organizations can be mastered and, I would argue as a consequence, tamed and turned to instrumental use in making organizations 'high-performing'.

The concept of mastery is one of Quinn's central arguments, and is a theory that he adopts from three streams of research by Streufert and Swezey (1986), Torbert (1987) and Dreyfus et al. (1986). Rather than taking the idea of mastery to mean something mystical or esoteric, as can sometimes be the case in more popular management literature (as pointed out by Dreyfus et al., 1986: 158), Quinn draws on these three developmental or evolutionary explanations of the way that judgment and grounded intuition matures in managers over time so that they can wield expertise, or mastery. In other words, as any professional progresses from novice, through competent practitioner to expert, they develop intuitive judgment, which allows them to go beyond the rules. They are able to recognize patterns, to develop in Bourdieu's terms a 'feel for the game' (1992) that they would be highly unlikely to be able to describe to anyone else, except other, similar experts, and which cannot simply be reduced to algorithms or rules.

The importance of mastery for Quinn is that it allows managers to develop an intuitive, holistic overview of organizational patterns, in this case contradictions or paradoxes.

Where rationalistic management approaches are helpful for more routine, logical management problems, holistic intuition is more helpful for the situations of uncertainty which he has previously described. Rational, or what he terms purposive management operates according to propositional logic and binaries, either/or, and so excludes things. For this reason it is unable to accommodate holistic management. On the other hand, holistic approaches are able to include purposive management thus doing away with the binary choice of either being purposive, or being holistic: it is possible to be both. A master manager uses both 'frames'. Notice here how Quinn draws on the idea of cognitive frames which were prevalent in psychological individualistic approaches to understanding paradoxes as well as the idea of wholes.

When managers achieve mastery, which they can do through experience and an explicit programme of self-development and discovery, they can then learn to manage paradoxes for the good of the organization. The programme of self-improvement is as conscious and calculated as the methods of managing competing values: a manager should analyse him/herself, note her strengths and weaknesses, set out a programme of change and enlist the support of others in achieving it, whilst being realistic about the costs of doing so. Equally, contradictory tendencies in organizations can be mapped and measured at each 'level' of the organization using a number of cobweb diagrams which punctuate the book. The paradoxes then need to be brought into 'balance' in order for the organization not to become trapped in a negative area.

Quinn's idea of mastery as applied to contradictory pressures in organizations is summed up as follows:

> Moving beyond rational management means using both frames [*purposive and holistic*]. It means moving through three steps. The first step is recognizing polarities. The second step is seeing the strength and weaknesses in each of the polar perspectives. The third, and most challenging, step is not to affix to one or the other but to move to a meta-level that allows one to see the interpenetration and the inseparability of the two polarities. This third step takes us to a transformational logic. It allows for simultaneous integration and differentiation. It allows us to understand management at a deeper, more complex and dynamic level – the level of the master.
>
> *(Quinn, 1988: 164–65; italicized inserted text is mine)*

Quinn has made a significant contribution to the literature by pointing out the importance of paradoxes in organizational life, but it seems to me that he has done so by reaffirming the rational management paradigm. There are a number of things to note about Quinn's understanding, which I would argue are paradigmatic of a particular and rational understanding of management.

First, Quinn's approach is both individually and cognitively based. So, for example, mastery is a rare and individual capability that a manager seems to be able to develop deliberately and alone, although with the contingent support of others. In the programme of self-development set out by Quinn, managers are able consciously to recognize their strengths and weaknesses and design a programme to address them. Equally, master managers can recognize polarities, and in recognizing them, choose a meta-position which is sometimes described as preserving their simultaneous differentiation and integration and sometimes described as bringing them into balance. This seems to be an entirely cognitive and frictionless exercise, described by him as 'effortless' and might be thought of as a kind of mysticism, despite claims to the contrary: where authors like Senge et al. (2005) explicitly appeal to Buddhism or some hidden order to the universe, Quinn is appealing to another, equally inexplicable faculty, that of pulling oneself up by one's bootstraps.

The move from 'either-or' thinking to 'both/and' thinking seems to me to split out the paradox, identifying first one pole, then the other, then assuming a meta-position. Master managers can turn their attention first to one, then to the other. Quinn gives us no clue how an individual manager can achieve this meta-position, although his thinking would be consistent with a functionalist understanding of organizations: the master manager can draw a boundary around one tendency and its opposite, and in stepping beyond it can take up a view from 'outside' the polarity. This is what the philosopher Thomas Nagel (1986) referred to as 'a view from nowhere' – how does a manager, even one who has achieved mastery, step beyond the bounds of the social reality they claim to bring into balance?

The second thing to notice is the way in which the exploration of contradictory tendencies is instrumentalized with the claim that harnessing paradox can improve organizational results. It is important to acknowledge that I go part way with Quinn: I would not be writing a book about paradox and contradiction if I did not agree that to pay attention to the way that organizational life is shaped by contradictions makes a helpful contribution to the way managers understand their jobs. However, recognizing the way that paradoxes constrain and enable work is not the same as taking the next step to claim that these can then be utilized for the good. My own claim is that this recognition, if and when it occurs, is much more provisional. This is particularly the case if you take the view that there is no stepping outside of paradox to take up a meta-position on it.

I mentioned previously that I considered Quinn's work paradigmatic in terms of the pattern that I notice of a particular research tradition in which there are scholars drawing attention to contradictions on the one hand, but attempting to subject them to rational splitting and management control on the other. Quinn's book is filled with elegant cobweb diagrams, which purport to offer a way of mapping organizational contradictions which can then be 'measured' and therefore manipulated or acted upon. This is a way of turning paradox into a metric: one might argue that it is trying to measure the unmeasurable.

So Quinn locates the ability to deal with the contradictions of organizational life in the individual – it is through personal mastery, developing, in Dreyfus and Dreyfus's (1986) terms, from novice to expert – which allows managers to assume a meta-position over and above contradictory pressures. Acquiring personal mastery is a rational process of self-examination and stepwise improvement, as is the mapping of contradictory pressures in organizations, which can be represented in one of Quinn's competing values spider diagrams. Quinn offers a functionalist understanding of organizational contradiction by drawing an implicit boundary around one organizational pressure and its opposite, beyond which Quinn places the expert manager.

There is little explanation as to how managers can achieve such an exalted position, a view from nowhere, except by force of will and self-scrutiny. A manager's mastery of the situation essentially dissolves the paradox to which Quinn is helpfully pointing and allows the expert manager to harness contradiction for increased performance. Quinn's work sits very much within the dominant discourse of instrumental management theory, which assumes that even paradox can be harnessed for the good of the firm.

Paradox: a relational view or a lens?

The next three pieces of scholarship I deal with are widely cited articles, and are written by scholars who would certainly not consider themselves as part of the dominant discourse on management. However, it seems to me that they stray towards some of the same assumptions.

Clegg et al. (2002) start out with the definition of a paradox which we have been working towards in this book, that it comprises two mutually contradictory elements, and then move swiftly to portray the whole of organizational life as a paradox. On the one hand organizations comprise autonomous human beings; on the other they are sites of order and control. They argue that the control pole of the paradox has figured most prominently in organizational literature, as we have seen in the treatment of Quinn's book in the paragraphs above. A paradox may present in three different ways, they argue. First, a paradox may manifest itself beyond the will or power of management, so there is little to do but acknowledge it. Secondly, it may present at different levels in the organization, in which case managers can only recognize and prepare for it. Or, thirdly, the paradox may reveal itself at different points in time in the authors' understanding of a Hegelian dialectic, with a period in organizational history contradicted by an opposite tendency.

From Clegg et al.'s reading of the literature, which for them is overly informed by a perspective of control, they argue that it suggests three ways to treat paradox: the first argues that managers must choose one pole; the second argues for striking a balance between the poles, and the third is for managers to integrate the opposite poles and resolve the contradiction. As an alternative, they argue that the tension in paradoxes should be sustained rather than resolved 'as a fertile ground for syntheses that improve the practice and understanding of management without replacing or attenuating the tensions that ground them' (2002: 489).

Their alternative is a 'relational' view of treating paradoxes, which is to bring them into bi-directional relation to enable some kind of synthesis between the poles. By synthesis the authors do not mean compromise or resolution, but some way of keeping the poles in constructive relation. This can only be done if they are treated in particular contexts and emerging from particular practices, they argue.

Clegg et al. are keen not to suggest that paradoxes can be resolved and their focus on practice and context is similar to the perspective taken in this book. However, my principal difficulty with Clegg et al.'s argument is that they seem mostly not to be talking about paradoxes at all, but dilemmas, particularly the ubiquitous explore/exploit dilemma, which is reproduced again and again in organizational literature. My second critique of their argument is that, despite their own contention that other organizational scholars move to resolve paradoxes, they do precisely the same thing themselves, only they call it a synthesis. Nor is it clear how a synthesis is arrived at or how a manager, or managers, intervenes to make the polarities of a paradox bi-directional. To paraphrase Norbert Elias, it seems to me that Clegg and his colleagues ultimately move to resolve a mystery with another mystery. This appears as a more gentle form of manipulation, where managers can somehow massage paradoxes for the good of the organization.

Meanwhile, Lüscher and Lewis (2008) draw on a two year action research study of a management reorganization at Lego in Denmark and notice how middle managers in particular are trying to make sense of seemingly contradictory imperatives. In this sense the study is interesting since it deals with a practical problem in real time in a company which is trying to make changes. The authors have an opportunity to make practical sense of their theorizing.

As a result of the confusion which arises in any change situation, Lüscher and Lewis notice that management meetings turn into what they term 'sparring sessions', where middle managers were able to think about how they were thinking about some of the contradictions which arose as a result of the reorganization. They develop a model of this problem-solving approach which they argue proceeds from a mess, an undifferentiated and fuzzy problem, to a specific problem with boundaries, to a dilemma to a paradox. They also group organizational paradoxes into three: paradoxes of belonging, paradoxes of organizing and paradoxes of performing. Moving to paradox enables managers to experiment with greater 'workable certainties', i.e. further opportunities for richer sense-making.

In stepwise fashion Lüscher and Lewis understand paradox to be a 'lens' which can be applied to particular organizational problems, and in choosing this metaphor they automatically place themselves outside the problem to be thought about, just as a natural scientist applies a lens to inspect an object in nature. The idea of a lens implies that managers can choose, or not, to apply paradox to understand a problem. According to the authors, moving to paradox enables managers to develop from one-dimensional to multi-dimensional understandings of the problems they are facing; however, the authors understand this as a process of transition from one stage to the next of their stepwise model, which requires their facilitation. This understanding is similar to the linear progression of paradox which we explored earlier when dealing with Quinn.

I share with the authors the insight that drawing attention to the paradoxical nature of organizational life can make managers more fluent with and skilful at dealing with some of the contradictory pressures of being a manager. I am more doubtful that a paradox can be sequenced and organized with a facilitator's intervention and that it is fully accessible by way of Argyris's (1993) double-loop learning model. This latter idea assumes that individuals make sense of the world by way of a representation, a mental model, which is stored in an individual mind. Argyris assumes that we can surface the mental model we are using and, by doing so, change it.

By taking a radically social view of mind, that it arises inter- and intra-subjectively, I am not assuming that we form individual mental representations of a world 'out there', but have argued instead that consciousness and self-consciousness arise through processes of mutual recognition. These social processes create unconscious drives which we are barely aware of, thus making it highly problematic to suggest that we can knowingly surface the way we make sense of the world and consciously change it.

Paradox as a dynamic equilibrium

Lastly, in this section I treat an article recently published in a leading management journal, the *Academy of Management Review*. The reason for doing so is because both scholars have made a reputation for themselves in writing about paradox, and I think as an example it helps us understand what is valued in management research and the kinds of assumptions it is based on, in particular that paradox can be instrumentalized by managers to unleash creativity and positivity, ideas which we previously encountered in the psychology literature.

In a wide-ranging article, Smith and Lewis (2011) try to synthesize 360 journal articles about paradox across 12 academic journals in order to increase conceptual clarity. They do so, they argue, in order to integrate the differing conceptions of paradox into an overall model to further organizational theorizing. Their aim is to 'leverage the potential' of different conceptions of paradox by developing a dynamic equilibrium model, understood in terms of biology, or systems dynamics, where opposing forces are maintained in terms of a fluctuating homeostasis.

They set out their own understanding of paradox as being the property of a system: 'First, paradox denotes elements, or dualities, that are oppositional to one another yet are also synergistic and interrelated within a larger system' (2011: 386). The paradox turns on the interrelationship of the duality across an internal boundary and defined by an external boundary, which binds the paradox and allows it to persist over time. The authors make a distinction between paradox and dilemma, and paradox and dialectic.

Dilemma is a tension between two competing alternatives, both of which have arguments for and against, and they understand dialectic to be the synthesis of competing tensions, which is then faced by another contradiction. In this latter definition they echo the conventional misunderstanding of Hegel's dialectic, thesis, antithesis, synthesis, which Hegel never used to describe his concept and which I have mentioned before. Both dilemmas and dialectics can have paradoxical properties if they persist over time, the authors claim. Smith and Lewis also reclaim what I have termed the explore/exploit dilemma as a paradox because the tension occurs simultaneously and can persist.

They also try to reconcile two views of paradox, that it is socially constructed or that it is a property of a system, by claiming that it is both. Inevitably the leader is central to the authors' idea of how paradoxes arise within the system and become salient for employees. It is because the leader makes choices about how the organization is to become that contradictions arise. In defining A, leaders are also defining a broad category not A. The systems and sub-systems which leaders create are complex and adaptive and are constantly changing to meet the conflicting demands of the environment. Equally, actors can make paradoxes salient by applying 'paradoxical cognition', by which I think the authors mean that actors either become aware of, or are able to construct a contradiction which was previously only latent.

The authors warn against the inevitable defensiveness which arises in actors when they are made anxious about the presence of contradictions, because of the desire for consistency and integration. This can have the opposite effect and cause vicious paradoxes. Instead, a strategy of acceptance of paradoxes by cognitive framing, emotional equanimity and organizational adaptability is more likely to promote virtuous circles, the authors claim. The response to paradox, then, occurs at two different 'levels': the individual responds with equanimity, whilst the organization, guided by the leader, responds by developing structures, cultures and learning approaches which better deal with the paradoxes. One way of dealing with paradoxes is to make choices in the short term, whilst remaining aware of the enduring contradiction over the longer term.

Dealing effectively with paradox, according to Smith and Lewis, through

> a dynamic equilibrium unleashes the power of paradox to foster sustainability. Individuals, groups, and firms achieve short-term excellence while ensuring that such performance fuels adaptation and growth enabling long-term success ...
>
> *(Smith and Lewis, 2011: 393)*

A dynamic equilibrium enables learning and creativity, it fosters flexibility and resilience and unleashes human potential: it can unleash positive energy into the firm and create organizational sustainability. Smith and Lewis argue that their dynamic equilibrium model allows managers to 'harness paradox for the good' of the organization. They contrast this with what they consider two previous ways of approaching managerial problems. First was the idea of one best way, either choice A or B. Then the development of a contingency approach allowed managers to ask in which circumstances one would choose A or B. As an alternative, a theory or paradox enables managers to try and sustain both A and B at the same time, not as an alternative to contingency theory, but as a complement to it.

One thing to notice in this article in an eminent academic journal is how hard it is for the authors to adopt a critical or dialectical position when writing for an academic audience. Instead of explaining and then negating some of the positions on paradox they find in other journal articles, the authors strive instead to bring them all into some kind of unified position. The problem that I see in this is that, in trying to give value to all positions they are in danger of adopting none themselves. So, accordingly, paradox is both a property of a system and is socially constructed; leaders can both temporarily split the paradox and be reminded of it over the longer term.

This also tells us something about the discipline of academic writing, particularly for journals, which privileges what is known in linguistics as agglutinative approaches. In other words, scholars are invited to acknowledge all previous scholarship, no matter how contradictory, and somehow make it all add up by adopting a meta-position in relation to it. Notice how it is possible, according to the authors, for leaders to be in control of the paradox they identify.

Actually, it would not be true to say that the authors have no position to speak of because it seems to me that they have quite an orthodox managerial perspective on paradox and organizational life. This is that paradoxes arise because leaders make choices, and they can join with managers in instrumentalizing them, creating mechanisms which turn paradoxes to the good, unleashing energy and creativity in the organization. Paradoxes appear at different 'levels' in the firm, as a property of a system, but at the same time the leader can take up a position in relation to them, presumably beyond the boundary of the system, which can utilize paradox in ways which optimize. There seems to me to be very little that is either new or different in these claims, which are simply a restatement of previous positions within the orthodox discourse on management.

Conclusions

Perhaps I am being harsh on contemporary management literature by pointing to its instrumentalizing tendencies, that no matter how complex and messy an area of human experience somehow it wants to bundle it up and present it as a tidy package at the disposal of managers and leaders. Management scholarship in its managerialist manifestation is after all an explicit ideology, which assumes that management theory is a stable and growing area of knowledge and that trained managers are a uniquely qualified cadre of professionals overseeing and promoting organizational change. It sits in a broadly modernist and positivist tradition which understands social life to be improvable and is committed to developing ways of understanding the complexities of organizational life, which managers will find helpful in doing their jobs.

Maybe instrumentalizing is exactly what we would expect the orthodox literature to be doing, and one way of thinking about it is that it is offering managers hope. Certainly the idea that our ability to conceive of one thing and its opposite can be brought into dynamic harmony, or can by synthesized, or can unleash creativity in the organization, may be partially reassuring to experienced managers who are painfully aware that their job is not easy.

There are also other examples in the literature where scholars investigate paradoxes in depth, investigate the ways in which other scholars suggest they may be resolved, and then themselves conclude that this is by no means the end of the story. For example, Poole and Van de Ven (1989) argue that: 'Resolutions of paradox in one aspect of a theory often create inconsistencies in another part of the theory. Thus, it seems unlikely that theorists can ever escape or resolve theoretical paradoxes completely. It has been suggested that at the heart of any theory that solves a paradox is another, different paradox, waiting to be discovered' (1989: 576). It is just this latter position which I am adopting.

I am conscious that when I suggest that paradoxes are unresolvable, by managers or by anybody else, and in turning to Hegel, the pragmatists and process sociologists for guidance in understanding what might be going on with them, potentially I am offering an anxiety-provoking alternative by leaving things hanging. I am critiquing a position without appearing to offer anything in its place. And, after all, many managers are probably doing a very good job most of the time and are highly unlikely ever to have heard of Hegel, Mead, Elias or speculative logic. The case for persisting with understanding paradoxes and contradictions differently is latent within the idea of paradox itself: I am putting forward a contrary view, not just for the sake of it but because in my opinion managerialism over-promises, and so could be accused of offering false hope.

Ironically, a tradition of thought which cleaves to realism and the discovery of scientifically provable laws at the same time tries to sustain a god's eye view of complex human experience to claim that managers and leaders can be in control of the very contradictions of which they are part, like the famous Escher drawing of two hands drawing each other. My critique of this position, then, is that realism is not quite realistic enough even in its own terms and leaves out precisely what managers need to focus on in order to make good sense of the uncertain, contradictory and paradoxical environments in which they often find themselves working.

In the rest of this book I will try and remain with the messy and complex reality of organizational life and develop arguments which set the mind moving. The intention is not necessarily to offer reassurance, at least not in a direct way, nor to offer any instruments of management. Instead I hope the reader will experience the movement of thinking, and the resonances of both similarities and differences which point to the ordinary and extraordinary nature of trying to get things done with other people. This is a kind of practical deliberation which assumes that thinking, talking and acting are inseparable aspects of human activity. I investigate organizational life as the complex responsive processes of human relating, where what we are doing together matters to us, and provokes conflict based on our engagement with each other and the world. My suggestion is that, by becoming more familiar, and perhaps at the same time more comfortable with organizational life's uncertainties and their own contribution to them, leaders and managers may at the same time become more skilful and perhaps more resourceful.

In the next chapter I discuss what I have previously termed the primary paradox of consciousness and self-consciousness and how this manifests as reflexivity. I use an example of everyday organizational life to think about how I and others are thinking about leading organizations and discuss what difference this might make to leaders and managers.

References

Argyris, C. (1993) *Knowledge for Action: A Guide to Overcoming Barriers to Organizational Change*, San Francisco: Jossey-Bass.
Bateson, G. (1970) *Steps to an Ecology of Mind*, Chicago: University of Chicago Press.
Bion, W. (1961) *Experiences in Groups*, London: Tavistock.

Bourdieu, P. (1982) *Leçon sur la Leçon*, Paris: Editions de Minuit.
——(1992) *The Logic of Practice*, Cambridge: Polity Press.
Clegg, S., Vierra da Cunha, J. and Pinha e Cunha, M. (2002) Management Paradoxes: A Relational View, *Human Relations*, 55(5): 483–503.
Csikszentmihalyi, M. (1996) *Creativity: The Work and Lives of 91 Eminent People*, New York: HarperCollins.
Dewey, J. (1929) *The Quest for Certainty: A Study of the Relation Between Knowledge and Action*, Gifford Lectures.
Dreyfus, H., Dreyfus, S. with Athanasiou, T. (1986) *Mind Over Machine: The Power of Human Intuition and Expertise in the Era of the Computer*, New York: The Free Press.
Farson, R. (1997) *Management of the Absurd*, New York: Touchstone Books.
Honneth, A. (1996) *The Struggle for Recognition: The Moral Grammar of Social Conflicts*, Cambridge: Polity Press.
——(2012) *The I in the We: Studies in the Theory of Recognition*, Cambridge: Polity Press.
Houlgate, S. (2008) Hegel's Logic, in Beiser, F. C. (ed.) *The Cambridge Companion to Hegel and Nineteenth Century Philosophy*, Cambridge: Cambridge University Press.
Kainz, H. (1988) *Paradox, Dialectic and System: A Contemporary Reconstruction of the Hegelian Problematic*, London: Pennsylvania State University Press.
Kets de Vries, M. (2001) *Organizational Paradoxes: Clinical Approaches to Management*, London: Routledge.
Koot, W., Sabelis, I. and Ybema, S. (1996) *Contradictions in Context: Puzzling over Paradoxes in Contemporary Organizations*, Amsterdam: VU University Press.
Luhmann, N. (1970) Soziologische Erklärung 1. Aufsätze zur Theoriesozialer Systeme, Opladen: Westeutscher Verlag, quoted in Joas, H. and Knobl, W. (2010) *Social Theory: Twenty Introductory Lectures*, Cambridge: Cambridge University Press.
——(1988) The Third Question – the Creative Use of Paradoxes in Law and Legal History, *Journal of Law and Society*, 15: 153–65.
——(1995) The Paradoxy of Observing Systems, *Cultural Critique*, 31: 37–55.
Lüscher, L. and Lewis, M. W. (2008) Organizational Change and Managerial Sensemaking: Working through Paradox, *Academy of Management Journal*, 51(2): 221–40.
Maturana, H. and Varela, F. (1980) *Autopoiesis and Cognition – the Realization of the Living*, Dordrecht: D. Reidel Publishing Company.
Nagel, T. (1986) *The View from Nowhere*, Oxford: Oxford University Press.
Newman, R. G. (1974) *Groups in Schools*, New York: Simon and Schuster.
Poole, M. S. and Van de Ven, A. (1989) Using Paradox to Build Management and Organization Theories, *Academy of Management Review*, 14(4): 562–78.
Quinn, R. E. (1988) *Beyond Rational Management: Mastering the Paradoxes and Competing Demands of High Performance*, San Francisco: Jossey-Bass.
Rasche, A. (2008) *The Paradoxical Foundation of Strategic Management*, Heidelberg: Physica-Verlag.
Rothenburg, A. (1979) *The Emerging Goddess: The Creative Process in Art, Science and Other Fields*, Chicago: University of Chicago Press.
Seligman, M. E. P. and Csikszentmihalyi, M. (2000) Positive Psychology: An Introduction, *American Psychologist*, 55(1): 5–14.
Senge, P., Scharmer, O., Jaworski, J. and Flowers, B. S. (2005) *Presence: Exploring Profound Change in People, Organisations and Society*, London: Nicholas Brealey Publishing.
Smith, K. and Berg, D. (1987) *Paradoxes of Group Life: Understanding Conflict, Paralysis and Movement in Group Dynamics*, San Francisco: Jossey-Bass.
Smith, W. K. and Lewis, M. W. (2011) Toward a Theory of Paradox: A Dynamic Equilibrium Model of Organizing, *Academy of Management Review*, 36(2): 381–403.
Streufert, S. and Swezey, R. W. (1986) *Complexity, Managers and Organizations*, Orlando, FL: Academic Press.
Torbert, W. R. (1987) *Managing the Corporate Dream: Restructuring for Corporate Success*, Homewood, IL: Dow-Jones Irwin.
Wood, A. (1990) *Hegel's Ethical Thought*, Cambridge: Cambridge University Press.

3

THE PARADOX OF INVOLVEMENT AND DETACHMENT

The importance of practical judgment

In this chapter I want to consider the ways in which managers and leaders are called upon to take a more detached, long-term view of the development of their organizations at the same time as they are caught up in daily processes of organizational life. And yet it is precisely these ordinary, everyday activities which can have a profound effect on how the organization will evolve over time. As I explained in Chapter 1 drawing on insights from the complexity sciences, I am assuming that organizations develop as a result of what everyone is doing and not doing in the organization, and because of their relationships with others in other organizations, developments which may or may not be anticipated or reflected in formal plans.

We are all subject to longer-term social processes and trends over which we have little control and which shape what we find ourselves talking about and having to respond to. At the same time, the precise way we participate together in making sense of particular social or organizational trends and the way these impact upon our pre-reflected plans, the way we cooperate and compete to get things done, is not predetermined. In other words, it is a paradox that we are shaping whatever it is that we have to deal with at the same time as it is shaping us.

I have been making the case in this book that what I have been calling the dominant or orthodox management literature pays much greater attention to the longer term and the more abstract aspects of organizational life, and assumes that the manager or leader is in control of these. Planning and strategizing are considered to be the most important parts of their jobs with the supposition that managers and leaders are better able to steer organizational futures than I think they are. The reason I question the notion of control is because my experience of work is that social life in general and organizational life in particular are both predictable and unpredictable: managers are both in control and not in control at the same time.

Indeed, sometimes our efforts to manage and direct bring about the circumstances that we seek most to avoid. The most obvious example of this is the creation of complex financial derivatives in the early 2000s. The idea was that designing highly abstract financial products could parcel up debt and spread it throughout the financial system, making risk almost disappear. Instead, it had exactly the opposite effect of distributing risk to the degree that none of the banks knew the extent of the risk they were exposed to.

I am certainly not saying that leadership and management in organizations are not required. I am merely encouraging a more measured discussion of what leaders and managers are capable of achieving. The alternative to doing so, it seems to me, is to leave leaders and managers in a vulnerable position of having highly unrealistic expectations about what they might accomplish with others, including the myth of the transformational manager.

As I have mentioned previously, the sociologist Norbert Elias was particularly interested in the way that the warp and weft of social life was driven by the interweaving of intentions, and how the past informs the present. In order better to understand the unique flow of social life, he argued (2001), we must adopt the perspective of both the airman and the swimmer. Unlike many objects in nature which are relatively unchanging, society is riven by tensions, disruptions and explosions. 'Decline alternates with rise, war with peace, crisis with booms' (2001: 12).

These disruptions are driven by the interweaving activities of highly social, interdependent people like ourselves competing and cooperating to get things done. Elias argues that it is only from the perspective of the airman that we are able to gain some detachment, a relatively undistorted view of the order of the long course of historical changes and the way we are forming and are formed by them. These long-term historical trends are extremely hard to resist, even by very powerful coalitions of people or groups.

However, there is nothing inevitable about our actions and reactions to the processes in which we find ourselves participating. Only by adopting the perspective of the swimmer, who is obliged to take action in the moment itself, is it possible to see how varied are the different pressures that are brought to bear on the particular circumstances in which we find ourselves acting, in order that we might create opportunities to bring about outcomes of a different kind.

Thinking about the implications of Elias's ideas for leaders and managers, then, it seems to me that he is suggesting the importance of our learning to be both involved and detached at the same time. Opportunities for doing something different, of responding to potentialities, only arise in the messy reality of the moment. However, moments are also inextricably linked in longer-term trends, which are very constraining. How might managers and leaders develop their dual focus?

Entrepreneurial leadership

I was reminded of Elias's thoughts on how we might make sense of the social when I came to reflect on a session that a colleague and I had recently run together. We had been invited to talk to a group of senior university managers about how they might aspire to being 'entrepreneurial leaders' and to explain the role that insights from the complexity sciences might play in helping them to understand the new demands that would be placed on them. The initiative arose from a decade-long discussion in higher education in the US and the UK about the changing circumstances of universities and the way they need to adapt to different expectations about their role.

In the UK in particular there has been a huge expansion of university provision, a big increase in the numbers of students attending and a decrease in the amount of money that government has committed to universities. This in turn has led to the charging of fees to students when previously higher education had been free in the UK, and concomitantly an increased marketization of the tertiary sector, with universities competing both for students and for different funding streams to compensate for their loss of income from the government.

One thread of this discussion, which is contested, with many points of view arguing for and against the changes in the sector, is that universities need to become more entrepreneurial. The suggestion is that it is no longer enough for universities to be 'ivory towers', but they must demonstrate their usefulness to the public and particularly to business. The idea is that universities need to become fluent with the 'triple helix' relationship between universities, government and industry (Etzkowitz, 2008) so that they might become more innovative, serving both public and private needs. They are moving from a Mode 1 model of autonomous academic discovery funded by government, to a Mode 2 model of being interdependent with a variety of stakeholders (Dooley and Kirk, 2007).

Navigating this interdependence, then, requires particular entrepreneurial skills and approaches which may have been lacking previously in the sector. As is usual in these types of discussions, there is a strong implication that leaders and managers in the sector need to 'transform' their practice in order to cope with the new realities, and with it an accompanying idea that some staff are likely to resist strongly.

Many of these debates are summed up in a joint publication between the National Council for Graduate Entrepreneurship and the Said Business School at Oxford University, which is entitled *Leading the Entrepreneurial University: Meeting the Entrepreneurial Development Needs of Higher Education Institutions* (Gibb et al., 2009), a report which formed the basis for the training programme that we were invited to join as contributors. The report reviews the debates about the changing role of the sector and concludes that the exceptional demands placed upon universities, with great complexity within universities and between them and other stakeholders, needs exceptional leadership capacity. If universities are to be entrepreneurial, then they require entrepreneurial leaders.

According to the report, the entrepreneurial leader in a university will be required 'gradually to build a culture of rewarding innovation in every department rather than a culture of defence' (2009: 23) and to 'to infuse departments with entrepreneurial values' (ibid). They will do this by being able to 'communicate a compelling vision', they 'will focus upon bottom up empowerment for ownership of innovation and experiment' and will have a 'strong strategic orientation' (ibid). The authors of the report agree that this model of leadership has a great deal in common with a much older notion of transformational leadership (Bass, 1990), but it is still 'distinctive'.

One of the distinctive features of entrepreneurial leadership is thought to arise for the environment of 'hypercomplexity' which pertains in the sector. The justification for uniting the two ideas, entrepreneurial leadership and the complexity sciences, was illustrated with the usual Cartesian two-by-two grid in the report. One axis of the grid plots the certain to the uncertain, the other plots the simple to the complex. According to the grid, entrepreneurial leaders have to be operating in the top right hand quartile entitled 'complex and uncertain'. How might entrepreneurial university leaders act in complex and uncertain environments in order to unlock the entrepreneurial talents of the staff they lead?

It was this area, the combination of complex circumstances and the requirement for university leaders to act into them in an entrepreneurial way, that my colleague and I were invited to address with a cohort of senior managers engaged in a year-long programme to turn them into entrepreneurial leaders.

Thinking about the invitation from the perspective of the airman and the swimmer

One way of understanding the whole exercise, for a moment from the perspective of the airman in Elias's terms, is as another example of a trend, now three decades old, where there is a valorization of transformational organizational change through the agency of leadership. The supposition that leaders have a unique role in helping to shape change has become a largely unquestioned assumption, which I have written about previously (Mowles, 2011) from a critical perspective, as have many others. The report I quote above repeats many of the tropes of conventional thinking about leadership that one might associate with the orthodox, taken-for-granted literature on leadership and management, particularly as it should be taken up in the public sector, which has been substantially critiqued elsewhere (Tourish, 2013; Martin and Learmonth, 2012; Ford and Harding, 2007; Khurana, 2007; Alvesson and Sveningsson, 2003; Rost, 1991).

For example, in their article describing the way in which the concept of leadership has become embedded in the discourse in the NHS, Martin and Learmonth (2012) compare and contrast the interviews which they carried out at the end of the 1990s with senior executives in the health service, with a study they undertook of Department of Health documents during the 2000s. The authors note the way in which many of their respondents had joined the health service as administrators at a time when this had not been thought of as a pejorative term, although at the time of the interviews it had become such, and was now negatively compared with management.

Equally, at the end of the 1990s senior executives made very little distinction between the term 'manager' and 'leader', using them interchangeably. Throughout the 2000s the Department of Health documents reviewed by the authors seem to mark a clear distinction between management and leadership as discrete realms of activity, and for the term leadership to be applied to a wider and wider group of stakeholders including front-line staff and even patients consulted about NHS reform.

The authors point to the contradiction between, on the one hand, the narrative of decentralization of power and distribution of leadership amongst a broader and broader constituency of groups of people contained in the official documents, whilst on the other hand the government was setting up more and more structures aimed at centralizing control and pulling more and more activity under its surveillance, with performance management regimes, audit and inspection agencies.

For Martin and Learmonth, the appeal to leadership is a form of rhetorical device, a kind of cooptation where local managers are invited to work with and support the process of greater centralization. The invitation of a critical mass of actors into the discussion of leadership and change in the NHS may be enough to minimize dissent, the authors claim, if the status and reward of being identified as a leader is enough to persuade actors that they are key contributors to change: 'The idea of "leadership" may make it more attractive for doctors to take on particular roles in organizations, and make them more sympathetic to policy changes of the kind traditionally opposed by the medical profession' (2012: 287).

The pervasiveness of the idea that leaders and leadership is central to public sector 'reform' has led to the creation of a Leadership Foundation in Higher Education (LFHE) in 2003, set up by the Department for Education and Skills, and the Leadership Academy for the NHS, which was set up in 2011. These in turn generate leadership training courses and literature and perpetuate what have become taken for granted ideas about visionary and transformational leadership. The NHS Leadership Framework bears many similarities to the entrepreneurial leadership framework developed for higher education set out in the report I quote. It also involves NHS leaders creating a vision and delivering on the strategy, encouraging innovation and facilitating transformation.

This kind of vocabulary is so extensive in ordinary discourse that it is very difficult to oppose or to think about the particular difficulties that different organizations face in any other way. It is often the vocabulary of first resort and, despite the claims to distinctiveness, the idea of the transformational leader is endlessly recycled.

Narratives about the imperative for change and the need for a different type of leadership/management are much less likely to value what organizations might already be doing to innovate so far, and tend to be relentlessly future-oriented, as I explore in the next chapter on stability and change in organizations. Business schools and the academics producing books and journal articles play no small part in buttressing the idea that particular new conditions require particular new responses, and that managers and leaders are a uniquely qualified cadre of individuals to help us survive the necessary transition from our current undesirable state towards some new ideal.

Developing entrepreneurial leaders

As part of the preparation for our own session, my colleague and I were invited to attend the prior session conducted by a forum theatre group who specialized in working with companies, so that we would be better able to speak into some of the themes that arose from it. As co-participants in the forum theatre event, both of us were obliged in the beginning to play the usual facilitators' games, which in my view are designed to bring about participant obedience. These usually involve plenty of games encouraging acts of personal disclosure, or semi-humiliating exercises ostensibly to alleviate self-consciousness but, in my experience, they often have the opposite effect.

Forum theatre is an improvisational theatre technique originally developed by Augusto Boal, a Brazilian theatre director, in the late 1960s and early 1970s (Boal, 1973/2008), as a technique of emancipation. Drawing on the ideas of his colleague and friend Paulo Freire (1996), an emancipatory educationalist, Boal developed theatre techniques to encourage particularly poor and marginalized communities so that they might stage plays describing the circumstances of their oppression. The idea is that they could improvise and experiment with ways of challenging it: the intention is to make the circumstances of their oppression more visible to them and to embolden them to develop different strategies for overcoming them. A wide variety of theatre groups have sprung up in the West which draw on Friere's ideas and Boal's techniques, and some of them also work with companies.

The way this particular company practised forum theatre was to borrow an idea from one of the participants about something that was going on for her at work, in this case having to break bad news to an employee about merging two teams, and to rehearse the playlet over and over again, demonstrating different 'behaviours' on the part of the person playing the manager, as well as trying to elicit particular 'behaviours' in the person playing the member of staff. The role play ignored the complex hinterland of the particular circumstances contributing to the role play, and concentrated instead on helping the manager to dominate. The main idea adopted by the two actors from the company was that the managers in the room could also learn to be actors and could present as being charming, convincing and empathetic towards their staff so that they would accept the (usually) bad news that they had to give them. We even spent some time trying to encourage the 'staff member' to be sympathetic to the manager for having to break bad news.

Inherent in this way of working was the idea of behaviouralism and linear cause and effect: a particular behaviour by the manager was bound to elicit a particular response from the managed. Additionally, the person being managed was supposed not just to accept the idea of change, even if it was to his or her disadvantage, but to be pleased about it. This was unthinkingly management as manipulation and the opposite of what we had been led to understand that 'entrepreneurial leadership' was all about, i.e. empowering others.

It was clear that some of the participants felt uncomfortable, both with some of the lessons that we were supposed to be learning about how to behave, but also as the degree of manipulation became more and more refined. Nonetheless, we all continued to participate, some enthusiastically, others out of politeness and from the constraint of not calling the game we were obliged to play into question.

In my experience of forum theatre, when used well it encourages a focus on experience, judgment, complexity and reflexivity. The audience is invited to contribute ideas about situations which they find particularly difficult, or perhaps oppressive, as a way of exploring with others how they might move forwards together. The participants do not come away with one lesson, one tool or technique, nor are they concerned to manipulate one another, but rather to find a way forward in often difficult circumstances, which sometimes neither the managers nor the managed are particularly enjoying. Where good forum theatre is dialogic, this was monologic; where good forum theatre evokes richness, this was very single track. Forum theatre can often evoke a subtle ethical complexity which confronts all players in a particular situation and resonates strongly with the audience as they are called to reflect upon their own work situations and find similarities and differences.

What was interesting was that a group of very senior managers in universities throughout the UK supposedly learning to become entrepreneurial leaders had quickly fallen into learning and developing techniques of disciplinary power (Foucault, 1991). This was seemingly completely at odds with the narrative of empowerment and creativity that is supposed to accompany the entrepreneurial activity of leaders in the sector trying to drag their colleagues into the opportunities of the twenty-first century in tertiary education.

When it was possible to do so, and because we could not bear any more of this, my colleague and I beat a hasty retreat so we could 'prepare our session'.

Taking the perspective of the swimmer

At the beginning of our own session with the same group of managers my colleague started by taking the perspective of the swimmer and talked about how he had experienced the previous event, as an uncomfortable lesson in manipulation. Talking about the emancipatory origins of forum theatre he noted how we had all just participated in practising it in exactly the opposite sense, as a way of oppressing others.

This led into his talk about dominant, often taken-for-granted ways of speaking about leadership and management and some of the alternatives, drawing on the complexity sciences. We started a discussion about how particular ways of talking about the role of managers and leaders have come to dominate and how one strong theme of contemporary leadership discourse privileges change and over-coming 'resistance' to change. This is what we had spent the last session acting out and having reinforced for us. Luckily, it was presented in such an extreme form that all of us could recognize what was going on as it was taking place, although none of us had found a way of disrupting it. We can link this directly to the daily experience of working in organizations where we are constantly called on to make judgments about how much to play the game and how much to call the game into question (Bourdieu, 1991: 58).

My colleague's disclosure led to others being able to say how they, too had experienced discomfort during the previous session and enabled them to reflect on some of the difficulties they were facing in their own universities, whether this involved their facing challenges that might be linked to the theme of entrepreneurial leadership or not. Ironically, their experience of one extreme interpretation of leadership and management had allowed them to reflect upon the subtleties and nuances of their own situations in contrast. This allowed me to question with the group whether there is such a thing as entrepreneurial leadership and to explore what we think leaders and managers might be doing when they try to go on in circumstances in which they themselves feel constrained, and in which none of the options may be good ones.

The society of individuals

The afternoon was a good example of what Norbert Elias (2001) was writing about in *The Society of Individuals* and how longer-term social trends are hard to resist and work against, even for the most powerful people. Everyone in the room, some of whom were very senior managers in UK universities, found themselves, for one reason or another, on a leadership development course, which attempted to inculcate what it had previously presented as distinctive skills necessary for a particular phase of development of the tertiary education sector. We were all, more or less, relatively willing subjects, yet we were drawn into ways of behaving which took us a long way from the rather idealized prescriptions for entrepreneurial leadership.

Similar leadership development courses have arisen over time as an irresistible development in contemporary organizational life and the kinds of leadership approaches one can learn are legion. To name but three of the sorts of leadership development courses that one might be exposed to, there are 'appreciative' leadership (Lewis, 2011), 'distributed' leadership (Spillane, 2006) and 'servant' leadership (Greenleaf, 2002), each with their particular prescriptions and models. The leadership phenomenon is one which Khurana (2007) and Tourish (2013) date back to the beginning of the 1980s, with the gradual separation of the concept of leadership from management. As we have seen from the examples of the health and education services in the UK above, public services in the UK have not been immune to the infection.

We might draw two differing conclusions from our experience from the perspective of the swimmer: either there is much more involved in entrepreneurial leadership than we might have been led to believe, i.e. there is a much less-discussed shadow side of the entrepreneurial university, which is not so positive and empowering for those members of staff the entrepreneurial leader is attempting to lead.

A new emphasis on a particular way of working is likely to be good for some staff and bad for others, and it is highly unlikely that all members of staff will fit the entrepreneurial mould. Or one might conclude the discourse on leadership is very overblown: despite the warm words about opportunity and creativity, the most obvious powers that leaders and managers have in organizational life is to scrutinize, discipline and punish, a point made by Ralph Stacey in his latest book on the tools and techniques of leadership (Stacey, 2012). Some staff may remain resolutely uninspired and untransformed and may actively resist organizational changes.

At the same time Elias is suggesting that there is no way of escaping longer-term trends, he also argues that the way these trends develop is neither automatic nor inevitable. Although one is highly unlikely to be able to avoid discussions about leadership or leadership development courses, this is not the same as saying that they play out everywhere the same, as the above example demonstrates. Elias calls upon us to notice the particular pressures that participating in these longer-term trends brings about and to explore what the possibilities are for different outcomes:

> Every large and complex society has, in fact, both qualities: it is very firm and very elastic. Within it scope for individual decision constantly appears. Opportunities present themselves that can either be seized or missed. Crossroads appear at which people must choose, and on their choices, depending on their social position, may depend either their immediate personal fate or that of a whole family, or, in certain situations, of entire nations and groups within them ... And whichever opportunity he seizes, his deed becomes interwoven with those of others; it unleashes further chains of actions the direction and provisional outcome of which depend not on him but on the distribution of power and the structure of tensions within this whole mobile human network.
>
> *(Elias, 2001: 49–50)*

Elias aspired to developing a different vocabulary for describing processes of social change which did not draw on mechanistic or static descriptions of what for him were constantly fluctuating figurations of power between people. For Elias, taking the twin perspective of the airman and the swimmer is one way of describing what it would mean to be more scientific about the social. Rather than assuming that we could ever be 'objective' about social processes which have formed us, Elias was optimistic that we could learn to be more detached about our involvement in social life (Elias, 1987).

The entrepreneurial leadership event that my colleague and I were invited to participate in has become a repeating and ubiquitous pattern of organizational life which has a history, and which has become unstoppable and virtually unquestionable. So, there is no ignoring the phenomenon, and usually no opting out, as my colleague and I found out. However, there are ways of engaging with it differently, potentially to call what is going on into question and to find different ways of talking about it.

Thinking about reflection and reflexivity

In order to notice and reflect upon what is going on in organizational life, and to work out what might be the implications for me, and for us, I would like to explore the concepts of reflection and reflexivity. These are the ways in which we can respond to Elias's invitation to notice 'opportunities ... which can be seized or missed', because to do so implies some degree of detachment from what is going on. I will define what I mean by the terms in more depth later, but for now I think these are important concepts for managers to address. At the same time it is also possible to over-promise the benefits of being reflective and reflexive, to present reflexivity as another 'tool' for managers to get on top of and control situations, or to assume that reflexivity is an unalloyed good.

As an example of the difficulty of getting firm hold of reflection and reflexivity, I think there are a number of problems with what I have done in the passage above. At the same time as setting out Elias's helpful analogy, I have done so in a way that suggests that it is possible consciously to adopt first one position, then the other, which makes it appear as though the two are distinct observational phases that one can embrace rationally and by choosing to do so. Instead, I would like to suggest that most of the time we are caught up in the game of organizational life mostly unreflectively, and we are so because we are invested in it, as I pointed out in Chapter 1. We play the game because it matters to us, and our commitment sometimes inhibits our ability to notice what we are doing (Bourdieu, 1997: 212).

There are also semi-automatically operating mechanisms, such as guilt and shame, which we are socialized into, and which cause us to reflect upon what we are doing, but which we largely do not choose to experience: embarrassing moments tend to choose us. In another treatise, his major work entitled *The Civilizing Process* (2000), Elias reflected upon both the conscious and unconscious triggers of what he referred to as our increased ability over time to take a 'detour via detachment', as well as consciously controlling ourselves, which were accompanied by what he described as 'an automatic, blindly functioning apparatus of self-control' (2000: 368).

Nor can we always tell what is a short-term concern, and what is more long term, so it is difficult to know exactly what perspective we are adopting on those rare occasions when we notice our involvement in the game. There is not always such a neat division between the perspectives of the airman and the swimmer, between our ability to describe a longer-term trend and the immediacy of what we have to deal with. They are both inextricably linked.

In the next few pages I will sketch briefly how we have come to understand reflection and reflexivity and the way it has been taken up in management research, as well as the potential benefits and drawbacks of each.

What are reflection and reflexivity and what might they help managers to pay attention to?

To start out with some definitions, I am claiming that reflection and reflexivity are two connected but separate activities. Where reflection is the ability to detach oneself from our involvement, and is a second order process, what Tsoukas (2009) calls 'self-distanciation', I am considering reflexivity as a third order process, where we are able to think about how we are thinking about how we are engaged. In reflecting we will be thinking and feeling deeply about something, possibly our own experience, whilst in becoming reflexive we are bringing that reflection back to ourselves and may be changed by it.

As we will explore later, the two processes are distinct, yet connected, and we are all capable of both to a greater or lesser degree. I am working on an assumption here that as social beings we are always acting mostly in a taken-for-granted way with others, and our activities are forming us, but also restricting us, in reflecting on, and being reflexive about the very social activity that we might want to think about.

We cannot start out by being aware of our prejudices. Reflexivity calls into question how we know what we know and how we have come to know it: as meaning-making animals we are also capable of trying to understand the meanings that we are making and how we are making them. We 'bend back' (*re-flectere*) our thinking on itself and on ourselves in order to call into question our own role in understanding what it is we are trying to understand. In other words, and according to management researchers Alvesson and Sköldberg (2009), we interpret our interpretations and this can be the beginning of a critique of what we are doing and how we understand what we are doing. It is the beginning of the exploration of what we take for granted and our habitual ways of thinking about the world, our prejudices if you like, which are invisible to us until we are brought hard up against them through the experience of difference.

Some commentators talk about 'radical' reflexivity, or even 'self'-reflexivity, but mean different things by it. For example, Pollner (1991) talks about radical reflexivity as a means of constantly drawing attention to the fact that: 'immutable or natural aspects of reality are of contingent, socio–historical construction' (1991: 379). In other words, reflexivity should never let things settle, but should point out continuously how history and context contribute to the meanings that we make. Meanwhile, Cunliffe (2003) thinks that radical reflexivity calls into question not only the phenomenon we are concerned about but also brings in ourselves; in other words, it should draw in the assumptions of the researcher/manager for discussion.

Lynch (2000) argues that radical reflexivity, particularly in science and technology studies, problematizes both the natural and social sciences and calls into question positive claims about progress, knowledge and professional autonomy. When I talk about reflexivity in this chapter I am already using it in the 'radical' sense and as an amalgam of some of the above definitions. I am assuming, after Mead (1934), that mind is a social phenomenon, and the consciousness and self-consciousness involves a conversation of gestures with oneself, which is the same but internalized process of gesturing and responding with others. We cannot help but be aware of ourselves in relation to others, which is why I am claiming that both reflection and reflexivity are already social activities. For me, to call the second order activity of thinking about how we are thinking about our involvement with others as 'radical' or 'self-reflexivity' is tautology.

I am also interested in organizational processes which encourage reflexivity amongst people working together. If we think of reflexivity as already being a social process because it involves an internal dialogue using the social medium of language, then promoting such activity in groups may help amplify the tendencies of people to be more conscious of their own practices in relation to others. This has particular relevance for the practice of management since it takes place in groups. What it might encourage is the ability to pay attention to what is currently going on and to consider how it might be linked to the longer-term trends to which it is contributing.

Some background to reflection and reflexivity

One of the most energetic exponents of the benefits of reflection, a tradition which dates all the way back to Socrates, was the American pragmatist philosopher

John Dewey. He took a radical and optimistic view of human intelligence, and argued against what he regarded as the unnecessary splitting of a researcher from the object of his or her enquiry when it comes to life and action, which is more usual when thinking about method practised in the natural sciences. In other words he was concerned to overcome the dualism of the subjective and the objective when we are considering problems that arise for us in everyday life. For Dewey there are not objects in the world on the one hand, and private states of consciousness which are unconnected to them on the other. Rather, because of our physiology, we are able to think about our involvement with objects in the world as we are involved with them – the subjective and objective are paradoxically intertwined.

When it comes to experience, which is messy, changeable and evolving, and involves us both as subjects and objects, there is no god's eye view of what is going on, and no certainty about what it means, he argued. It is this god's eye view that he referred to as a spectator theory of knowledge (2008: 163) and which I mentioned earlier. He is making the case that we cannot form abstract theories about what we should be doing without also paying attention to what we are doing as actors, including our feelings, values and imaginative involvement. From a management perspective, then, it is important not to get carried away with our abstractions about what we might achieve in the future, or become inordinately wrapped up in our schematic representations of work or the ubiquitous two-by-two grids which proliferate in business schools.

As far as experience is concerned, Dewey was sceptical that we could ever establish timeless and unchanging certain knowledge because experience itself is always changing. However, he was optimistic that we could develop skills more patiently to pay attention to the everyday. Dewey argued that intelligent reflection, and he makes no distinction between reflection and reflexivity, was a very helpful and appropriately scientific way of enquiring into everyday life and the problems which afflict us there, with a view to learning how to act differently.

The aim of reflection is always practical, to deal with an obstacle which prevents our progress. He was striving for a consonance between the method of inquiry and the object enquired into: where experience is constantly changing and evolving, so too should be the method of appraising it. The intelligent person needs to develop an eye for context and consequences. For him reflection was a method suited better to understanding the everyday messiness of getting things done together, since in reflecting we create more objects for reflection; experience becomes enriched and more adequately described (1958: 7). The process of reflection creates more opportunities for thinking about our thinking and so promotes our understanding and enjoyment of what we are doing, particularly if we constantly link back to original experience itself:

> Thus we discover that we believe many things not because the things are so, but because we have become habituated through the weight of authority, by imitation, prestige, instruction, the unconscious effect of language etc. We learn, in short, that the qualities we attribute to objects ought to be imputed

to our own ways of experiencing them, and that these in turn are due to the force of intercourse and custom. This discovery marks an emancipation; it purifies and remakes the objects of our direct primary experience.

(ibid: 14)

Dewey is concerned that we try to liberate ourselves from our own habits and thought patterns when they have ceased to be useful and to try through reflection to become more aware of our taken-for-granted assumptions. This is not to say that habits are unhelpful: habits form, he argues, precisely because they develop as shortcuts to accomplishing routine behaviour. They can be very useful, but they may become inhibiting over time. He constantly points out that the way we understand the world is inextricably linked to the way we have been socialized – there is no entirely objective viewpoint about our activities. Managers, then, could usefully find time to reflect upon how they have become habituated to understanding things in a particular way, and to question whether these habits of thought are still helpful.

Reflection may sound like a very passive activity which is the opposite of acting, but this is not the way that Dewey meant it. This is an important thing to bear in mind in organizational life where there is often a bias towards action, and talking about what is going on is treated as some kind of luxury. For Dewey, thinking, feeling and forming intentions were all varieties of action, and when we can bring them under scrutiny, they can better prepare us for acting more intelligently in the world. He argues that when things are uncertain and indeterminate it would be foolish to rush around acting without thinking; it would be much better to participate in the very practical activity of thinking about what we are doing as a way of doing it better:

A disciplined mind takes delight in the problematic and cherishes it until a way out is found that approves itself upon examination. The questioning becomes an active questioning, a search. The scientific attitude may almost be defined as that which is capable of enjoying the doubtful; scientific method is, in one aspect, a technique for making a productive use of doubt by converting it into operations of definite inquiry.

(Dewey, 2008: 183)

I am reminded of the emphasis in many organizations on what has come to be termed 'delivery' – the previous government in the UK even had a delivery office, by which was meant that once leaders had determined a course of action what was needed was lots of implantation activity, but sometimes very little thinking.

Dewey is making a strong case for what it means to be scientific about the social, which is an active mobilization of doubt, a process of continuous enquiry. One way of better understanding Dewey's method here is to notice the way he brings into play a number of paradoxes: we can only become more certain by investigating uncertainty; when we have cause to doubt this can lead to a line of definite questioning; and we can be more objective about social life if we include our subjective experience. In this way Dewey is trying to hang on to the generative tension of a concept and its opposite, in the same way that Elias does in his analogy of the airman and the swimmer.

Dewey considered his approach to exemplify experimental method, where we mobilize doubt and disciplined enquiry, are concerned not to jump to conclusions too early and rush into action, and try out our temporary conclusions in a practical way to see if our deliberations have made a difference. This was no different as far as he was concerned when dealing with moral and value-based aspects of social life. On the one hand, he did not imagine that we should or could simply abandon our religious and moral traditions partly because he regarded human beings as being quite conservative. Nor did he think we should just take a leap into moral relativism. However, on the other hand, he was also insistent that we should not blindly apply moral laws as though they were inflexible and relevant in all circumstances:

> A moral law, like a law in physics, is not a thing to swear by and stick to at all hazards; it is a formula of the way to respond when specified conditions present themselves. Its soundness and pertinence are tested by what happens when it is acted upon. Its claim or authority rests finally upon the imperativeness of the situation that has to be dealt with, not upon its own intrinsic nature – as any tool achieves dignity in the measure of tools served by it.
>
> *(ibid: 222)*

Dewey was heavily influenced by both Hegel and Darwin and took a radically evolutionary approach to understanding the social. For him, it is not just experience that changes, but so do the norms and categories by which we try to interpret experience. If we assume that standards outside experience can be brought to bear unproblematically on the situation under consideration, then we may find that we are too rigid and inflexible in our thinking, and our standards may not serve us well. The means and methods we employ are as important as the ends we aspire to – for Dewey there is no separating means and ends. Our value judgments and standards need to keep pace with the way what we would like to judge is evolving over time.

Readers will be reminded about what I was saying about Hegel's speculative logic in Chapter 2, that not only the content of thought changes, but the categories by which we order thought may also change. For managers I think the implication is that previous experience is very important in making sense of what is going on for us now in organizational terms, but in novel circumstances our experiences may blind us to what we need to see.

To push the point even further, the dangers of not thinking about how we are thinking are not just that we might be too rigid or inflexible in trying to work together, but that being unreflective prevents us from seeing the moral or human aspects of what we are dealing with. Another philosopher writing in the same pragmatic philosophic tradition as Dewey, Richard Bernstein, writes extensively about the importance of considering our perspectives on the world as fallible, in development and thus worthy of continuous enquiry.

During his life he got to know the political theorist Hannah Arendt and wrote a book about her work (Bernstein, 1996), as a way of grappling with the importance of reflecting and thinking about what we are doing, because this concerned her too. Bernstein's book on Arendt dwells in particular on her coverage of the Eichmann trial for *The New York Times*, which she wrote up in a report entitled 'Eichmann in Jerusalem: A Report on the Banality of Evil' (2006), because of the storm of protest it created at the time and subsequently. Arendt was struck by Eichman's defence that he was 'just doing his job' in ordering the mass killing of Jews. The significance of the defence for Arendt were its implications for all of us: she did not consider him a uniquely evil monster, but as someone, caught up in a totalitarian ideology, who had lost the ability to take himself as an object to himself, and to think about what he was doing in relation to others.

Of course, in Nazi Germany he was not the only one. By describing evil as 'banal', according to Bernstein, she by no means meant to mitigate the seriousness of what he and others did, nor to absolve him and others from moral responsibility. Rather, she wanted to point to the potential in all of us to lose sight of what we are doing because of the loss of the ability to think and make reflective judgments in our daily lives. Bernstein tries to expand her argument as follows:

> Thinking must not be confused with knowing ... The type of thinking that Arendt is speaking about is not something that is the prerogative of philosophers or 'professional thinkers', but one that can be practiced by everyone. Thinking involves an internal dialogue – what Arendt calls a 'two-in-one' – in which there is a dialogue between me and myself ... It was the ability to judge, to tell right from wrong in particular circumstances that was lacking in Eichmann.
> *(Bernstein, 1996: 171–72)*

In Eichmann's case, he seemed to have lost the ability to make judgments and to feel guilt and shame about what he did, particularly with the defence he mounted. Evil resulted, according to Arendt, because Eichmann could neither think and judge, nor feel shame. He was unable to make the link between the particular and the general and to work out the implications for himself and for others.

Arendt, Bernstein and Dewey are pointing to the fact that in our daily lives we will encounter all kinds of new circumstances in which our moral precepts may only be a partial help. There are not necessarily any rules to appeal to, and/or simply following the rules that we have may propel us into all kinds of moral hazard. What is important, then, is to pay attention to the particulars of the specific situation into which we find ourselves acting with others and to find ways of discussing what this means for us. Arendt, Bernstein and Dewey are all appealing to the importance of reflection and reflexivity, of thinking and judging. And of course, they are also pointing to the importance of reflexivity as a generator of civilized behaviour, since thinking about how we are thinking may also produce shame and embarrassment, socially formed and semi-automatic mechanisms which cause us to have a conscience about what we find ourselves caught up in.

The importance of reflection and reflexivity for managers

Why might any of this be important for managers? What relevance do arguments arising from particularly bleak periods in human history have for thinking about management?

Much is made in contemporary management literature and political discourse about the increasing complexity of organizational life, and how staff in organizations are subjected on a daily basis to constant change and uncertainty. The ability to become reflexive about these changes and how they are affecting working practices and people's capacity to get the job done, must be one way for managers to make sense of the uncertainty into which they are obliged to act. Reflexivity is not a hedge against uncertainty, nor does it make the complex simple, but it is an opportunity to think more critically about what is the same and what is different about the particular situation under review, and how the nature of the work is evolving. It opens up the prospect of thinking about whether the way things have always been done best serve current conditions and whether our habits of thought are justified.

Additionally, organizations are both political and moral spaces where particular practices become accepted, routine and widespread. There are always consequences of our actions, both good and bad, anticipated and unforeseen depending on one's viewpoint. In the UK, and in addition to the financial collapse which began to take significant effect in 2008, we have had a number of banking scandals where large numbers of managers have either encouraged or colluded in the fixing of the inter-bank lending or LIBOR rate, or misselling mortgage protection insurance, or laundering money from criminal gangs. Prior to this a large number of British Members of Parliament (MPs) were exposed as having fiddled their expenses. Quite often their defence was that they had done nothing wrong and were simply following the rules.

The examples I am quoting are not all the same and do not all have the same implications: so rigging the LIBOR rate and asking too few questions about laundered money has always been illegal, whereas in the case of the MPs sometimes they were encouraged to massage the rules by staff in the very office who paid them their expenses. However, and despite encouragement to do so, some MPs still refused to claim more than the absolute minimum they were entitled to, so over-claiming was not a universal phenomenon.

Nonetheless, the fact that these illegal, immoral or dubious practices continued over periods of time and involved substantial numbers of people raises questions about how such patterns arise in groups of people, and what prevents them from either noticing or changing their behaviour. One way of explaining what was going on, drawing on the arguments we have been identifying from, namely Arendt, Bernstein and Dewey, is the suggestion that in each of these cases the ability to raise doubts and questions publicly was severely curtailed.

Of course, this is not to argue that some of the people engaged in these activities were necessarily unaware of what they were doing, as Lewis's account of the current financial crisis (2011) seems to suggest. To a degree, it is impossible for human beings not to reflect on, and be reflexive about what they are doing. However, there is no guarantee that this translates into anything different from the prevailing practice. Lewis argues that many people in banks and other financial institutions showed an irrational belief in the financial models they were using, but there must have been others who had come to doubt them but who nonetheless saw advantages for themselves and/or their colleagues in continuing to play the game to their advantage. Equally, with British MPs, just because some made the argument that they felt that they had done nothing wrong does not mean that they all whole-heartedly believed this, even as they were saying it.

Part of the case for encouraging reflection and reflexivity in organizational life, then, is that it offers opportunities to make greater sense of uncertainty and change; it offers a chance to ask whether routines which have developed over time are still relevant to new circumstances, and to notice the way in which colleagues may have become caught up in the game. It allows for questioning of what may have become harmful practices, although this is not to imply that questioning is either easy to do, or will necessarily be effective.

Rather than just relying on scrutiny from outside the organization, which is increasingly the case in the public sector in the UK, where hospitals and schools are not trusted to declare how they are performing but are exposed to inspections from statutory agencies, the invitation to reflect and be reflexive can be a form of self-generated scrutiny. It has the potential for being a much more thorough way of judging the value of work, too, since it is grounded in the everyday reality of what people are doing, rather than proceeding from some general and pre-reflected standard.

Deflating some of the claims for reflection and reflexivity

Having made the case that it is important to call things into question it is time to subject the idea of reflexivity to the same treatment. To do otherwise would perhaps demonstrate too little reflexivity about reflexivity. As I pointed out in the opening chapters of this book, my argument proceeds dialectically, putting one side then the other, as a way of opening the question up further.

And perhaps this is the beginning of a critique of reflexivity, that it is hard to know when to stop being reflexive. When is it helpfully problematizing, and when does it simply undermine your own argument until you disappear into your own critique? For the critics of reflexivity, the idea that it is at the heart of enquiry into organizational life has the potential for not allowing anything to stand and so makes it extremely difficult to make solid claims about what is happening. They consider that it is relativizing and is in danger of pulling the questioner into infinite regress; in expressing doubt or questions about what is going on, the questioner then begins to doubt their own doubt, and so on. In organizational life you can see how this might lead to dithering.

Additionally, it is not always helpful or timely to call things into question, and reflexivity might become overly self-conscious. On the one hand, being reflexive can call attention to the game in which we find ourselves caught up, thus decentring the activity, and on the other hand the process can call attention to itself, so that the reflexive questioner themselves becomes temporarily the centre of attention. Alvesson et al. (2009) point to the irony that a reflexive attitude that claims to point out the weaknesses of other people's involvement is also something of a claim to superiority, of having access to a greater truth to undermine the taken-for-granted truths of those caught in the critical spotlight.

The narrative I set out at the beginning of this chapter shows how reflexive questioning was both destabilizing and disruptive, although it allowed participants in the workshop to engage in a different conversation than the one they thought they were going to have. Reflexivity can puncture the smooth running of organizational activity by introducing doubt and perhaps even mistrust and anxiety into groups of people trying to get things done together, especially if they are not particularly habituated to being explicitly reflexive together. Radically calling into question what is going on can be a shocking and exposing experience for people who are asked suddenly to bump up against themselves and their involvement.

And because this experience of exposing taken-for-granted assumptions may leave people feeling destabilized and vulnerable, many organizations have developed ways of avoiding the pain to which this might give rise. Another way of thinking about this avoidance is to understand it as an evasion of a challenge to authority or existing power relations. For example, in another article by the critical management scholars Mats Alvesson and his colleague André Spicer (2012), both explore the notion of what they call organizational 'functional stupidity'. By this they mean the number of different devices and methods that have become institutionalized in contemporary organizations through management theory and the practice of managers to render more difficult asking of questions and expressing doubt. This can be done through a variety of ways: by insisting that everyone be positive and constructive, for example.

The idea that we should be 'appreciative' and only accentuate the positive has become quite widespread in organizational life and takes shape in a particular form of consultancy called 'appreciative inquiry' (Cooperrider and Srivastva, 1987), which draws on the positive psychology movement in North America. Appreciative inquiry (AI) is informed by social constructionist thinking, which assumes that we already create our social worlds, that we are caught up in a web of our own weaving. AI then takes the next step with this thinking by arguing that if the social world is constructed and not found, then we can intend to create a social world of our own choosing: by being positive with one another we can construct a positive and appreciative environment in organizations. However, even AI practitioners have begun to notice how this way of working can restrict what it is possible to say publicly, and can provoke the very opposite of what it intends (Fitzgerald et al., 2010).

Another aspect of organizational functional stupidity is the variety of persuasive techniques that managers and leaders have learned to encourage employees to pay attention only to a narrow range of organizational concerns and to trust in an often heroic and idealized narrative about managers and 'visionary' leaders. Alvesson and Spicer consider this to be a form of identity manipulation, where employees are persuaded to develop a sense of self more in line with particular definitions of what is best for the organization. In other words, it attempts to perpetuate a particular configuration of power.

The function of functional stupidity is to facilitate the smooth operation of organizations and to maintain control, to work against the disruption that we have identified as one of the potential outcomes of reflexivity. Of course, if organizations are to achieve things then a degree of control will be necessary. As we have noted above, it is impossible to call everything into question all of the time. To a degree, functional stupidity 'works' because it reduces organizational uncertainty and time spent in calling things into question. It is, in Alvesson and Spicer's words, the 'pillar of organizational order' (2012: 1213).

A further set of doubts about reflexivity comes from Lynch (2000), who attempts to deflate the claims for the disruptive potential of reflexivity in organizations. He does so as a response to critics of reflexivity, who argue that the problem with it is that it is potentially relativizing and therefore is in danger of producing infinite regress. To argue that reflexivity could cause infinite regress in reasoning, he says, is to credit it with too much power. It may not be the devastating technique that its proponents claim for it, he argues.

In creating a typology of reflexivity, Lynch tries to demonstrate that it is both ubiquitous and unavoidable: it is part of being human. Nor is reflexivity necessarily challenging. Reflexive insights can be trivial and inconsequential, and are no more likely to lead to truth than the aspiration to 'be objective' is. According to Lynch: 'A self-consciously reflexive pronouncement may not necessarily strike others as profound and revealing. It may just as easily seem pretentious, silly or evasive' (2000: 47). Other scholars have also pointed out how reflexivity can be coopted by a particular organizational regime as a way of harnessing employees' reflective powers to sustain and enhance what they are doing, rather than challenging it.

Concluding thoughts on reflection and reflexivity

I began this chapter with a narrative about how a colleague and I had been asked to present some thoughts on an entrepreneurial leadership course attended by many senior managers from the UK higher education sector. By drawing on the sociology of Norbert Elias I pointed out how such courses have become an unstoppable trend in organizational life over the last 30 years connected to the proliferation of the discourse about leadership and leaders. Many organizations put on leadership courses for their staff which involve even the lowliest employees because it has become taken for granted that leadership is the key to organizational success.

In this particular incident my colleague and I were expected to say something about 'entrepreneurial leadership', which was presented as a novel development in the leadership discourse. It was supposed to be particularly relevant to senior managers in this sector trying to make the necessary transition from managing universities as ivory towers to 'bringing them into the twenty-first century', i.e. making them more responsive to communities and specifically to business. Entrepreneurial leadership was presented as being a unique conceptual response to the management of complexity, which would equip leaders in the sector with the necessary skills to 'transform' their institutions.

However, and coincidentally, when we attended the session prior to our own, which involved practising ways of convincing staff that organizational changes were 'good for them', we were made uncomfortable by what we took to be the promotion of techniques of manipulation and disciplinary control. Although managers and leaders are bound to be involved in the politics of everyday organizational life, and may have to do all kinds of things which leave them feeling uncomfortable, it struck us at the time that what we had experienced seemed to have little to do with the new transformational concept touted as entrepreneurial leadership.

In starting our own session afterwards we took the risk of drawing attention to what had just happened as a way of beginning a conversation about what we might mean by leadership, and whether entrepreneurial leadership was really offering anything new. We had not planned to do it this way, but we combined the perspective of Elias's swimmer, reflecting on the detail of what we had found ourselves doing together with the longer-term trend of developing such leadership courses, trying to contextualize this event in the way we understood longer-term trends.

One of the claims I am making about managing in organizations, then, from a complex responsive processes perspective is that it is not enough to engage with management in the abstract, but we must engage with the particular details of how longer-term organizational trends are functionalized, made practical, in everyday life. It is important to take the perspective of both the airman and the swimmer, to be alert both to the diachronic and synchronic nature of the event we are concerned with. That is to be alert to the longer-term perspective, as well as the specific circumstances themselves. Of course, this is easier said than done. We are not always capable of noticing the ways we are caught up in the game because, quite often, it is a game we care about and in which we are invested.

It is here that reflection and reflexivity may prove useful. In this chapter we have explored the ways in which both capacities are both ordinary, in as much as everybody is capable of being reflective and reflexive, and extraordinary. The ability to take ourselves as objects to ourselves makes us uniquely human and offers us the possibility of applying ourselves intelligently to practical problems that beset us in the hope that we can make better judgments about what to do next.

In this chapter I have taken what other scholars have called a radical view of reflexivity, since I am assuming that humans are social through and through. We become ourselves in responding to a world of other selves, so my assumption is that reflexivity inevitably links the self and others. I noted how Dewey, Bernstein and Arendt all made great claims for the systematic application of intelligent reflection and judgment to keep us alive to the particular and unique circumstances that we may be facing, and by applying ourselves to them, to appreciate their full complexity and, in doing so, to undertake more thoughtful action.

Past successes may not prepare us for the exigencies of the present, and for Dewey and Arendt we need to be alive to the limitations of the norms and categories that we bring to bear on lived experience. Reflexive questioning, I am arguing here, brings in the important dimension of the group: it enables the opportunity to ask what the implications are for us of what we find ourselves doing together. It allows us to talk about who we might be becoming and in doing so it keeps moral questions alive and perhaps it also carries the potential of allowing us to act with greater intelligence.

However, although the capacity to reflect and the ability to develop reflexivity in groups of staff in organizations has potential benefits, it can also be disruptive, anxiety-provoking and shaming. This is why, according to some scholars, management scholarship has developed a raft of techniques to bring about cultures of persuasion, in order to maintain control and to ensure that only a narrow range of questions become possible to ask. Contemporary organizational life can be relentlessly upbeat, a superficial celebration of the benefits of strong organizational management and leadership.

Reflexivity in its turn might just produce superficial explorations of what is happening and may produce nothing helpful or insightful. Alternatively, it can produce insights which call into question the very nature of what is being promoted; for example, whether there is such a definable concept as 'leadership' in general, let alone a specific manifestation of it known as 'entrepreneurial leadership'. On these occasions reflection and reflexivity can profoundly unsettle taken-for-granted assumptions and can call into question the inevitability of the circumstances we find ourselves facing together.

Although it would be impossible to get things done if everything was called into question all of the time, there has to be a role for the thoughtful exploration of our involvement with each other in organizational life. To do so obliges us to negotiate a number of paradoxes. We take risks in order to feel more secure in what we are doing: by probing uncertainty we may become more certain about what we are doing, at least for the next few steps. We strive to be more detached in order to appreciate a fuller quality of our involvement in what we are trying to do with others. It is part and parcel of organizational life that institutions should oblige us partially to conform to their requirements, but in order to exercise our judgment and freedom it behoves us to call these invitations to conform into question and to probe the legitimacy of what it is we are being asked to do or to believe in. From time to time we need to puncture what is presented as both normal and inevitable, and to resist simplifications of what we know to be much more complex concerns.

The question arises, then, as to how people in organizations acquire these abilities to reflect together, to become reflexive and to make judgments. The answer can only be that they do so through practice, through talking and experimenting together and by taking risks in uncovering some of the assumptions that they are making in undertaking the work. In doing so, they find themselves engaging with the messy uncertainties of the here and now of their work situation, and the contradictions and paradoxes that are inherent in it. As a result of this, they may be able more intelligently to take the next step together in their complex responsive processes of relating.

References

Alvesson, M. and Sveningsson, S. (2003) The Great Disappearing Act: Difficulties in Doing 'Leadership', *Leadership Quarterly*, 14(3): 359–81.

Alvesson, M. and Sköldberg, K. (2009) *Reflexive Methodology: New Vistas for Qualitative Research*, London: Sage.

Alvesson, M. and Spicer, A. (2012) A Stupidity-Based Theory of Organizations, *Journal of Management Studies*, 49(7): 1194–220.

Alvesson, M., Hardy, C. and Harley, B. (2009) Reflecting on Reflexivity: Reflexive Textual Practices in Organization and Management Theory, *Journal of Management Studies*, 45(3): 480–501.

Arendt, H. (2006) *Eichmann in Jerusalem: A Report on the Banality of Evil*, London: Penguin Books.

Bass, B. M. (1990) From Transactional to Transformational Leadership: Learning to Share the Vision, *Organizational Dynamics*, 18(3): 19–31.

Bernstein, R. (1996) *Hannah Arendt and the Jewish Question*, London: Sage.

Boal, A. (1973/2008) *The Theatre of the Oppressed*, London: Pluto Press.

Bourdieu, P. (1991) *Language and Symbolic Power*, Cambridge: Polity Press.

——(1997) *Pascalian Meditations*, Stanford: Stanford University Press.

Cooperrider, D. and Srivastva, S. (1987) Appreciative Inquiry in Organizational Life, *Research in Organizational Change and Development*, 1: 129–69.

Cunliffe, A. (2003) Reflexive Inquiry in Organizational Research: Questions and Possibilities, *Human Relations*, 56(8): 983–1003.

Dewey, J. (1958) *Experience and Nature*, New York: Dover Publications.

——(2008) *The Quest for Certainty: The Later Works 1925–1953, Vol 4, 1929*, Carbondale: Southern Illinois University Press.

Dooley, L. and Kirk, D. (2007) University–Industry Collaboration. Grafting the Entrepreneurial Paradigm onto Academic Structures, *European Journal of Innovation Management*, 10(3): 316–32.

Elias, N. (1987) Problems of Involvement and Detachment, in Elias, N. and Schröter, M. (eds.) and Jephcott, E. (trans.) *Involvement and Detachment*, Oxford: Basil Blackwell.

——(2000) *The Civilizing Process*, Oxford: Oxford University Press.

——(2001) *The Society of Individuals*, Oxford: Oxford University Press.

Etzkowitz, H. (2008) *The Triple Helix, University–Industry–Government: Innovation in Action*, London: Routledge.

Fitzgerald, S., Oliver, C. and Hoxsey, J. (2010) Appreciative Inquiry as a Shadow Process, *Journal of Management Inquiry*, 19(3): 220–33.

Ford, J. and Harding, N. (2007) Move Over Management: We Are All Leaders Now, *Management Learning*, 38(5): 475–93.

Foucault, M. (1991) *Discipline and Punish*, London: Penguin.

Friere, P. (1996) *Pedagogy of the Oppressed*, London: Penguin Books.

Gibb, A., Haskins, G. and Robertson, I. (2009) *Leading the Entrepreneurial University: Meeting the Entrepreneurial Development Needs of Higher Education Institutions*, London: NGCE.

Greenleaf, R. (2002) *Servant Leadership: A Journey into the Nature of Legitimate Power and Greatness*, Mawah, NJ: Paulist Press.

Hegel, G. W. F. (1807/1977) *Phenomenology of Spirit*, Oxford: Oxford University Press.

Khurana, R. (2007) *From Higher Aims to Hired Hands: The Social Transformation of American Business Schools and the Unfulfilled Promise of Management as a Profession*, Princeton, NJ: Princeton University Press.

Lewis, M. (2011) *Boomerang: Travels in the New Third World*, New York: W. W. Norton.

Lewis, S. (2011) *Positive Psychology at Work: How Positive Leadership and Appreciative Inquiry Create Inspiring Organizations*, Oxford: Wiley Blackwell.

Lynch, M. (2000) Against Reflexivity as a Virtue and Source of Privileged Knowledge, *Theory, Culture & Society*, 17(3): 26–54.

Martin, G. and Learmonth, M. (2012) A Critical Account of the Rise and Spread of 'Leadership': The Case of UK Healthcare, *Social Science and Medicine*, 74: 281–88.

Mead, G. H. (1934) *Mind, Self and Society from the Standpoint of a Social Behaviourist*, Chicago: University of Chicago Press.

Mowles, C. (2011) *Rethinking Management: Radical Insights from the Complexity Sciences*, London: Gower.

Pollner, M. (1991) Left of Ethnomethodology: The Rise and Decline of Radical Reflexivity, *American Sociological Review*, 56(3): 370–80.

Rost, J. C. (1991) *Leadership for the 21st Century*, Westport, CT: Praeger Publishers.

Spillane, J. (2006) *Distributed Leadership*, London: Jossey-Bass.

Stacey, R. (2012) *Tools and Techniques of Leadership and Management: Meeting the Challenge of Complexity*, London: Routledge.

Tourish, D. (2013) *The Dark Side of Organizational Leadership: a Critical Perspective*, London: Routledge.

Tsoukas, H. (2009) A Dialogical Approach to the Creation of New Knowledge in Organizations, *Organization Science*, 20(6): 941–57.

4

ATTEMPTS TO CHANGE ORGANIZATIONAL CULTURE

The paradox of the local and the global

It has become axiomatic that organizations need to change their cultures in order to reform or modernize, or to adapt to a changing world, or to bring about some kind of improvement in performance. Implicit (and sometimes explicit) in this kind of thinking is the idea that certain organizational cultures are more conducive to success than others, and that adopting a particular culture is likely to lead to organizational improvement. I wrote about this in connection with stimulating entrepreneurial leadership in universities in the last chapter. It has become a way of talking as though organizations can 'have' a culture which can be identified and changed from one state to another. Culture becomes reified, or 'thing-like', and is capable of being shaped and manipulated. Usually there is a close link in the discourse to values which are thought to relate causally and directly to behaviour. Restating the values required of staff, usually ones chosen by the chief executive or the senior team, is supposed to lead to improvements in the workplace.

Just as it has become a reflex whenever something goes wrong in an organization to assume that the culture needs changing, so employees have become used to preparing themselves for enquiries into their commitment and values. The danger is that the endless and invasive activity can lead to cynicism amongst employees and a sense of disappointment or hopelessness amongst managers. What is the strength of the argument that changes in organizational culture lead to improvements in performance?

This chapter will explore this contemporary discourse on culture change and will question how helpful it is to think about culture as arising in one organization and as being manipulable, even in a big organization. Rather, it will suggest that culture is a very rich concept which arises in the paradox of the local and global, and in an iterative and cyclical understanding of time. The past informs us in the present as we anticipate the future: social life is both repetitive and flexible, it changes, yet stays the same. I consider how broader social themes and questions of identity and belonging arise in particular organizations at particular times, and meld together with local practices which have a specific history.

The chapter explores the contemporary discourse on culture as being primarily about regulating people's conduct (Alvesson and Willmott, 2002), as a disciplinary project, which is likely to call out a range of responses in people, from the compliant to the rebellious. I suggest that the complex interplay of the particular and the general, the local and global, the *habitus*, is a phenomenon which no group of managers, no matter how powerful, can control, even if they can to a degree control behaviour. I consider some of the assumptions that repeat themselves again and again about the programme of culture change in organizations, which usually suggests the need for integration, convergence and stability. As a contrast I will put forward the idea that equally important are processes of subversion, explorations of difference, and the paradox of stable-instability.

This involves trying to develop an understanding of what we might mean by culture, drawing on a range of scholars who have tried to do exactly that, and to explore the way it contributes to identity and practice. I then intend taking a particular case study, the National Health Service (NHS) in the UK, which has been the object of much hullabaloo about the need for culture change. Concerning the NHS I look at the case made for culture change, inspired by the British Government, and a contemporary critique of it.

Some pervasive ideas about the connection between leadership and culture

Let me give an example of the kind of thinking that links managerial activity and organizational culture. A colleague with whom I sit on a trustee board recently sent me a questionnaire as part of her 360 degree appraisal evaluating her leadership skills. I was invited to respond as someone who knew her professionally, but was not part of the very large organization in which she worked: this was a 'view from outside' as part of the 360 degree appraisal. Although she was very senior, this colleague managed very few people directly, so could only be considered to be a leader in the broadest sense. I have aggregated some of the questions in the questionnaire together since it was quite long, but for each question I was asked to score her on a Likert scale assessing whether she was able to:

- promote teamwork and collaboration
- embrace/encourage/generate change and innovation – taking risks and standing by them (but not too many)
- be confident, positive and a risk-taker
- have an aspiring, compelling vision
- be able to communicate positively, stating clearly what he or she believes, conveying complex ideas with brevity
- create the right culture where people enjoy high morale
- acknowledge conflict and different positions and be able to reconcile them and concentrate on high performance and metrics for performance.

There are a variety of aspects of this questionnaire which are of interest, but which I deal with in other chapters, such as the preoccupation with change, for example, or the insistence on the importance of being positive and inspirational. What interests me more in this chapter is the world view that the questionnaire implies, with the leader (and in this instance the subject of the questionnaire led very few people directly) prevailing over and steering an orderly workplace in which other staff members are bit-part players. The leader creates a culture, in the questionnaire's terms the 'right culture', which will directly affect morale and productivity, will acknowledge difference but avoid conflict. The leader creates and controls a convergent world which exists mostly in a stable state, and is predicated on unity and positivity.

Leadership and culture

There is a great deal of organizational literature which supports this way of thinking, and investigating it briefly may give us some insight into how more orthodox scholars frame the link between leaders and managers and organizational culture. For example, Edgar Schein, an eminent organizational scholar who has written about organizational culture over a number of decades, cleaves to a dual position that, on the one hand, organizational cultures have natural life-cycles of birth, maturation, crisis and regeneration or death, like organisms in nature, whilst on the other hand he argues that leaders have a principal role in shaping them. He states this very explicitly: 'In this sense culture is ultimately created, embedded, evolved and ultimately manipulated by leaders' (2010: 3), although he intends this to mean culture understood at the level of the organization.

For Schein has a systemic understanding of culture, that is to say for him it operates at different levels of society at the national, ethnic, occupational and organizational levels, and in microcosms. He maintains the levels are interconnected, although he does not go on to explain how they are so. In organizations, the leader's role is to intervene in the natural evolutionary cycle, perhaps to speed up the process of evolution to ensure a continuous fit with the organization's environment. Notice how he draws on biological and evolutionary metaphors on the one hand, which have instinctive appeal, whilst appealing to the idea of rational managerial control on the other. Organizations evolve, according to Schein, but there is nothing deterministic about their evolution.

Despite the fact that the term culture denotes an abstract concept, he argues, the way it functions tends towards integration:

> But if the concept of culture is to have any utility, it should draw attention to those things that are the product of our human need for stability, consistency and meaning. Culture formation is always, by definition, a striving toward patterning and integration, even though in many groups, their actual history of experiences prevents them from ever achieving a clear cut unambiguous paradigm.
>
> *(ibid: 18)*

Culture is a set of shared assumptions and practices of a group and tends towards stability and equilibrium, sometimes overly rigid stability, which will come to need the attention of a leader or manager to shift. It is a phenomenon which makes things predictable and meaningful to staff. Throughout the book Schein argues that working with culture involves leaders constantly correcting disequilibrium that arises in organizations, which he feels militates against predictability and meaning-making. In this respect Schein draws directly on the sociological tradition of Talcott Parsons (1923/1991), where values and culture are considered to be part of the integrating function of a system which is tending towards equilibrium.

Schein sets out the processes through which he thinks culture evolves naturally in organizations as a way of offering leaders a conceptual tool to analyse the state of the organization so that they can intervene more effectively and manage culture towards desired outcomes. Culture arises on the basis of shared understandings or assumptions which function similarly to rules in organizational life. He argues that changing culture involves both unlearning established ways of doing things and relearning new ones, thus drawing directly on the work of Kurt Lewin (1951) and his idea of unfreezing and refreezing, as well as the idea of the organization understood as a *gestalt*, or whole.

After Lewin, Schein also draws on spatial and systemic metaphors to argue that leaders embed culture 'in' an organization through primary and secondary embedding mechanisms. He argues that the most straightforward way of influencing culture is through charisma, although he regards it as unfortunate that this is 'unreliable … because leaders who have it are rare, and their impact is hard to predict' (2010: 235). Primary embedding mechanisms are to do with who gets promoted or sacked, what and who the leader rewards and pays attention to, how resources are allocated. Secondary mechanisms are more symbolic, including work and building design. In using the concepts he does, Schein is making a twin appeal both to nature and to reason: culture is a natural given, but it is malleable to rational intervention at the same time, partly because it exists discretely at different 'levels' in a society understood as a whole.

Schein's book argues for bringing the organization understood as system into balance: balancing the individual versus the group, competition versus collaboration, top-down versus bottom-up, a dynamic learning culture versus a stable predictable culture. Implicit, then, is the idea of feedback to optimize the organization understood as system.

I have chosen just one book to illustrate this way of thinking, but it would be possible to draw on many others. For example, Cameron and Quinn's (2011) latest volume on *Diagnosing and Changing Organizational Culture* (an update of Quinn's (1998) book which I refer to in Chapter 2), both of whom are eminent American academics. The book contains many of the same assumptions: that changes in culture can be linked to organizational success and improvement; that culture is a mixture of the tangible (rules, behaviour, rewards) and the intangible (symbols); that culture can exist in an organization and in sub-units within an organization; that it can be 'diagnosed' and changed (with Cameron and Quinn's downloadable

Organizational Culture Assessment Instrument), in this instance with a nine-step programme moving from existing to preferred cultures; that it is often precipitated by a leader having an inspiring vision. Cameron and Quinn argue that 'targeting' culture is a prerequisite for successful organizational change, and involves dealing with both organizational and individual goals and values.

The culture change literature as an example of culture change

I have been setting out the case that in contemporary organizational life it is often taken for granted that we are able to design the culture we want using tools and techniques and that this will bring forth the kind of outcomes that we expect. This is a perspective which is relatively recent in organizational theory, and more broadly in society as a whole. What Schein, and Cameron and Quinn argue for, the technologizing of social life with the promise of predictable results of improvement, is an idea which has taken root and come to be accepted as a given only in the last decades of the twentieth century. It has not always been this way and it might be worth making a short digression to reflect upon how this way of thinking has developed and what the consequences are. What does it enable, and what does it inhibit in organizational terms?

A seminal article by Linda Smircich (1983) noted the way that notions of culture, symbols and ritual migrated to organizational literature from anthropology. This, she argues, first took the form of comparative management, which compared and contrasted, say, Japanese management techniques with those in the West. Then, according to Smircich, came the concept of culture understood as a boundaried phenomenon within organizations particularly during the late 1970s and early 1980s, and both were taken up within a systemic understanding of organizational life. The appeal of the concept of culture was that it provided a way of linking the 'micro and macro levels of analysis', for those interested in strategy, as well as scholars interested in organizational behaviour. Smircich noted both the trend to adopt culture as another tool in the manager's armoury, but also pointed to a critical current within organizational research in reaction to this movement of thought:

> Some, however, genuinely question whether organization culture is indeed manageable. Much of the literature refers to an organization culture, appearing to lose sight of the great likelihood that there are multiple organization subcultures, or even countercultures, competing to define the nature of situations within organizational boundaries. The talk about corporate culture tends to be optimistic, even messianic, about top managers molding cultures to suit their strategic ends. The notion of "corporate culture" runs the risk of being as disappointing a managerial tool as the more technical and quantitative tools that were faddish in the 1970s. Those of a skeptical nature may also question the extent to which the term corporate culture refers to anything more than an ideology cultivated by management for the purpose of control and legitimation of activity.
>
> (Smircich, 1983: 346)

Since this article drew attention to the growing expansion of the literature about culture in organizations, and despite the note of caution and scepticism that Smircich sounds, some organizational scholars have amplified the discourse about culture as a managerial tool. They have quickly identified and emphasized the importance of its ideological power and can sometimes tend towards the messianic, as Smircich warns: for example Collins and Porras (2005) argue that organizations should create a 'cult-like' culture as a way of including and excluding staff. The idea that organizations should develop a 'strong' culture has become very pervasive. In his most recent book Dennis Tourish (2013) explores at length the disasters which can arise from developing cult-like cultures in organizations, where dissent is eliminated and culture is 'totalised'.

As an alternative to this way of thinking, Smircich goes on to describe ways of understanding culture as something an organization 'is' rather than something it 'has': that is to say, one way or another organizational culture is produced and reproduced multiply by employees trying to reconcile and make sense of competing needs, wishes and aspirations. She identifies a number of different schools of thought in this second way of writing about culture in organizations: from a cognitive perspective, where organizations arise as a system of thought; from a symbolic perspective, where attention is given to interpreting symbolic action which creates and maintains a sense of organization; from structural anthropological and psychodynamic perspectives, which have an interest in penetrating the surface appearances to discover the workings of the unconscious mind.

In what follows I try to develop Smircich's second approach to culture, understanding it as something an organization is. The appeal to me, as with other organizational researchers, is that culture enables the linking of the paradox of the micro and the macro, the particular and the general. I will reflect on the idea of culture as history and identity with the sociology of Norbert Elias, and then turn to thinking about how it emerges in practice from the perspective of moral philosophers Alasdair MacIntyre and Hans-Georg Gadamer. In doing so I try to overcome the split between theory and practice that I detect in more conventional management and organizational theory, and to challenge the idea that culture takes place within the boundaries of a discrete organization, or at different 'levels' of society. I hope to call into question the possibility of manipulating organizational culture, the practices of a group referred to in Schein's work.

Culture as history and identity – longer-term social processes

As we have explored elsewhere, Norbert Elias takes a highly social view of human beings. We are who we are because we are members of specific groups and live at a particular moment in history where social relations have evolved in particular ways. To a degree we take on national characteristics as well as personal ones according to our position in the social networks of the country, time and place in which we live. We participate in the *habitus*, the habituated life process of our society, which is both firm and elastic at the same time: we form it just as it is forming us.

Elias studied the *habitus* of particular societies, especially Britain, France and Germany, as a form of enquiry into how specific national characteristics evolved as a consequence of longer-term historical processes, how cultures emerged. For Elias these broader social processes were contributory factors in helping to explain how certain historical conditions, for example the rise of fascism in German, became possible. The evolution of highly interdependent societies also forms us psychologically: we develop a sense of self, with both an 'I' layer and a 'we' layer. However, in contemporary life, he argues, there have been significant changes in the I/we balance, with the 'we' layer of our personalities having been pushed markedly to the background. We have become convinced that we are autonomous, separated individuals cut off from other, similar individuals. Most famously, such thinking is summed up by a British prime minister, who declared that there is 'no such thing as society'.[1] Our sense of we-ness is most likely to come to the foreground at times of national crisis or celebration.

In a book tracing the historical development of Nazi Germany, Norbert Elias (1997), himself a German Jew, reflects upon how nationalism came to take such a strong hold on the German bourgeoisie throughout the nineteenth century leading up to the First and Second World Wars. What interests Elias, and is key to our argument here, is how ways of thinking evolve and change over many decades, becoming part of the competition and cooperation between different groups in society, and then, as some come to dominate, they come to be taken for granted as natural and given national or class characteristics. They become a way of thinking which is unquestioned because it is part of the group and/or national identity: certain notions become part of a society's 'we-identity', the self-beliefs and values of a whole group of people. This is not to suggest that these ideas are uncontested, or experienced everywhere the same, but what is intriguing for Elias is to see the

> persistence with which certain patterns of thinking, acting and feeling recur, with characteristic adaptations to new developments, in one and the same society over many generations. It is almost certain that the meaning of certain key-words and particular undertones embedded in them, which are handed from one generation to another unexamined and unchanged, plays a part in the flexible continuity of what one otherwise conceptualizes as 'national character'.
>
> *(Elias, 1997: 127)*

I want to draw attention to two aspects of Elias's argument. One is that 'patterns of thinking, feeling and acting' arise in the cooperative/competitive relationship between groups in particular societies (and I explore the paradox of cooperation and competition in Chapter 6), although some may come to dominate. Secondly, he regards national character, or culture, as both flexible and continuous. In other words, it arises as the consequence of struggle between groups which calls out both regularities and differences. I revisit these ideas again later in this chapter.

For Elias, nationalism is an important social phenomenon characteristic of large industrial state societies of the nineteenth and twentieth centuries. Later on in this chapter I discuss the National Health Service (NHS) in the UK in terms of the concept of culture, which one might consider as a particular institutional manifestation of the national characteristics of Britons. For, according to Elias, a nation's history produces specific national beliefs, doctrines and institutions, as well as patterns of conscience and ideals, which become influential in people's identities.

To continue with the argument, Elias comments on the barely understood processes of mutual identification which take place in highly developed mass societies. When people live together in large, highly differentiated populations, overseen by the same framework of governmental and administrative organizations, the links between them are much more complex than in simpler societies. Instead, he argues, they are woven together with symbolic emotional ties:

> So, the emotional bonds of individuals within the collectivity which they form with each other crystallize and organize themselves around common symbols which do not require any factual explanations, which can and must be regarded as absolute values which are not to be questioned and which form focal points of a common belief system. To call them into question – to cast doubt on the common belief in one's own sovereign collectivity as a high, if not the highest possible value – means deviancy, a breach of trust; it can lead one to become an ostracized outsider, if nothing worse.
>
> *(ibid: 146)*

This is Elias's particular formulation of what Griffin (2002) has written about elsewhere, drawing on Mead's idea of 'cult values': collectively held ideals the conformity with which one decides whether one will be included or excluded from a group. Here idealized symbols of social solidarity, such as nationalist language and symbolism, act as norms of inclusion and exclusion. It seems to me that it is precisely this that the more orthodox writers on organizational culture want to stake a claim to: they would like managers to set and be in control of what Bourdieu (1986) refers to as symbolic capital as a form of disciplinary control in organizations.

If one really could command it, it would be a big prize, because the symbols around which people identify provoke very strong feelings in people:

> These symbols and the collectivity for which they stand attract to themselves strong positive emotions of the type usually called love. The collectivity is experienced and the symbols are represented as something apart from, something holier and higher than, the individuals concerned ... whatever else it may be, it is also a form of self-love.
>
> *(Elias, 1997: 151)*

However, for Elias there are two principal difficulties related to the control of shared symbolic affiliation. First, if the numbers of people caught up in the phenomenon are large, it can take on a self-amplifying momentum all of its own, which goes beyond the ability of any individual to influence. Secondly, when symbols get taken up as group norms, disciplining individual members of the group as well as acting as a form of self-discipline through guilt, they can have contradictory effects: they can bind people to each other as well as uniting them against others, depending on the degree to which the norms are shared. In this sense they have both integrating and disintegrating effects. Nor is it always the case that shared symbolic values experienced as norms are all of a piece: they may well be contradictory and pull in opposing ways.

Elias recognizes, as does the orthodox management literature, the importance of mediating symbols in social life, symbols which can also be represented in particular people (for example, the Queen of England, or perhaps the CEO of a company). They contribute to our sense of individual and collective identity. However, for Elias they can have paradoxical effects: they both include and exclude, unite and divide. Nor can these symbols and the collective ideals and values they call out, and which provoke strong feelings in people, be controlled by anyone, since they can take on a dynamic of their own 'through a self-escalating dynamic of mutual reinforcement' (ibid: 150).

In this way I think Elias's descriptions of the processual and evolutionary nature of culture undermine the idea that it exists in some kind of equilibrium state, or that it is always integrating. It seems to me that he argues that it is constantly evolving and that the evolution is driven by the constant flux of integration/division cooperation and competition between groups. Cultures change as much by conflict as by convergence, as I explore in Chapter 6.

Already, then we can see some of the difficulties arising for organizational scholars who claim that culture, whatever they understand by it, can be harnessed and manipulated for the good of the company. First, in Elias's terms, it is a kind of voluntary and collective identification involving affect: since it is freely given, identification is a hard phenomenon to oblige someone to give. Secondly, it both integrates and divides at the same time. Even if leaders and managers were able to manipulate culture, it would still play out in contradictory ways. Tourish gives a variety of examples where leaders have systematically applied Schein's (1961) concept of 'coercive persuasion', for example in Enron, in order to create a culture of obedience and conformity. But it was precisely this environment of cut-throat and competitive conformity which led to widespread corruption and fraud.

Culture as practice – the paradox of the particular and the general

I noted in the first paragraphs of this chapter how more orthodox management scholars write about culture as something separate from what people are actually doing together. They take the view that people's daily activities form something above or outside of their interactions, which can be analysed and operated on, reformed and optimized. For me this is a way of separating out theory and practice and giving managers a god's eye view of what everyone is creating together. Moreover, it also gives an impoverished account of what practice is, unless the term is used merely in the vernacular to mean people's everyday actions. I am going to explore the idea of practice as an internally regulated, self-replicating process which is self-consistent. Readers may remember that these are the characteristics of fractals, which I referred to in Chapter 1.

To do so I turn to MacIntyre, Gadamer and Eikeland to reframe theory and practice as paradoxically informing each other, the abstract informing the practical, and the practical the abstract, which unfolds in particular contexts shaped by history. All three philosophers write in an Aristotelian tradition, where they are trying to explore what exercising practical judgment, what Aristotle and Plato referred to as *phronesis*, means in a contemporary setting. All three cleave to the idea that practice is a social, cooperative and contextual activity, which cannot simply be imposed from the outside, according to generalized standards of what the good is taken to be.

MacIntyre (1985) defines a practice as 'any coherent and complex form of socially established co-operative human activity' and argues that it is important to understand practice in terms of submitting to a discipline and joining a tradition of thinking and acting. A practice, which for MacIntyre includes playing chess through to working as a nurse or physician, is a continuing discussion between those engaged in it as to what they collectively take to be standards of excellence and how these might be extended over time:

> A practice involves standards of excellence and obedience to rules as well as the achievement of goods. To enter into a practice is to accept the authority of those standards and the adequacy of my own performance as judged by them.
>
> *(MacIntyre, 1985: 190)*

So a practice is a discipline, which involves self-discipline, and arises from subjecting oneself to the highest standards of the practice which have been set so far, but not to be limited by these. It means entering into a relationship with current practitioners, but also with past practitioners who have established the discipline. In other words, it is an engagement with a tradition, one which is continued through institutions. Development of the practice will, for MacIntyre, always involve deliberation about the good, virtues such as truthfulness, justice and courage, if the practice is to avoid becoming corrupted. It is a complex and highly social interplay between practitioners and their traditions of thought and action, the institutions which extend them over time, manifested in ongoing discussions of the good.

But it is difficult to engage in a critique of the practice until one has become an accomplished practitioner. I think what Macintyre is arguing here is that the practice develops and evolves as a consequence of the intense engagement between committed practitioners reflecting on, and talking about, their practice. This is not the same as saying that a practice can be improved or optimized by managers and leaders taking a view from without. The Aristotelian scholar Olav Eikeland (2008) expresses the idea similarly:

> We, as knowers, are *inside* praxis. Practical ways of knowing are not *about* something external to themselves, which they try to represent, explain, predict, use, manipulate, and control from the outside. Instead, praxis-ways of knowing organise and structure the competence of their carriers, within a certain field, or in general, and become primarily a qualification of their carriers themselves (individually and collectively) ...
>
> *(Eikeland, 2008: 304, emphasis in the original)*

It is hard to get away from the spatial metaphors of inside and outside, but what I think MacIntyre and Eikeland are pointing to is that the goods and standards of excellence involved in any practice are self-generating, paradoxically arising from practice and informing practice, both at the same time. Eikeland draws on Aristotle to point to two different ways of knowing about the world arising from the ancient Greek concepts of *theoresis* and *theoria*:

> On the one hand there is theory and science based on distant, disengaged, and non-interfering perceptual observation (*theoresis*). On the other hand there is theory and science based on deep involvement in, participation in, and practical observation of the activities studied (*theoria*) ... What *theoria* explores and searches for, then, are existential and basic historical concepts, practical concepts that we live and enact, receiving them first from our culture, societies and traditions through habituation and socialization, later sorting and sifting them critically and dialogically, acquiring them anew in a different, more distinguished way. *Theoria* is not only knowledge *for* practice. It is knowledge *from* practice, and necessarily so in order to be knowledge *for* practice.
>
> *(ibid: 305–7, emphasis in the original)*

Eikeland opposes some of the more inflated statements made about practical judgment by some other scholars (see, for example, Flyvbjerg, 2001), who have claimed that it is quite distinct from scientific knowledge. For Eikeland, it would be impossible to exercise practical judgment without drawing on abstract, scientific knowledge, but as a guide to action which needs particularising in a concrete situation at a particular time. This inevitably involves a discussion and a negotiation about what 'we', those of us involved in the particular situation, take to be the good. It cannot be reduced to rules and prescriptions, otherwise practice becomes mechanical and absorbed in ticking boxes. However, it emerges from culture and informs how we proceed to re-enact it: it is self-referencing.

Similarly, Gadamer was also concerned with the idea of practice and what we might mean by it as a way of questioning how amenable it might be to rational control. In a chapter entitled 'What Is Practice? The Conditions of Social Reason', Gadamer (1993) reflects on what practice might mean in a scientific age, and concludes that in our time theory and practice have become separated. He argues that we have come to think of practice arising as the result of applying scientific thinking and we assume that we develop theory, then apply it as practice. So in this formulation, thinking comes before action. This split between theory and practice has evolved since the Enlightenment and the development of science, Gadamer argues, and has arisen from the way that natural science manipulates relationships in the abstract using isolated experimental conditions. This abstract manipulation of relationships is then reintroduced into society as technology, and in contemporary life as social technology:

> The old relationship of the products of the arts and crafts with the models furnished by nature has thus been transformed into an ideal of construction, into the ideal of nature artificially produced in accord with an idea.
>
> *(Gadamer, 1993: 70)*

On the one hand, manipulation and the ideal of construction, disassembling phenomena into parts and whole, then reassembling them, have led to enormous achievements in terms of conquering nature and making our lives comfortable. On the other hand, they have inverted our relationship with technology: instead of bending it to our use, we instead find ourselves bending and adapting to the requirements of technology. This is particularly the case with the media and technology-based social networking. By responding to technological requirements we relinquish some of our freedom to act and we in turn are manipulated. Gadamer argues that in technological society and in the long term the adaptive power of individuals is rewarded more than their creative power: we advance in contemporary society by being obedient.

So is practice, what Gadamer elsewhere calls practical philosophy, a science, and how is it different from a technological approach? As we found in Eikeland, for Gadamer practice involves deliberation with others and an assessment of the good in particular concrete situations. It is neither theoretical science, like mathematics, nor is it mere knowledgeable mastery of technical procedures. Rather, it involves questions of ethics and of politics:

> Practical philosophy, then, certainly is a 'science': a knowledge of the universal that as such is teachable. But it is still a science that needs certain conditions to be fulfilled. It demands of the one learning it the same indissoluble relationship to practice it does of the one teaching it. To this extent it does have a certain proximity to the expert knowledge proper to technique, but what separates it fundamentally from technical expertise is that it expressly asks the question of the good too ... It does not merely master an ability, like technical expertise, whose task is set aside by an outside authority: by the purpose to be served by what is being produced.
>
> *(ibid: 93)*

Practice for Gadamer is primarily a social activity that is driven by internal goods of concrete situations, rather than requirements or standards imposed from the outside. Practice draws on universal theory but requires an assessment by people in a given situation about what is reasonable, rather than what is rational. Practice involves a paradox of the general and the particular, how more universal themes are to be taken up in particular situations with others.

From the perspective of management, the idea that we can engineer a more rational society has become pervasive to the extent that we think we can make intentional plans to bring it about. In these circumstances we privilege the role of the expert and what Gadamer calls the functionary (by which term I assume he means managers):

> In the scientific, technical, economic, monetary processes, and most especially in administration, politics, and similar forms, he [*sic*] has to maintain himself as he is: one inserted for the smooth functioning of the apparatus. That is why he is in demand, and therein lies his chances for advancement. Even when the dialectic of this evolution is sensible to each one who asserts that ever fewer people are making the decisions and even more are manning the apparatus, modern industrial society is oppressed by immanent structural pressures. But this leads to the degeneration of practice into technique and – through no fault of the experts themselves – to a general decline into social irrationality.
>
> *(ibid: 74)*

What I take Gadamer to mean here is that the maintenance of the increasingly technical areas of organizational life has taken precedence over what often makes sense in human terms. The pressure to maintain 'the apparatus', to feed the beast, means that employees in organizations are asked to do more and more irrational things in terms of what their work requires. What is good for the organization does not always make sense in local contexts where employees are obliged to improvise creatively with each other in order to get the work done. Rather than being invited to make appropriate choices, to exercise practical judgment, to act in solidarity with others, we are increasingly rewarded for conforming and agreeing to be manipulated by the perceived needs of the organizations we work for understood in abstract terms.

A good example of what I am talking about is the tyranny of targets, where employees are rewarded first and foremost for conforming to targets often set many removes from the *locus* of the work. For Gadamer this is likely to lead to a lack of a sense of identity and a failure of imagination. The extent of the technologization of social life leads both to modernity's strength and its current crises, he argues.

Alasdair MacIntyre (1985) picks up the same theme in *After Virtue*, that the role of the modern manager is mostly concerned with manipulation and technique:

> The manager treats ends as given, as outside his scope; his concern is with technique, with effectiveness in transforming raw materials into final products, unskilled labor into skilled labor, investment into profits ... They are

> seen by themselves, and by those who see them with the same eyes as their
> own, as uncontested figures, who purport to restrict themselves to realms in
> which rational agreement is possible – that is of course from their point of
> view the realm of fact, the realm of means, the realm of effectiveness.
>
> *(MacIntyre, 1985: 30)*

The manager focuses on the needs of the organization. In doing so questions of
politics, what we take the ends of our activities to be, are considered irrelevant, or
even irrational aspects of what a manager is responsible for, so discussion focuses
merely on the means of achieving them. This MacIntyre terms 'emotivism', the
idea that questions of value and politics are beyond contestation: it is taken for granted
that society is best served by focusing on effectiveness, efficiency and economic
growth.

The link I am making to the discussion of the rational planning of culture found
in Schein, and Cameron and Quinn's work is that this proceeds with the split
between theory and practice, between ends and means which Gadamer and
MacIntyre identify as a taken-for-granted in contemporary life, and then assumes
that culture, the practices, beliefs and shared understandings of employees, are like
objects capable of manipulation towards a pre-reflected ideal of a higher performing organization. In other words, the perceived needs of a particular organization
for a 'changed culture', come to dominate people's working life when they are
formulated in terms of targets to meet, rules to follow and proscribed ways of
behaving.

From Gadamer's perspective this ignores the situated, context-specific quality of
practice, which brings together both the particular and the general in a deliberation
about the good. Gadamer is questioning whether practice can ever be designed
and, if it can, whether this simply reduces to a series of techniques which value
conformity and obedience to the rules. In turn this conformity produces patterns of
social irrationality, where the requirements of the 'apparatus' take precedence over
what makes sense in a particular work situation. More than this, it means that people's
sense of identity, how they find themselves in their work, becomes destabilized. Here
I think Gadamer is suggesting that attempts to rationalize social life bring about the
opposite of what they promise. Rather than producing employees who are obedient
to a certain way of thinking and acting it may leave them disoriented and unable to
do the work which is required. I am sure that we can all think of examples from
contemporary organizational life where a process of rationalization or systematization
has led to bizarre consequences for undertaking the work.

As an example, in my own organization, finance colleagues have decided to
streamline and control purchasing with the noble intention of cutting costs. This
means that any member of staff wanting to buy something has to fill in a form
justifying the purchase and explaining why he or she is using the particular chosen
provider. The form designed by purchasing colleagues clearly has in mind those
members of staff ordering stationery or perhaps chairs, since there are questions to
be answered about which catalogue and which page the item is on, which colour is

to be ordered, and where the item should be delivered. Be that as it may, all members of staff have to fill in the same form.

I wanted to invite a theatre company to work with a group of postgraduates so that they could rehearse problem situations at work and how they might deal with them. This is an innovative technique which encourages reflection in the moment and improvisation, and which I write about in more depth in Chapter 3. In order to get the theatre company paid I had to write a justification for why I was using this group as opposed to one of the university's 'preferred suppliers'. In this box I simply argued that the question was irrelevant since there were no preferred suppliers of theatrical services. The form was returned to me because it had 'insufficient justification' for adding the group's name to the university payment IT system: without such justification the auditors might complain.

Summary of the argument so far

By drawing on Elias, MacIntyre, Eikeland and Gadamer I have tried to develop the idea of culture as a complex social phenomenon. It involves history, collective identification around symbols, self-amplifying processes of integration and division, and a contextual understanding of practice as a tradition. In highlighting practices as central to the transmission of culture, I share a great deal with Nicolini (2012) with his suggestion that social life is created and recreated by human bodies engaged in power and politics. Where we disagree centres on his retention of a systemic perspective, which still privileges the individual and his suggestion that practice is a theoretical 'lens'. As I stated earlier, I am trying to gain insight into practice from within practice itself.

If we take these arguments seriously then we would see that culture shapes who we are and how we see the world (even to the degree of believing that we can predict and control culture), so that there is no independent position outside of our culture from which we can view it, partly because there is no 'it' to view. Culture, or what Bourdieu (1977) also referred to as *habitus*, is written on the body and is a disposition to think and act in a particular way. Whatever we take to be national and cultural characteristics, these result from processes of cooperation and competition between groups, until over time certain ideals, values, practices and ways of thinking come to be taken as natural and given. These can be called out by powerful collective symbols which exist in every society, and can provoke highly emotive responses in us of mutual identification, but can also promote division as 'we' unite against 'them'.

No one can be in control of this powerful affect because it is self-referencing and sometimes self-amplifying. History shapes us, the way we think and act, the values that we have, indeed perhaps this process turns on its head the idea that we 'have' values; rather that values, as a heightened sense of identification with the collective, take us over. Practice, if we intend by it anything more than just a simple word meaning everyday activity, becomes institutionalized over time, and is also a highly social process, which is informed by an ongoing discussion of values, and what engaged practitioners in a particular discipline take to be the good: it involves argument and contestation and often struggles over power between different groups. A practice develops from within practice itself and in response to the demands of taking up something that is generally understood but exercised in specific contexts.

Trying to rationalize practice according to ideals conceived outside of the practice itself is likely to lead to organizational irrationalities, organizational requirements which inhibit the ability of staff to respond creatively in their contexts. This, according to Gadamer, may make it more difficult for people to find themselves in their work, to develop a sense of professional identity.

As the idea of culture has migrated from anthropology to organizational theory, so it has become highly instrumentalized and reified. It is another example of the hubris of managerialism, which claims to be able to analyse, predict and control the intangible, and with the result that it can bring about the opposite of what it intends. In other words, with the intention of ensuring that employees are more committed to their work and are more productive, repeated culture change programmes can have the effect of inducing cynicism or resistance in staff (McKinlay and Taylor, 1996). With an insistence that staff align their values with those of the organization, what may result is gaming strategies on the part of staff to cover over what they really think and feel (Jackall, 2009).

However, leaders and managers do of course have control over the more tangible aspects of organizational life, what Schein refers to as 'primary embedding mechanisms', i.e. who gets rewarded and promoted, and how resources are allocated. Conversely, this would include who is publicly shamed, who has resources taken away from them, who is excluded. In other words, and to a degree, leaders and managers have some control over conduct through disciplinary measures and rewards. This has been amplified in the public sector in the UK over the last few years by governments of all persuasions creating league tables and hierarchies of achievement, with a tendency to 'name and shame' those who are perceived to be failing.

In the next section I discuss a particular example of intended organizational culture change in a very large organization as a way of investigating how it is conceived and articulated. This will involve looking at the change which is planned for the NHS, understood as a whole organization which comprises over a million employees. After this I will set out a critique of the proposed changes drawing on some of the ideas I have set out above, as well as some contemporary critiques of the way that managerialism manifests itself in the NHS at the moment.

Cultural change within the NHS in the UK

The Department of Health (DH) and the NHS Commissioning Board have issued a new strategy and vision for nurses, midwives and care staff in the NHS. This is in response to a perceived crisis in the values of caring following a number of scandals about the standard of care in hospitals and care homes. The intention is to reinforce the existing values which underpin caring for vulnerable and sick people, but the strategy also intends to change culture: 'There is also growing recognition in all levels of the health, care and support system, that we have to change our culture if we are to change our care' (2012: 12).

At the heart of this strategy are what the document refers to as 'the 6 Cs': care, competence, compassion, communication, courage and commitment. Compassion is understood to be 'how care is given through relationships based on empathy, respect and dignity. It can also be described as intelligent kindness and is central to how people perceive their care'. I will return to the idea of intelligent kindness later on to look at the provenance of the idea because I think it opens up areas of discussion not covered by either Schein or the Department of Health. Meanwhile, these 6 Cs will inform everything that caring staff do, will be communicated vigorously in collaborative working relationships with others, will form the basis of training, promotion and performance management and will be instrumental in whole organizational culture change. Each of these areas of organizational activity is intended to fit neatly over the others to form a coherent whole of overlapping and reinforcing organizational change, and is amplified through reward and recognition.

This strategy is currently being implemented across the health service. All front-line workers are considered to be 'change champions', and leadership is expected to occur at 'every level' of the organization, although staff designated as leaders and managers are thought to have a particular role in the process:

> Leadership is key. Leaders and managers need to create supporting, caring cultures, within teams, within organizations, and in the system as a whole in the way that organizations relate to each other. Leaders at every level have a responsibility to shape and lead a caring culture.
>
> *(DH and NHS Commissioning Board, 2012: 11)*

In a similar way to Schein, then, culture is considered to be a set of conditions or shared attitudes and mindsets which are manipulable by leaders and managers towards a desired end-state. The NHS requires a new equilibrium state of a culture of compassionate caring, where all workers feel empowered to speak out courageously to make the changes that patients need. The document talks of local organizations developing 'cultural barometers' to measure the success of the changes being implemented.

In what follows I want to explore some of the difficulties that NHS leaders and managers might encounter in being set the task of changing organizational culture. Additionally, I would like to think a bit more broadly about the theme of culture and how it emerges both locally and more broadly in the NHS, emerging as it does from the wider environment of British society.

The NHS as an institutionalization of British values

Whether you think the NHS is a millstone around the necks of British taxpayers or an example of all that is good about the welfare state, the institution figures large in the symbolic imagination of many British people. To give a prominent example, a significant section of the Olympic opening ceremony in 2012 was given over to a performance celebrating the genesis of the NHS, which even those who are opposed to state provision found it difficult to criticize. To a degree, then, the NHS still has the status of a cult value, which makes it difficult to denigrate publicly because it provokes very strong feelings in people.

In using the word 'cult', I am referring to GH Mead's use of the term, and the reference to values that I discussed above in the passage on Elias and the collective symbols of nationalism. Similarly, and from a social anthropological perspective, and after Mary Douglas (1986/2012), the NHS is to many people a sacred object, which evokes fervent emotional responses in those who consider it to be under attack. Whatever we might take the problematic term 'British identity' to mean, it is clear that a strong attitude towards the NHS, for or against in its current state, forms a part of what Norbert Elias referred to as the 'we' layer of the British personality structure. It is an important part of who British people are and is the institutionalization of a particular attitude of caring, that health provision should be free at the point of delivery for all citizens.

The strong symbolic value of the NHS and its role in identity formation in the discussion of what it means to be British has a powerful influence on how debate about the institution's future can be framed. It also explains why there is such a struggle over the future of the institution since broader political disagreements in the national context become particularly heated when enacted within and about such an important organization. Disagreements for British people revolving around who we think we are, and what we would like to become are reflected in changes to the NHS. The sacred nature of the NHS conditions the arguments of even those who would like to dismantle it and replace it with privatized provision because they are obliged to do so, whilst publicly claiming that the NHS is very dear to their hearts and is safe in their hands.

The current coalition government in the UK came to power averring that there would be 'no more top down reorganizations of the NHS', and only declared and implemented its changes after it had formed a government. However they are using the word 'reform', politicians and health policy analysts are obliged to argue that reform is necessary because the NHS is so important and central to the British way of life.

Culture and idealization

The cult-like status of the NHS leads to idealization, which is both understandable and occasionally unhelpful. The difficulty with idealization is that it can quickly flip over into its opposite, denigration. The extreme polarities make it very difficult to talk sensibly about the difficulties of managing the complex process of caring for people's needs in large numbers because it can lead to simplistic dualisms.

But these matters matter to us. Returning to the current debate about care in the health service to which the strategy discussed above is a response, scandals have involved the most idealized 'angels', the nurses and care staff, of an already idealized institution. The high esteem with which we generally hold nurses is commensurate with our shock and surprise at stories which emerge when they appear not to have adhered to basic standards of care and compassion. They are two sides of the same coin and, as I argued earlier in this chapter, no one can have control over the strong emotions which cultural symbols evoke.

A book alluded to in the Royal College of Nursing strategy with its reference to 'intelligent kindness' tries to grapple with the complexities of cultural change in the NHS. In this volume, Ballatt and Campling (2011) argue that a split in values has evolved in contemporary society, one side of which privileges individualism, self-reliance, entrepreneurialism and competition, whilst the other emphasizes kinship, solidarity and interconnectedness. This is exactly the kind of struggle over competing values that Elias alluded to in his book on the *The Germans* outlined above.

Ballatt and Campling argue, along with psychoanalyst Adam Phillips and historian Barbara Taylor (2009), that the former set of values has come to dominate over the latter, with ideological overtones that being competitive and individualistic is a form of tough and rugged realism, whilst the latter is a soft-hearted, amateur luxury. That we are 'consumers' and what we care about most is 'choice' has come to be accepted as axiomatic and natural. There are a variety of contemporary critical publications making very similar claims that the predominance of markets has changed us socially and psychologically; see for example Verhaeghe (2012) and Sennett (2005), particularly through the use of language (Mautner, 2010).

Ballatt and Campling understand intelligent kindness to be a kind of practice which arises from the ability to see the person in the patient and to form a 'therapeutic alliance' with them. This is a term borrowed from psychotherapy and counselling and describes a relationship of trust, where the therapist or carer is believed to have the client/patient's best interests at heart. The authors adduce research which suggests that a strong therapeutic alliance, where the client/patient feels that he or she matters to the therapist or carer, leads to better treatment and improved outcomes, and a virtuous circle of improved organizational effectiveness and productivity.

Ballatt and Campling are not so naïve as to think that this is an easy process. Although they agree with the Harvard philosopher Michael Sandel's (2012) observation that compassion is like a muscle and gets stronger with exercise, they nonetheless draw attention to a number of phenomena which impede the virtuous cycle that they hope for. They point out that health professionals' encounters with ill-health can provoke mixed feelings of anxiety, guilt and inadequacy that the standard of care can ever be good enough, or equally it can encourage over-identification with the sick person. Although the practice of kindness is predicated on relating to the 'other' as though they are kith and kin, it is sometimes difficult to do so if the experience of extreme illness can make patients truculent, rude or unpleasant in other ways.

For Ballatt and Campling the hospital is a theatre of love and hate and will call out both strong and mixed feelings in medical staff. They also draw attention to the pressures of being a member of a group, and how this can provoke anxiety and irrational behaviour in group members, such as the tendency to deny poor practice or other unwelcome evidence that is contrary to what the group is trying to achieve, as well as collusion and competitiveness with other groups. The authors recommend reflective discussions as a means of establishing affiliative relations between colleagues, using the same principles that establish generative relations between patients and carers.

The reason for exploring the book at some length is that I think it gives a much more realistic account of what is involved in the daily routine of caring for vulnerable others. In highlighting the contrasting pressures of health and ill health, individuals and groups, love and hate, and persistent anxiety against a background of profound political contestation the authors help to explain how it is that health care is provided in conditions of stable-instability.

Ballatt and Campling point to other inhibitors of caring approaches. They argue that the industrialization of medicine, regimes of benchmarking and standardizing, have led to the spread of mediocrity. Requiring rigid adherence to standardized tools does not always recognize expertise which has already developed beyond the rules. I think this is a critique similar to the one I alluded to above, drawing on Gadamer: that schemes for the rationalization of practice driven by organizational imperatives often make little sense to experienced practitioners drawing on a tradition of practice, and may even make their jobs harder to do.

Additionally, Ballatt and Campling argue that the marketization process has led to a commodifying of the spirit of voluntarism, which until recently has pervaded medicine as a vocation. They give as an example the way that the new GP contracts have obliged them to count all the hours that they work as units of pay, whereas previously they would have worked for free. Despite the fact that their pay has increased, so too has their dissatisfaction at having to itemize and claim for every minute they are working to justify their claims. In addition, the move to inspection, intense monitoring and 'naming and shaming' supposedly poorly performing hospitals leads to an environment of suspicion, which has a tendency to set up defensive relations between care staff and the public they serve.

The daily life of health professionals, then, involves struggles over power and influence, and intense emotions of love, hate and potential shame. It encompasses globally political and locally practical themes and shows how fraught caring can be because it brings professionals face to face with the extremes of what it means to suffer, as patient and as carer: hospitals can be fora for the playing out of very strong and mixed emotions. The authors demonstrate how 'reform' is never a technical and neutral word and it can be used equally easily by politicians and managers to bring about diametrically opposite changes. They argue that latterly changes to the health service have reflected a particular ideology and have resulted in instrumentalizing relationships between people.

That the cleavage of left and right, individualism and solidarity, pro and asocial behaviour shows up at the heart of one of Britain's principal institutions can be no surprise. Questions of what it means to change the NHS also involve themes concerning what it means to be British, since the institution symbolizes one very central way of collective belonging and identity. Culture, approached from within an emblematic institution, is also an expression of who we are and who we would like to become.

Nonetheless, as important as their contribution is in identifying some of the processes which militate against mutual recognition, to a degree, Ballatt and Campling could also be critiqued for idealizing intelligent kindness and the extent to which it can contribute to a 'virtuous circle' in health care. They are setting out an alternative equilibrium model based on the idea of stabilizing and integrating 'for the good', where organizational culture is still manipulable. From a complex responsive processes perspective, whatever we take organizational culture to be, the *habitus*, will always be both stable and unstable at the same time as staff navigate the contradictory processes of finding the 'I' in the 'we'. In drawing attention to the neglected pole of competition/cooperation they have to an extent lost the paradox between the two, and may be in danger of over-claiming, particularly when they start to argue that their understanding of intelligent kindness can be equally efficient and effective. Efficiency and effectiveness are much more problematic terms if one assumes that the interactions between human beings are non-linear: creativity and learning may only be possible in situations where there is a certain amount of redundancy of both time and/or resources.

Concluding thoughts on culture

What the relationship is between the individual and society is probably still the most enduring question in sociology, usually known as the agency/structure problem. It turns on the conundrum as to the extent society determines people's actions, as opposed to the degree to which individuals can influence the social through their plans and activities. Norbert Elias took a paradoxical view of this particular question:

> The root of the misunderstandings on the relation of individual and society lies in the fact that while society, the relations between people, has a structure and regularity of a special kind that cannot be understood in terms of a single individual, it does not possess a body, a 'substance' outside individuals.
>
> *(Elias, 2001: 61)*

What I take him to mean here is that it is neither one nor the other, neither the individual nor the social predominates: recognizable regularities arise from people's daily interactions, and at the same time the regularities influence what people do. It is the paradox of the 'I' in the 'we'. But their relations with each other produce nothing outside of themselves, nothing that is analysable as a 'thing' and manipulable in the way that even powerful groups of people in society would intend:

> The long-term planning of individuals, compared to the multiplicity of individual purposes and wishes within the totality of the human network,

and particularly compared to the continuous interweaving of individual actions and purposes over many generations, is always extremely limited. The interplay of actions, purposes and plans of many people is not itself something intended or planned, and is ultimately immune to planning ... The interweaving of the needs and intentions of many people subjects each individual among them to compulsions that none of them has intended.

(ibid: 62)

We can of course have plans to influence other people: in fact we make such plans all the time. But as we have seen from the NHS example, there are plenty of other things going on in organizational life informed by broader political and social questions, as well as matters of values and identity, over which no single person, or group of people, has control. Working with ill and dying patients goes to the heart of what it means to be human and how we think about institutionalizing our relations of caring.

A question remains for me, however, as to why managers and management and organizational scholars should be so preoccupied with questions of culture. I would of course expect leaders and managers to encourage high standards of work and a generous attitude to colleagues and clients. There is a difference, however, when a concern for the environment in which people do their work and the standards they maintain, shades into an invasive attempt to oblige people to conform to something often highly idealized, where culture blends into cult. We have already discussed the ways in which systematic attempts to mould culture rationally can often bring about the very opposite of what they intend: they can produce irrational requirements on employees, who then have to subvert the very rules they are obliged to follow in order to get the job done. However, it is important not to ignore the totalitarian overtones of some of these schemes for whole-organizational change, no matter how well intended. I think that this is something that Hannah Arendt was alluding to in her major treatise on totalitarianism:

Total domination, which strives to organize the infinite plurality and differentiation of human beings as if all of humanity were just one individual, is possible only if each and every person can be reduced to a never-changing identity of reactions, so that each of these bundles of reactions can be exchanged at random for any other.

(Arendt, 2004: 565)

What concerned Arendt, and which also concerned Gadamer and MacIntyre, is the application of technological ways of thinking to close down on human spontaneity, what Arendt termed 'natality': the human ability to create and begin things anew. For her, human beings cannot be reduced to being objects of technological, or ideological, manipulation without violence. There is much to be troubled about in the contemporary fixation with changing culture, particularly in its more orthodox form.

From a complex responsive processes perspective leaders and managers are particularly powerful players in the game of organizational life. They can set rules, they can move bodies, they can scrutinize, cajole, persuade and coerce. What they are unable to do, however, is to control predictably the fluctuating social patterning, to which they themselves contribute, and which engender identity and collective belonging.

Note

1 Mrs Thatcher talking to *Woman's Own Magazine*, 31 October 1987.

References

Alvesson, M. and Willmott, H. (2002) Identity Regulation as Organizational Control: Producing the Appropriate Individual, *Journal of Management Studies*, 39: 619–44.
Arendt, H. (2004) *The Origins of Totalitarianism*, New York: Schocken Books.
Ballatt, J. and Campling, P. (2011) *Intelligent Kindness: Reforming the Culture of Healthcare*, London: Royal College of Psychiatrists Publications.
Bourdieu, P. (1977) *Outline of a Theory of Practice*, Cambridge: Cambridge University Press.
——(1986) The Forms of Capital, in Richardson, J. (ed.) *Handbook of Theory and Research for the Sociology of Education*, New York: Greenwood, 241–58.
Cameron, K. and Quinn, R. E. (2011) *Diagnosing and Changing Organizational Culture: Based on the Competing Values Framework*, London: John Wiley and Sons.
Collins, J. and Porras, J. (2005) *Built to Last: Successful Habits of Visionary Companies*, New York: Random House.
Department of Health (DH) and NHS Commissioning Board (2012) *Compassion in Practice: Nursing, Midwifery and Care Staff. Our Vision and Strategy*, London: Department of Health and NHS Commissioning Board.
Douglas, M. (1986/2012) *How Institutions Think*, London: Routledge.
Eikeland, O. (2008) *The Ways of Aristotle: Aristotelian Phronesis, Aristotelian Philosophy of Dialogue and Action Research*, Bern: Peter Lang.
Elias, N. (1997) *The Germans: Power Struggles and the Development of Habitus in the Nineteenth and Twentieth Centuries*, Cambridge: Polity Press.
——(2001) *The Society of Individuals*, London: Continuum.
Flyvbjerg, B. (2001) *Making Social Science Matter: Why Social Inquiry Fails, and How it Can Succeed Again*, Cambridge: Cambridge University Press.
Gadamer, H.-G. (1993) *Reason in the Age of Science*, Cambridge, MA: MIT Press.
Griffin, D. (2002) *The Emergence of Leadership: Linking Self-Organization and Ethics*, London: Routledge.
Jackall, R. (2009) *Moral Mazes: The World of Corporate Managers*, Oxford: Oxford University Press.
Lewin, K. (1951) *Field Theory in Social Science; Selected Theoretical Papers*, Cartwright, D. (ed.) New York: Harper & Row.
MacIntyre, A. (1985) *After Virtue*, London: Duckworth.
McKinlay, A. and Taylor, P. (1996) Power, Surveillance and Resistance: Inside the Factory of the Future, in Ackers, P., Smith, C. and Smith, P. (eds.) *The New Workplace and Trade Unionism: Critical Perspectives on Work and Organization*, London: Routledge.
Mautner, G. (2010) *Language and the Market Society*, London: Routledge.
Nicolini, D. (2012) *Practice Theory, Work and Organization*, Oxford: Oxford University Press.
Parsons, T. (1923/1991) *The Social System*, London: Routledge.
Phillips, A. and Taylor, B. (2009) *On Kindness*, London: Penguin.
Quinn, R. E. (1988) *Beyond Rational Management: Mastering the Paradoxes and Competing Demands of High Performance*, San Francisco: Jossey-Bass.

Reynolds, M. and Holwell, S. (eds.) (2010) *Systems Approaches to Managing Change: A Practical Guide*, London: Springer.

Sandel, M. (2012) *What Money Can't Buy: The Moral Limits to Markets*, London: Allen Lane.

Schein, E. (2010) *Organizational Culture and Leadership*, London: Wiley, 4th Edition.

Schein, E., with Schneir, I. and Barker, C. (1961) *Coercive Persuasion: A Sociopsychological Analysis of 'Brainwashing' of American Civilian Prisoners by the Chinese Communists*, New York: Norton.

Sennett, R. (2005) *The Culture of the New Capitalism*, New Haven, CT: Yale University Press.

Smircich, L. (1983) Concepts of Culture and Organizational Analysis, *Administrative Science Quarterly*, 28(3), Organizational Culture: 339–58.

Tourish, D. (2013) *The Dark Side of Transformational Leadership: A Critical Perspective*, London: Routledge.

Verhaeghe, P. (2012) *What About Me? The Struggle for Identity in a Market-Based Society*, London: Scribe Publications.

5

ON THE PREDICTABLE UNPREDICTABILITY OF ORGANIZATIONAL LIFE

Change and innovation

I was invited to give a keynote speech at an academic conference on innovation at a university in Scandinavia. A variety of academics, business people, representatives of local and national government attended and participated in two and a half days of interesting discussion in the five thematic tracks in the conference. There were a large number of papers presented and often detailed discussion followed, which seemed to me to set out two broad narratives about change and innovation, which are interconnected, one could even say interdependent, but through a relationship of negation. I will argue below that it would be impossible to understand innovation and change without taking both views into account, but at the same time it seems to me that one narrative threatens to cover over the other one completely.

Narrative 1 was the dominant as well as the majority narrative in the conference, which I will term the management narrative, which also has strong and urgent moral overtones of the kind I alluded to in the last chapter about the imperative of change. Narrative 2, which arose in people's reflections on their papers or in their less formal discussions on how difficult it was to undertake innovation in their organization or context I will term the contingency narrative about how innovation happens. Both bring with them their own perspectives on the world and, I will argue, their own methods. Both arise as a consequence of trying to undertake innovative projects or change programmes in organizations which I argue are in paradoxical tension.

For the sake of discussion, the two narratives are over-drawn, but I do so in order to point to the tensions that I perceive in thinking and writing about how change comes about in organizations and to question how much we can plan it, tensions which are not always evident from academic papers or text books on the subject.

Narrative 1: The managerial narrative on innovation and change

Narrative 1, the managerial narrative, portrays a world of conscious choosers. So, in order to get hold of this difficult concept, 'innovation', a number of the less nuanced presenters asserted, it needs to be defined explicitly along with concrete ways of achieving it. It has to be made a target, usually involving a strategy, perhaps with an 'innovation champion' to safeguard it. Innovation arises from plans and solutions can be designed to innovation problems. This narrative privileges the idea of rational, conscious choosing managers who are designing innovation, and in order to do so they require models which tend to be fixed, explicit and abstract.

Narrative 1 presupposes that managers have to invent explicitly to 'be original', to put something in place which has never been there before. Doing so involves an effort of will, of driving the change that managers want to see 'going forwards'. It is a moral imperative. Innovation and change are thought to be the polar opposite of what is currently happening in organizations, stability, which is considered simply repetitive and routine.

The management narrative acknowledges that there are tensions in this process, which one presenter referred to as dualisms. Speed of product development has to be traded off against inclusion of customers; internal business coherence has to be balanced against external input, new product development has to be reconciled with the production of the existing product range. The managerial innovator strives to balance one pole of the dualism with the other. I deal with these dualisms in more depth later on in this chapter in the review of the literature on innovation.

However, innovation arises because managers are acting on others to bring something about. Sometimes this narrative turns into a heroic tale of managerial achievement fuelled by anxiety and evangelism. It is also a moral tale which was retold by one of the other keynote speakers at the conference. So the story goes something like this: we live in exceptional times, there's so much change going on at a faster and faster pace. If companies, governments, health services don't keep up they will be left behind. There is an imperative to innovate now (or be taken over by Brazil, Russia, India, China or South Africa, the BRICS countries). This requires a revolution in practice and in thinking – it needs a change in 'mind set'. We have to change our 'mental models', just as we need to produce new models of working.

I noticed a combination of optimism about the ability to design innovation processes but a degree of pessimism about people working in organizations who were portrayed as being against change. This is why it needed the urgency of evangelism and moral imperative, in case people do not grasp or react sufficiently quickly to the need for change.

Narrative 2: Innovation and change as practical, everyday politics

Narrative 2, which I am terming the contingency narrative, occurred when the technical and rational narrative of innovation broke down, either through reflection or as people accounted for the fact that things had often not turned out as they had expected. In reflection there was sometimes a retreat from the heroic to the mundane and different accounts showed how innovation and change were emerging constantly from the blockages and impediments that researchers experienced in trying to get their ideas implemented, what one might think of as the politics of everyday life. Sometimes existing practices confounded or cut across what the researchers were trying to achieve. New practices did emerge, but they were not always changes that they had anticipated.

When presenters departed from their academic papers to talk about the unexpected, the contingent and the unwanted consequences of what they were trying to achieve, what emerged was a more detailed description of people trying to cooperate and compete to get things done, often tripping each other up or blocking each other, for good reason and bad. When researchers or managers described how they were trying to do whatever they had planned to do to innovate, they found themselves constrained and enabled by existing power relationships in the organizations where they were working. It was the negotiation and exploration of the blockages, misunderstandings, lacunae, the intersection of stability and change, that led to the possibility of new things emerging. One of the most profound changes occurring, then, was in the way that people understood themselves and what they were doing.

Tales of what people actually encountered trying to pursue their goals of innovation and change seemed to demonstrate that organizations and the people working within them were sometimes impervious to them. In these organizations subversive activity, deceit, greed, good and bad intentions all emerged on a daily basis between individuals absorbed in that particular game of organizational life. Both new and predictable things were arising constantly in the interactions people were describing with each other, many of which they did not immediately recognize and could only make sense of retrospectively; and this retrospective sense-making sometimes provoked a crisis, such as the imperative to consider more radical change.

From the perspective of narrative 2, the contingency narrative, what was termed an 'innovation' often reflected an ideological choice. People were improvising all the time as they struggled to get the work done together, but the improvisations which were recognized and pursued as innovations reflected who could decide what was innovative and what was not. From the perspective of narrative 2, innovation was not fixed in models or abstractions but in the way that people following the elusive concept of innovation found themselves having constantly to explore with each other what it was they thought they were doing and were finding out together in pursuit of the model. The most obvious change occurring was in self-perception and mutual understanding.

Drawing the narratives together

To sum up these two over-drawn narratives of innovation: in narrative 1, the overwhelmingly dominant tendency in the conference understood innovation to arise from conscious acts of managerial planning, which may have involved recombining what already existed to produce novelty. The important thing seemed to be to change constantly. This narrative was largely optimistic, future-oriented, and predicated on will, the will of the managers 'driving change', often change for other people. It was a deliberate act of prediction and control combining different groups, making things inclusive, getting 'the whole system in the room', planning, developing tools and techniques, and perhaps even compliance techniques so that employees were scrutinized to see that they were being innovative enough.

I recognize here some very familiar themes drawn from other aspects of management, such as strategy development, which involves the idea of generating a vision, of getting people to align and agree. There is a linear understanding of time stretching from the here and now into a semi-predictable future. Innovation was thought to arise from the alignment of people's plans and intentions, a phenomenon which we have explored elsewhere in this book.

Narrative 2 more readily presented innovation as originality, by which I mean going back to the origin of what was happening and exploring this in some detail, leaving behind the idealization. According to this narrative, innovation or change arises as a consequence of the struggle between people engaged in the ongoing, active participation in the exploration of what they thought they were doing together in organizations or communities, and the paradox of stability and change. Rather than being predicated on the developing models, these narratives were accounts of surprising things emerging between highly engaged people, often when the models broke down in the contingency of everyday life.

In the conference, people described an iterative understanding of time where they had to keep interpreting their plans in the light of opposition, or unintended consequences: they were constantly adapting in relation to the circumstances they encountered and in the ways these obliged them to revise what they thought they were doing. It would be possible to argue that these narratives tended towards the pessimistic, or perhaps, the realistic appraisal of the traps, difficulties and hardships that people encountered along the way of trying to be innovative.

Both of these narratives of innovation arose in the conference, but the first, heroic narrative tended to eclipse the second. Type 2 narratives were often offered ruefully, and with a degree of embarrassment: they were exceptional accounts, war stories about what can go wrong in the process of trying to undertake necessary innovation. They also usually provoked laughter and gestures of recognition from the audience, who had all experienced similar things themselves.

Recognition, shared insight, may also be considered to be a process of change and innovation. However, one might understand the two accounts as interdependent narratives, constantly negating each other, but in the discourse on innovation and change the first, in my experience, definitely crowded out the second. It was easy to come away with the impression that innovation is best undertaken as a deliberate and planned activity involving others, often driven by managers or leaders but resisted by employees, and that successful innovation depends upon overcoming such resistance.

The origins of innovation talk

In contemporary organizational life there is often a huge preoccupation with innovation and change and the role that leaders and managers have in bringing it about. This is a reflection of a much broader discourse promulgated by public figures, government ministers and business leaders about the need for improved economic competitiveness driven by continuous transformation and innovation, and which has evolved over the past three decades.

As I explore briefly in this chapter, the competitiveness discourse is seen by some scholars as a response to the rise of neo-liberal economics as an orthodoxy, and increased globalization. According to this perspective, business imperatives are now everyone's imperatives, no matter in which sector they might find themselves working, and this has led to widespread introduction of market forces into all sectors of the economy, even into those areas which were previously protected, such as the NHS in the UK (Politt, 1990, 1997). It is now largely taken for granted that all organizations should be adapting and changing, innovating continuously, in order to enhance a particular nation's ability to compete in the global market. This way of speaking creates particular contradictory pressures for leaders and managers since it relies to a degree on the fantasy of predictability and control.

In the exhortatory rush to innovate and change, there is little reflection on the relationship between stability and change, however. If innovation is taken to mean the introduction of a new product, idea or way of working, a change in something, then to call something innovative is to make the distinction with its opposite, continuity, stability or an existing practice. Continuity and change are in paradoxical and dynamical relationship, which implies that neither of them is a static state: sometimes we may need to innovate to keep things the same. It would be impossible for social life to continue if things were changing all of the time, and nor is there necessarily anything reactionary about stability; some of our enduring traditions and practices make us who we are and allow us to recognize each other.

It would be unwise, then, to assume that all innovation is necessarily a good thing as even a moment's reflection on events of the twenty-first century, where a range of highly innovatory financial products were developed by banks in North America and Europe to parcel up debt and distribute it throughout the financial system, might suggest. Innovation and change are much talked about but little understood. There is an additional irony that change and innovation talk is highly repetitive and unimaginative, revolving as it often does around familiar tropes and exhortations.

Talk of innovation and change creates an enormous and, one might even say, self-perpetuating pressure on managers to demonstrate that they can command innovation and change in organizations for the good. There has been a proliferation of scholarly work focused on innovation, and a restive search for managerial approaches, tools and formulae which can bring about this rather elusive organizational goal. The stakes are high for management as a profession if it ascribes to itself a unique ability to bring about innovatory developments which, apparently, we all crave.

Thinking about innovation and change and the role of managers

One of the principle claims of what I have been calling the dominant discourse of management, usually referred to as managerialism, is that managers and leaders have unique and appropriate skills and sets of techniques for bringing about predictable organizational change or innovation, and that change is obvious and desirable when it occurs. Moreover, there is a strong claim, too, that bringing about innovation and change is a manager's central role. I examine the strength of these claims, particularly in light of the fact that even scholarship supportive of the idea of wholesale change or innovation programmes often laments the fact that results are often very mixed. Usually, uneven success is attributed to the fact that managers have been insufficiently systematic or they have been half-hearted, or have not followed the evidence on how to do these things well, or that employees have resisted and subverted what was unavoidable and good for them because they are essentially resistant to change.

Instead, I explore the idea that wholesale programmes of change are inevitably both predictable and unpredictable, that innovation is likely to be hit and miss, and both will evince a variety of responses in staff working in organizations, which are supportive and resistant, leading to expected and unexpected consequences. This is partly because employees in organizations are to a greater or lesser extent convinced by the need for change, given that they are not always positively affected by it. So change, and resistance to change are intimately tied up with relations of power.

I am putting forward the case that there is always both continuity and change in organizations, and always has been, and that the job of the manager is to work as creatively as possible with that paradox. Nor am I arguing that managers can somehow control the paradox, as some scholars suggest, which we will discuss in more detail below. I argue that stability and change are dynamic states, and that it sometimes takes as much improvisation and effort to keep an organization stable as it does to change it. I question whether change and innovation are automatically a 'good thing' in and of themselves and look at the provenance of what we might think of as the discourse on change and innovation, the constant talk of transformation. I would like to go into more depth about why social life is both predictable and unpredictable at the same time, which will involve thinking about some differences between the natural and social worlds.

First, it might be helpful to contextualize briefly the discourse on innovation and change, and to understand how it is located in broader political and economic changes. We might then briefly consider how these developments during the last 30 years or so have affected the role of managers and management, and how they have come to be discussed.

Thinking about innovation as a change in power relations between groups reflected in discourse

As we have noted, and for a variety of socio-economic reasons, the discourse of change is ubiquitous in contemporary organizational life, and is manifest in its more heroic form as transformational change and innovation. No aspect of the workplace and no area of the economy is thought to be immune from the change-oriented attentions of leaders and managers, from organizational structures and everyday ways of working, through to employee values and what is referred to as organizational culture (Chapter 4).

As du Gay (2003) has pointed out, the rhetoric of change is often presented in apocalyptic and dualistic form: either you 'embrace' change or you are left for dead, and a good deal of scorn is reserved for those who cannot recognize the multiple opportunities that change presents. Du Gay describes the ways in which change is presented as both homogenous and linear: all of us are said to be facing change at this particular epoch in time in a unifying global process, no matter in what organization we work. This discourse produces an ambition for naïve wholesale change, which is in danger of covering over the specific and differing contexts in which work occurs, he argues, and can be experienced as a form of tyranny.

Moreover, it also has a tendency to hide the political complexion of the change that is being recommended, which in the case of the public sector is often mar-ketization of services as a preparation for privatization. Much of this is presented, in the UK at least, as public sector 'reform'. When it is presented as such, by gov-ernments of a variety of different persuasions, then it is much more difficult to oppose and to appear to be against 'reform'.

The change narrative, predicated on constant innovation in pursuit of ever greater competitiveness, is a discourse that the political economist Philip Cerny has been following for the past 20 years or so in a body of work charting the rise of what he calls the 'competition state' (Cerny, 1990, 2005, 2010). He argues that with the ascendancy of neoliberal economics and globalization the role of the state has changed dramatically, particularly in Western Europe. Instead of governments acting to decommodify and protect areas of the economy, such as, for example, public services and health care, to some extent shielding them from economic imperatives, their role instead has been to expose the domestic economy to trans-national competition, to internalize external pressures. Economic growth through efficiency, competition and innovation is promoted above all else, and the discourse of change and transformation has become all-pervasive.

Whereas previously there was a very strong notion of a sovereign state, where politics stopped at the nation's shores or boundaries, now the state plays a strong role in opening up society and the economy to the influence of the global political economy. Borrowing and developing the idea of 'governmentality' (government rationality) from Foucault (2008) to explain this change, where previously the role of the government, *la raison d'État*, was to promote the sovereign state, Cerny argues now that governments have developed a *raison du Monde*. That is, they have a paradoxical role of, on the one hand, actively hollowing out state provision by exposing it to market forces and privatization and, on the other, taking a strong and centralizing lead in privileging economic development above all else and creating the conditions where this can be brought about. They have been setting the tone for discussions about, and the conditions for the practice of innovation and change.

This has had consequences both for what governments consider their role to be, but also for the governance and management of organizations and has contributed to the pervasive discourse of innovation and change and the proliferation of scholarship about the same.

From a management perspective, Rakesh Khurana (2007) has charted the way that neo-liberal economic thinking has taken hold in American business schools, changing both the curriculum and the way that the role of manager is understood and promoted. In his book *From Higher Aims to Hired Hands*, he describes how 'ordinary' management came to be seen as an impediment to transformational and necessary changes if the economy was really to be driven by competitiveness. The reframing of the role of management and the inauguration of the idea of leadership as an alternative, he argues, was coterminous with the rise of neoliberal economics informed by the monetarist Chicago School (Friedman, 2002).

Economic disciplines gradually came to colonize what was taught in the curricula in business schools, and there was a shift away from anything that was not measurable and quantifiable in economic terms. From the early 1970s onwards, Khurana claims, there was a gradual discrediting of the idea that managers should try to meet the needs of the multiple stakeholders in firms (shareholders, employees, the local community). It was thought instead that the most economically measurable, and therefore 'objective', indicator of managers' performance was to increase the value of the firm for shareholders.

However, it was confusing to try and meet the needs of multiple stakeholders; instead, the rise of agency theory (Sen, 1977) put forward the case that the role of the leader was to act as the agent of shareholders. It became more routine for leaders' interests to be more closely aligned with the value of the firm through stock options and bonuses, so they were much more predisposed to make decisions about strategy, which increased the value of the company in the short term. Management, if it meant being deliberative and balancing a variety of interests, came to be seen as a constraint on the permanent revolution that was needed to drive up shareholder value.

Khurana understands the 1970s and 1980s as the start of the discourse on the need for transformational and innovatory management and leadership, which has escalated and expanded to give rise to a great deal of scholarship, governmental attention and conferences such as the one I attended in Europe. It has also led to detailed surveillance of staff who are obliged to conform to performance metrics to demonstrate that they are making a contribution to the profitability of the firm (Ghoshal, 2005; Power, 1997).

The restructuring of the global economy over the last three decades has led to a reconfiguring of the role of managers, and a change in emphasis on what they should be doing and how they should be practising. It has led to a change in the way of speaking about managerial concerns, a change in discourse which reflects a broader change in the power relations between groups. Drawing on Cerny,

Khurana and Ghoshal, one might make the case that managers have been coopted into the project of globalization and radical competition, which is supposedly brought about through constant change and innovation, as well as tighter and tighter scrutiny of the performance of staff measured against highly reductive metrics. This has affected both how managers are educated to do their jobs, their sense of professionalism and identity and what they find themselves involved in doing as managers. One of their principle roles is thought to be to champion innovation, by designing, implementing and supervising the necessary transformational changes that will guarantee competitive advantage.

The effects of the change agenda on organizational life

As a consequence it seems to be a common experience amongst employees in a variety of sectors that they are condemned to endless rounds of changes, which appear to them to be pointless, and which seem to be organized on the principle that things have to be constantly changed in order for managers to appear to be dynamic, a trend I alluded to above. This is a consistent danger for incoming CEOs, who can come under enormous pressure to show that they are doing something in their first 100 days. One commentator has called this persistent change obsession 'repetitive change syndrome' (Abrahamson, 2004).

In my view, it is important both to examine and to deflate the change narrative, given that in every epoch people consider themselves to be in the grip of unprecedented and unusual change, which is claimed to be in response to particular crises. Taking change seriously will involve paying attention to the quality of the changes being either recommended or experienced and the kinds of often hyperbolic rhetoric that accompanies them, what Alvesson (2013) in his most recent book refers to as an economy of persuasion. It will also involve making more complex the reductive binaries of positive change or negative stability that try to crowd out more subtle discussion. I intend to try to denaturalize the change narrative, and argue that it is not inevitable, a point of view expressed by Foucault who was alive just long enough to notice the rise of neoliberalism and globalisation as it was occurring:

> pure competition is not a primitive given. It can only be the result of lengthy efforts and, in truth, pure competition is never obtained. Pure competition must and can only be an objective, an objective thus presupposing an indefinitely active policy. Competition is therefore an historical objective of governmental art and not a natural given that must be respected ... There will thus be a sort of complete superimposition of market mechanisms, indexed to competition, and governmental policy. Government must accompany the market from start to finish.
>
> *(Foucault, 2008: 120–21)*

As usual, Foucault reminds us of the fact that there is nothing inevitable or even natural about the discourse of innovation and change driven by competition. It is a discourse which results in particular practices, and particular ways of describing the world. It makes us subjects in the sense that we are subject to these pressures, but at the same time they give us a sense of identity and purpose; we become who we are. However, it arises as a result of what everyone is doing, stitching together the project of globalization and liberalization as a form of what Cerny (2010) refers to as *bricolage*.

It seems to me that there is a great deal at stake for managerialism in its claim to be able to be in charge of and to be able to predict and control change, given that this is one of the principle ambitions of management understood as a social science (Flyvbjerg, 2001; Glynos and Howarth, 2007: 18–48). There is a strong tradition of scholars aspiring to develop management as an evidence-based social science (Rousseau, 2006; Pfeffer and Sutton, 2006), which we explored in Chapter 1 and which turns on the idea that it is possible to accumulate 'variables' and good practices that measurably affect organizational outcomes.

The practice of management, then, is the gathering of more and more practices that 'work', and which can guarantee organizational success. As with any discipline, there is an aspiration to acquire a stable body of knowledge which bestows professionalism and expertise on those who claim to be in possession of it. If managers cannot successfully design and implement the required change and turn organizations round for the good, then what are they there for?

Although the idea of uncertainty is often mobilized in the discourse of innovation and change, nonetheless even this is sometimes presented as being governable. Contradictions, the dualisms which I alluded to, can be organized to bring about ends which are predictable in advance, and which can be forecast to turn out to be beneficial for organizations. Much of the more orthodox management discourse acknowledges that change and uncertainty are disturbing, but this is a necessary unsettling, which is the precursor to achieving a new and more satisfactory organizational state. Some of the more orthodox literature, which I explore below, argues that in the change process it is the manager or leader who can surf the tides of change, whatever their uncertainties, and turn instability to their organization's advantage.

In what follows I call into question the idea of managerial control by considering the limits of management as a social science.

Sources of unpredictability in social life

Earlier in the book I drew attention to the ways in which the sociologists Norbert Elias (2000, 2001) and Pierre Bourdieu (1977, 1990) gave an account of the stable instability of social life. In this section I want to examine how the moral philosopher Alasdair MacIntyre assesses strengths and limitations of the social sciences for investigating these regular irregularities. He makes an important argument that the social sciences will never develop the predictive power of the natural sciences because of the unique and anticipative/responsive characteristics of human beings and because of the intervention of fate and contingency in our lives. We make our way together, he argues, in the paradox of predictable unpredictability.

For MacIntyre there are four sources of unpredictability in human affairs. First, he calls into question the idea that humans can ever plan to innovate, a question I raised at the beginning of this chapter, and one which goes to the heart of the managerial project. He argues that any plan to call into being something radically innovative already contains within it the idea of the innovation. He illustrates this by drawing on an analogy offered by Karl Popper. Two Stone Age people are standing together predicting that in 10 years' time someone will invent the wheel. Together they have already just invented it. So the notion of the prediction of some innovation is itself conceptually incoherent. Innovations, he argues are a form of discovery and are a surprise, which is not to argue that they are inexplicable after the fact.

This observation will no doubt be obvious and will provoke ironic recognition in anyone who has had to apply for funding from a grant-maker or an innovation fund for a research or a development project which needs to demonstrate in advance that it is going to be original or innovative.

The second area of unpredictability is one which MacIntyre describes as a trivial truth with substantive consequences – that I cannot always predict what I will choose from a variety of options in social life. My inability to predict my own choosing has consequences for others whose choices are, to a degree, dependent on my own. Even if it could be argued that those close to me might be able to predict my choices better than I could myself, they are in the same position as me: where their own preferences are partially obscured to themselves. This argument is in many ways similar to Mead's (1934) theory of the social self: that we are always emerging as selves in response to the gestures of other selves. We cannot realize ourselves until we see ourselves reflected back in the actions of others.

The third area of social unpredictability is the game-theoretic nature of social life. Despite the original optimism that game theory, based on the idea of rational calculation, could produce rule-like generalizations this has not proved the case in more complex situations of imperfect knowledge. In effect, we have to anticipate the anticipations of others when, as in the last point in the paragraph above, we are often unable to predict how we would behave ourselves. MacIntyre observes that the difference between a game modelled on a computer with a determinate set of players and determinate constraints, is that life is open-ended and there may be multiple games being played at the same time. This is a similar observation to the one made by Norbert Elias (1978), that social life consists of a game of games. Rather than gaining advantage through rational calculation, Elias argues that the best that can be achieved is to predict two or three moves ahead in the game through a process of detached involvement.

Fourthly, we must acknowledge pure contingency, he argues, with illustrations from great events in history. What if Cleopatra had been ugly and Anthony had not fallen in love with her? What if Napoleon had not had a cold at the battle of Waterloo and had not delegated command to Ney? We are all exposed to fate, or what the philosopher Martha Nussbaum (2001) has termed the fragility of good-ness in human affairs. There is no guarantee that our acting with good intentions will necessarily play out as such because of contingent circumstances, and nor is there any guarantee that good ideas will survive in an environment crowded with other options. Sometimes timing and happenstance are all.

Having set out the unpredictability of social life, MacIntyre then turns to the more predictable aspects. The first arises from the necessity in highly interdependent, developed societies to coordinate activities and to have regular routines, from the timetabling necessary to run bus and train services through to the regularities of what Mead (1934) termed elsewhere the social objects. Without such regularities social life would break down.

Society also demonstrates statistical regularities, MacIntyre argues. So we know that suicide rates increase at Christmas, that mental health problems are higher in Ireland than in Denmark and that homicide rates are higher in the USA than in the UK. But these regularities are relatively independent from causal knowledge about why such regularities exist. Just as unpredictability does not mean we cannot find explanations after the fact, so predictability does not mean that we necessarily know the causes. We also have knowledge of the causal predictability of nature: that snowstorms cause chaos, viruses cause disease and that diet will affect our health chances. The impact of statistical and natural regularity has a large effect on the making of plans and our ability to make choices between the relative success of one course of action over another.

As we navigate social life, then, we encounter the peculiar ways in which the unpredictable and more predictable aspects of social life interlock and affect each other. We would not achieve very much if we moved aimlessly from one isolated episode of life to another unconnected by what MacIntyre calls threads of large-scale intention to develop and perpetuate human institutions. However, our intentions and plans are profoundly affected by the fragility and contingency of human life, in which luck, bad timing and specificities may play out to thwart what we intend. It is necessary for life to have meaning, he argues, for us to engage in long-term projects and to try to render the future predictable. Equally it is necessary for us to be in charge of ourselves and not just to be the objects of other people's projects. Consequently, we are actively engaged in trying to make others predictable to ourselves by developing generalizations to capture their behaviour, whilst we try to make ourselves unpredictable to others by eluding their generalizations of us.

To what degree does MacIntyre think we can we generalize from social life? First of all, he thinks that generalizations will never have the law-like predictability of generalizations from the natural sciences. We will always be obliged to limit the scope of what we are claiming since there will always be counter-examples. They will take the form of 'characteristically, and for the most part ... '. Additionally, fate, contingency and our inability to anticipate our own responses, let alone those of others, will always play a strong role in how things will turn out.

Similar arguments about the way in which theories tend to draw unsustainable aggregate conclusions from particular examples have been made in social science literature in general (Starbuck, 2006; Fish, 1989) and organizational literature in particular (Sandberg and Tsoukas, 2011; Weick: 2003, 2007). Tsoukas (2009: 295) puts forward the idea that organizational research can most helpfully produce what he calls 'heuristic generalizations', which are generalizations abstracted from empirical data, but ones which are open to further specification and adaptation depending on context.

If the future is unknowable and if social life arises in the interconnection of the regular and the irregular in our social interactions, then the idea of a predictably efficient and effective organization is a contradiction in terms as far as MacIntyre is concerned. Mapping out the future would imply not just predicting the future but would involve attempts to control it in a totalitarian way, to develop projects which try to overcome the unpredictability of others. History presents us with a number of examples of precisely this kind of totalitarianism, which was of particular interest to the political theorist Hannah Arendt, whom I introduced in Chapter 3 on reflexivity.

What then, is the expertise of the manager, if there are no law-like generalizations to be made about organizational life, and what is the claim to legitimacy? MacIntyre argues that the manager's claims to expertise are false and that the best manager is the best actor, the one who can appear to others as though they are in control even though they never can be. Nonetheless, this does not prevent them from producing a variety of tools and techniques which do claim to control the social world, as we shall explore in the next section.

MacIntyre argues that both quantitative social scientists and managers/administrators have much in common and act ideologically by making strong claims to be able to predict and control social life. They do so by developing classificatory schemes which suit their purposes but which often make no reference to rival arguments about alternative forms of classification; they aspire to producing evaluatively neutral variables and assume that change is brought about causally by them – for the quantitative social scientist this is necessary in order to draw on statistical methods, and for the manager to claim that their policy intervention 'works'. Both quantitative social scientists and managers believe that the social world is manipulable, that they can engineer change in social structures in predictable ways. But they do so by simplifying the world and the selection of hypotheses about the world so that they are only paying attention to contexts where there is an assumption of defined regularity:

> Methodology then functions so as to communicate one very particular vision of the social world and one that obscures from view the fundamental levels of conceptualization, conflict, contestability, and unpredictability as they constitute and operate in the world.
>
> *(MacIntyre, 1998: 64)*

In this way, MacIntyre argues, the entwining of bureaucratic authority and quantitative methods acts ideologically, by presenting a particular conception of the world not as a partial view, but as the way things are, as 'the facts'. Sometimes the appeal to scientific management is also an invitation to avoid politics and contestation, as though we could produce improvements to the way that work gets done which everyone would accept because the facts speak for themselves, which was also an aspiration of one of the original fathers of scientific management theory, Frederick Taylor. In contemporary society we are constantly reminded of this in the way that we are deluged by statistics, league tables, rating systems and 'facts' about how a particular government's policies are helping to improve the performance of the public services.

MacIntyre's views are important to bear in mind as we assess the claims of management scholars to be able to offer ideas of substance to managers wishing to pursue innovatory or change projects. The idea of improvement is an important one, according to MacIntyre, but our plans are highly unlikely to work out as we intended. We are more likely to be able to recognize innovation after the fact, but much less likely to be sure that we can be innovatory before we act, or to be able to predict the consequences of what we are doing.

The idea of managing paradox and contradiction in processes of innovation and change

In the following section I will consider two scholarly approaches to innovation and change which accept that it is a probabilistic undertaking. In other words, the scholars I assess critically have already gone beyond the idea that managing change is a matter of simply having the right plans and strong determination to change reluctant 'mind sets'. In their own separate ways they each directly address the paradox of stability and change, but do so very differently.

In this book we have been examining whether exploring the contradictions, paradoxes and ambiguities of work can support managers better to understand the work they are doing, and there are a large number of other scholars who previously have asked the same question. The two pieces of scholarly research try to contend with contradiction from the perspective of theory and models of change, and from a perspective based loosely on ideas of complexity.

Attempts to model contradiction implicit in innovation and change

An example of a recent attempt to gain some purchase on the connection between innovation and contradiction is Rosenkopf and McGrath's article attempting to retheorize innovation (2011). The article is helpful in many ways because it reviews a great deal of recent scholarship on innovation and change and seeks to sum up what we might learn from this. The article covers what we might understand as the strong tendency in much managerial research to develop models, frameworks or formulae for guaranteeing organizational success through innovation.

The authors seek to redefine the idea of novelty by reviewing the way that previous scholars have attempted to generalize about innovation using a variety of concepts and models. Many of these take an industry-specific, or sector-wide approach and try to generalize from it. Drawing on March's seminal article (1991), which discussed the dualism of exploration, i.e. finding new things to do, and exploitation, once novelty has been discovered, then turning the discovery into products or services, Rosenkopf and McGrath review past literature which argues either that the two be brought into balance, or points out that firms often undertake them both at that same time to try and demonstrate 'ambidexterity'.

The question remains, however, how do they bring them into balance and in what proportion? Do they sequence first one then the other, or do so both at the same time, i.e. having different units in a business responsible for exploration or exploitation? Following a review of the literature, the authors reflect upon the different concepts, often borrowed from the natural sciences, to find ways of talking about 'balancing' exploration and exploitation. For example, Burgelman (2002) borrows the concept of 'punctuated equilibrium' from evolutionary theory to explain how organizations have long periods of stability punctuated by periods of frenetic activity.

Rosenkopf and McGrath review the empirical studies, the modelling, including set theory and NK modelling and ubiquitous two-by-two grids, and the search for 'mechanisms' which have been taken up by different scholars to conclude that there is little which is generalizable from one context to another, with many scholars undertaking sector-specific studies which seem to have few implications for another sector. The concept of novelty, the authors argue, is a multifaceted one, where there is a difficulty defining exactly what it is that we are talking about: there is a problem around construct. What do we call innovation, and to whom is it innovative?

In conclusion, and as is often the case in papers which have reviewed previous attempts to generalize from a complex area of organizational life in highly general and abstract terms, the authors call for more research in order to bridge what they see as the divide between theory and practice. The appeal for a formula or a two-by-two heuristic to help with 'balancing' contradictory pressures seems to have been a vain one, and there is nothing solid to recommend to firms wanting to find a formula that will guarantee producing higher performance.

As with the search for evidence-based management, which I referred to in Chapter 1, what emerges is a patchwork of partially helpful, incomplete, often sector-specific scholarship, which has struggled in vain to produce observations of a generic and stable kind which would be universally helpful to managers. The authors have not given up on their search, however, but argue that further research will produce deeper insights into the relationship between contexts and mechanisms which will prove helpful when generalized.

Contradiction as complex arrangements

The second approach to understanding how novelty develops in organizations is typified by an in-depth study carried out by Garud et al. (2011) on the company

3M Corporation. There were a variety of reasons for the researchers choosing this company to study, not least because of one of the researcher's long-term association with it, but principally because they felt that the firm personified sustainable innovation. The researchers interviewed a large number of employees as well as trying to trace how products were developed over time in terms of their 'innovation journey'. The researchers conclude that sustainable innovation arises from what they call 'complexity arrangements', which they categorize as follows.

First, the researchers think they have identified what they term 'relational complexity' in the ways in which employees, technologies and devices continuously interacted, and how new employees were socialized into the broad spread of technologies across the firm. Secondly, they notice 'manifest' complexity from the numbers of patents, developments, products and applications that are emerging at any one time in the company. Thirdly, they draw attention to what they call 'regulative' complexity, such as an injunction to employees to spend 15 per cent of their time exploring new avenues not necessarily directly connected to their mainstream jobs.

Next, Garud et al. describe 'temporal complexity' in the way that the company encouraged employees to take advantage of serendipitous moments: although they were invited to take advantage of 15 per cent of their time to pursue their own projects, they were not obliged to do so all at once, but at times that made sense to them. Employees were encouraged to think of what they were doing in the moment, as well as in the longer term, both synchronous and diachronous time scales. Equally, the researchers note how seeming dead-ends and false starts may have proved innovative over the long term: sometimes employees in 3M created products which were in search of a market, rather than the other way round.

All of these complex arrangements are woven together by what Garud et al. identify as a predisposition to tell company narratives, which tie together different histories and keep past achievements and breakthroughs alive in the present. This is an important and complex understanding of the importance of time to understanding organizational becoming, although I am interpreting more into the article than perhaps is made explicit by Garud et al. That is, the past, present and future are woven together in the way that employees at 3M understand what it is they are doing: past achievements influence current practice in anticipation of future innovations. The complexity of narrative structure allows for the connecting of different actors, different phases of product development and complex configurations which are distributed throughout the company.

Garud et al.'s overview of the conditions pertaining in 3M point to a way of overcoming the dualisms that arise in a great deal of management literature discussing innovation and change by describing a variety of organizational arrangements, including a strong company narrative about achievements in innovation and retrospective sense-making, that allow for what they call 'multiple agentic orientations', by which I think they mean the ability to entertain many contradictory pressures at the same time.

Summary of the two approaches to understanding contradictions in change

Rosenkopf and McGrath perform a very useful service for us by showing a huge variety of ways in which scholars have struggled with novelty and innovation, trying to produce helpful theories or grids and frameworks which might be useful to managers. Unfortunately, Rosenkopf and McGrath argue that the concept is too unclear, the examples incommensurable and the research too partial for managers to draw much in the way of general conclusions in terms of being able to plan to innovate, and by doing so to reconcile some of the organizational contradictions which arise in the process. In other words, they point precisely to what MacIntyre was arguing in his assessment of the lack of predictive power of the social sciences. According to MacIntyre, the best that can be achieved in the social sciences is to argue 'characteristically, and for the most part'. Talk of innovation and change is contingent on the circumstances in which it is carried out. What the authors call for is more practice-based examples to make the concept of producing novelty more robust, and to narrow the gap between theory and practice.

Finally, Garud et al. take a historical and a social view of how staff in one organization, renowned for its continuous innovation of products over time, account for the way that this has proved possible. The authors conclude that this is due to what they refer to as complex arrangements: a variety of ways of socializing new employees and exposing them to different parts of the company and what they are doing along with general encouragement to develop their own ideas in their own time. 3M seems to be a company which is capable of taking the long view, more relaxed about whether innovation will necessarily lead to some concrete return immediately. Moreover, a main part of the socialization process is the company narratives which get told and retold about the development of products which creates what Elias and Scotson (1994) referred to as a 'heroic "we" identity' amongst employees.

As Garud et al. point out, narrative also has a complex structure (Czarniawska, 1998; Tsoukas and Hatch, 2001), bringing together the past, the future and the present, and often with a variety of points of view of the actors in the narrative. In many ways it is no surprise to find narrative at the heart of Garud et al.'s account of the 3M experience given that they claim that 3M encourages 'multiple agentic orientations', the ability to face in many different directions at once. Garud et al. make more complex Quinn's simple binaries, which we explored in Chapter 2, which can be transcended from a meta-position and set out a more convincing social account of innovation. They also take a long-term view, suggesting that innovation arises as a form of regular practice between people with a history of working in particular ways. This is not an account of heroic leaders coming into an organization and transforming it, but rather a description of particular practices into which new members of the company become inducted.

Nonetheless, there are still difficulties inherent in Garud et al.'s account of the complexity arrangements at 3M, although there is much in the article which moves the discussion on from either the simplistic narrative of managerial prediction and control, or Quinn's idea of the individualistic master manager.

First, the authors still present an overly ordered account of organizational life which renders no insight into the breakdowns, misunderstandings and sometimes open conflict that arise from processes aimed at innovatory change (and may sometimes even lead to it). Both MacIntyre and Elias have pointed to the fact that managers' intentions are not the only game in town as they try to anticipate the anticipations of others. In an organization which is serially innovative we gain no insight into who gains and who loses as one group's intentions impact upon another's. The encounter with the intentions and plans of others brings us hard up against our own intentions and plans: we have to reconsider them and rethink what it is we are doing. Power relationships, self-understanding and identity are all closely related.

The fact that Garud et al.'s account may be over-orderly and gives little insight into power relations may have something to do with the privileged access they were given to 3M and the nature of organizational research, where there may be a tendency always to present an explicitly named research subject to the good. What we are left with, then, is a convincing account of cooperation, but with very little understanding of competing claims for resources and managerial approval and the inevitable lacunae, misunderstandings and conflicts of everyday organizational life, which may also lead to innovation. Rosenkopf and McGrath's question as to who gets to decide what innovation is and in what circumstances is still unanswered. Nor can we understand the paradox of stable instability: how do managers at 3M routinize innovation and how is 'innovation' related to the everyday improvisational practices which are necessary to achieve the work in an ensemble performance?

What Garud et al. refer to as regulative complexity, by which I think they mean some kind of constraint on employees, is the proposal that employees should take 15 per cent of their time to develop their own projects. This is not equivalent to the kinds of constraints that conference participants were describing in their off-record debriefings – the unconvinced senior manager, the resistance of employees, rearguard action by the accounts department, what Elias has referred to as the interweaving of intentions which are mediated by power relations.

Secondly, Garud et al.'s account suggests that 'harnessing' complexity arrangements can help to sustain innovatory practice, but this seems to me to stray exactly into MacIntyre's territory, where we can only say that in general, and for the most part the kinds of arrangements that they describe are likely to lead to better innovatory performance. It also places the manager or researcher outside the arrangements which are affecting everyone else, in some kind of meta-position. 3M is 120 years old, and the arrangements the researchers elucidate have evolved over decades: this evolution presumably involves both planned organizational development as well as responsiveness to what the authors describe as serendipity, surprise and the unexpected, recognition after the fact that particular working arrangements have proven more productive than others.

Activity informs working arrangements but equally, and paradoxically, working arrangements affect activity. This is exactly the same story that the researchers tell about the development of products, and in this sense there is a degree of consistency between product development and organizational development. To what extent, though, can other companies learn from this experience? 3M has its own history and its own particular arrangements, which are directly related to its development.

Concluding thoughts on the paradox of stability and change

In my own institution a new Vice Chancellor was appointed who came into the organization claiming that he was not necessarily going to change anything: he was simply going to listen and understand what was already working well. Within the first six months the trustees of the university were asking him what he was going to change to make his mark and within no time the organization was embarking upon a change programme which the top team called 'Agile'. The Agile programme, amongst other things, aimed to strip out a number of tiers of management so that the top management team could have a clear 'line of sight' and communication with the rest of the organization. Better communication and reduced hierarchy was intended to make the organization more agile and flexible.

One of the aspects of Agile was to reduce the number of deans of school as well as the number of schools. The number of schools was reduced but, as an indirect consequence, and for reasons unimportant to go into here, the number of senior middle managers increased, which was not part of the original plan. One way of understanding the changes is that there are still the same number of managers reporting to the senior management team, although now they are configured slightly differently. There was enormous disruption over a number of months, and quite a few colleagues were obliged to apply for a reduced number of jobs at particular grades in the organization, although the number of senior middle managers remains about the same.

It is far too early to know whether this organization-wide change programme has had the desired effect of making the university more agile, but almost everyone in the more than 2,000 staff complement has been affected by it. It is a very good example of what Foucault was referring to as discourse, how a particular way of talking about the world creates practices which shape social life, which in turn informs discourse. In Foucault's terms (1991), power is not exercised by 'them' over 'us', but we discipline ourselves and each other. Even the Vice Chancellor of a university is not in a position only to command, but is also commanded, as in turn is the board of governors who will have its expectations shaped and formed by the environment in which it finds itself acting.

In this chapter I have investigated some of the reasons why managers may be caught up in a particularly febrile discourse on change and innovation, which I have argued has been informed and shaped by longer-term socio-economic trends. This is a self-perpetuating and self-amplifying discourse which privileges one pole, change, over the other pole of what I am presenting as a paradox, stability, and in my view severely over-estimates the ability of even very senior managers to bring about innovation and change in the way that perhaps they would like. It is a largely unnuanced discourse which assumes that all change is for the good, and that constant innovation, transformation even, applies equally across all sectors of the economy in similar ways. It also assumes to a certain extent that change is for other people, and not for the controlling managers. It often gives little account of the way in which managers themselves are changed by the projects they have unleashed.

I have also noted the way that innovation talk can cover over political projects of marketization and privatization and has colonized management education and poses a direct challenge for managers who are assumed to have unique abilities in commanding change for the good of the organization. The discipline of management can make strong claims to be able to predict and control social life, which are unfulfillable in practice.

Of course, as experience shows, managers are in charge but not necessarily in control. They will inevitably be called upon to make changes in organizations since, as MacIntyre observes, longer-term shared projects to make the future less unpredictable are an inevitable part of being human. However, as he advises us, because of fate and contingency, because of the interweaving of intentions as we try to discover things about others that we strive equally hard to conceal from them as we try to anticipate the anticipations of others, because generalization takes a different form in the social sciences than in the natural sciences, we may only succeed 'characteristically, and for the most part'. The claim to be able to guarantee positive change for the good of the firm is either, according to MacIntyre, good acting, or the road to tyranny where we impose our conceptions of the good, irrespective of the resistance we are likely to meet.

Management scholarship that takes the complexity of stability and change seriously follows a number of pathways. Like Rosenkopf and McGrath, it may review the plethora of approaches that have tried to pin down and systematise innovation only to conclude that the concept is still rather elusive and our ability to generalize about it may be limited. Alternatively, after Garud et al. it may conclude that innovation arises from a variety of complex, interdependent practices which develop over time, and which are sustained and regenerated by organizational story-telling and an iterative understanding of time: how we reinterpret the past in the present in expectation of the future. Even then, the story of 3M is a relatively ordered and sanitized tale which contains little of the accounts of disappointment, frustration and sometimes open conflict that arose in the narratives of researchers and managers giving presentations at the conference to which I was invited.

From a complex responsive processes perspective, stability and change, innovation and continuity are two sides of the same coin. Both are created or maintained dynamically in everyday activity as people improvise together in an ensemble performance to achieve whatever they set out to achieve together. To a degree, then, employees are always being innovative even if it is to keep things relatively stable. What becomes established as an innovation involves a value judgment informed by ideology and is reflective of a configuration of relationships of power.

Elias would go further and argue that changes in the balance of power between groups lead to the production of knowledge which is sometimes to no one's benefit. To understand the innovation discourse in this light may enable more reflective managers to take a more detached attitude towards the exhortation constantly to innovate and change, although there will certainly be no avoiding it. However, our bright and transformative innovations of today are provisional, and are always open to reinterpretation.

As Mead observed: 'The pasts we are involved in are both irrevocable and revocable' (1932/2002: 36), by which I take him to mean that each passing generation inevitably reinterprets the past in order to imagine a different future in the present. Organisations have always been, and always will be, sites of both stability and change with managers in the critical position of trying to straddle and make judgments about the generative tension between the two. Managers are likely to be changed as much as changing others, and one of the principal changes taking place in organizations is in self-understanding in the fluctuating relationships of power brought about by the interweaving of intentions.

References

Abrahamson, E. (2004) Avoiding Repetitive Change Syndrome, *MIT Sloane Review*, 45(2): 93–96.
Alvesson, M. (2013) *The Triumph of Emptiness: Consumption, Higher Education, and Work Organization*, Oxford: Oxford University Press.
Bourdieu, P. (1977) *Outline of a Theory of Practice*, Cambridge: Cambridge University Press.
——(1990) *The Logic of Practice*, Cambridge: Polity Press.
Burgelman, R. A. (2002) Strategy as Vector and the Inertia of Coevolutionary Lock-in, *Administrative Science Quarterly*, 47(2): 325–57.
Cerny, P. G. (1990) *The Changing Architecture of Politics: Structure, Agency and the Future of the State*, London and Newbury Park, CA: Sage.
——(2005) Political Globalization and the Competition State, in Stubbs, R. and Underhill, G. R. D. (eds.) *The Political Economy of the Changing Global Order*, Oxford: Oxford University Press, 3rd Edition, 376–86.
——(2010) The Competition State Today: From *Raison d'État* to *Raison du Monde*, *Policy Studies*, 31(1): 5–21.
Czarniawska, B. (1998) *A Narrative Approach to Organization Studies*, Thousand Oaks, CA: Sage.
du Gay, P. (2003) The Tyranny of the Epochal: Change, Epochalism and Organizational Reform, *Organization*, 10(4): 663–84.
Elias, N. (1978) *What Is Sociology?*, New York: Columbia University Press.
——(2000) *The Civilizing Process*, Oxford: Oxford University Press.
——(2001) *The Society of Individuals*, Oxford: Oxford University Press.
Elias, N. and Scotson, J. (1994) *The Established and the Outsiders*, London: Sage.
Fish, S. (1989) *Doing What Comes Naturally*, Oxford: Clarendon Press.
Flyvbjerg, B. (2001) *Making Social Science Matter: Why Social Enquiry Fails and How It Can Succeed Again*, Cambridge: Cambridge University Press.
Foucault, M. (1991) *Discipline and Punish*, London: Penguin Books.
——(2008) *The Birth of Biopolitics: Lectures at the Collège de France, 1978–1979*, trans. Graham Burchell, London: Palgrave Macmillan (French edition 2004).

Friedman, M. (2002) *Capitalism and Freedom (40th Anniversary Edition)*, Chicago: University of Chicago Press.

Garud, R., Gehman, J. and Kumaraswamy, A. (2011) Complexity Arrangements for Sustained Innovation: Lessons from 3M Corporation, *Organization Studies*, 32(6): 737–67.

Ghoshal, S. (2005) Bad Management Theories Are Destroying Good Management Practices, *Academy of Management Learning and Education*, 4: 75–91.

Glynos, J. and Howarth, D. (2007) *Logics of Explanation in Social and Political Theory*, London: Routledge.

Khurana, R. (2007) *From Higher Aims to Hired Hands: The Social Transformation of American Business Schools and the Unfulfilled Promise of Management as a Profession*, Princeton, NJ: Princeton University Press.

MacIntyre, A. (1981) *After Virtue: A Study in Moral Theory*, Notre Dame: Notre Dame Press.

——(1998) Social Science Methodology as the Ideology of Bureaucratic Authority, in Knight, K. (ed.) *The MacIntyre Reader*, Cambridge: Polity Press.

March, J. G. (1991) Exploration and Exploitation in Organizational Learning, *Organization Science*, 2(1): 71–87.

Mead, G. H. (1932/2002) *The Philosophy of the Present*, New York: Prometheus Books.

——(1934) *Mind, Self and Society from the Standpoint of a Social Behaviorist*, Chicago: Chicago University Press.

Nussbaum, M. (2001) *The Fragility of Goodness: Luck and Ethics in Greek Tragedy and Philosophy*, Cambridge: Cambridge University Press.

Pfeffer, J. and Sutton, R. (2006) *Hard Facts, Dangerous Half-Truths, and Total Nonsense: Profiting from Evidence-Based Management*, Boston, MA: Harvard Business School Press.

Pollitt, C. (1990) *Managerialism and the Public Service: The Anglo American Experience*, Cambridge, MA: Basil Blackwell.

——(1997) Managerialism Revisited, in Peters, B. G. and Savoie, D. (eds.) *Taking Stock: Assessing Public Sector Reforms*, Montreal: McGill-Queens University Press.

Power, M. (1997) *The Audit Society: Rituals of Verification*, Oxford: Oxford University Press.

Quinn, R. E. (1988) *Beyond Rational Management: Mastering the Paradoxes and Competing Demands of High Performance*, San Fransisco: Jossey-Bass.

Rosenkopf, L. and McGrath, P. (2011) Advancing the Conceptualization and Operationalization of Novelty in Organizational Research, *Organization Science*, 22(5): 1297–311.

Rousseau, D. (2006) Is There Such a Thing as 'Evidence Based Management'?, *Academy of Management Review*, 31(2): 256–69.

Sandberg, J. and Tsoukas, H. (2011) Grasping the Logic of Practice: Theorizing Through Practical Rationality, *Academy of Management Review*, 36(2): 338–60.

Sen, A. (1977) Rational Fools: A Critique of the Behavioural Foundations of Economic Theory, *Philosophy and Public Affairs*, 6: 317–44.

Starbuck, W. H. (2006) *The Production of Knowledge: The Challenge of Social Science Research*, Oxford: Oxford University Press.

Tourish, D. (2013) *The Dark Side of Transformational Leadership: A Critical Perspective*, London: Routledge.

Tsoukas, H. (2009) Craving for Generality and Small-N Studies: A Wittgensteinian Approach Towards the Epistemology of the Particular in Organization and Management Studies, in Buchanan, D. A. and Bryman, A. (eds.) *The Sage Handbook of Organizational Research Methods*, London: Sage, 285–301.

Tsoukas, H. and Hatch, M. J. (2001) Complex Thinking, Complex Practice: The Case for a Narrative Approach to Organizational Complexity, *Human Relations*, 54(8): 979–1013.

Weick, K. E. (2003) Theory and Practice in the Real World, in Tsoukas, H. and Knudsen, C. (eds.) *The Oxford Handbook of Organization Theory*, Oxford: Oxford University Press, 453–75.

——(2007) The Generative Properties of Richness, *Academy of Management Journal*, 50: 14–19.

6

THE PARADOX OF COOPERATION AND COMPETITION

Conflict and the necessary politics of organizational life

Managers spend a great deal of their time dealing with uncertainty, moderating differences, negotiating and responding to the unexpected. There are often conflicting demands and points of view about what is important and how it should be dealt with. However, you would be hard pushed to find much of this reflected in the majority management literature, except in writing which argues that conflict happens in organizations but that it, too, can be managed and harnessed to the good. This is in keeping with the general claim that most areas of human experience can be managed (projects, time, risk, anger) so orthodox organizational literature offers a variety of tools and techniques to identify, analyse and treat organizational conflict so that it is harnessed towards increasing organizational performance.

In this chapter I investigate this last thread of organizational theory more thoroughly to argue that there is no standing back from the hurly-burly of organizational life; rather, and perhaps counterintuitively, I suggest that the most productive way of dealing with it is to participate in organizational struggle as fully as possible.

However, the appeal to the idea of a rational treatment of contested areas of life is increasingly made in broader policy circles, in government and local government, say, where ministers of officials stake a claim for the legitimacy of what they are doing in the name of science or research. There is something instinctively convincing about it. The appeal to reason is based on the idea that 'the data speak for themselves' and point in only one direction, the direction the particular minister or official has already chosen. I am not in any way trying to imply that politicians or managers should ignore evidence or data, merely that all research comes with assumptions, may answer some questions but raise others, and is unlikely to say anything about what should be done as a result of the research. In any situation where there are competing goods with no obvious way of sifting or choosing between them, the way forward is likely to be contested. Finding ways to explore these competing conceptions of the good is at the heart of organizational life and life in general. Staking a claim to the moral high ground of truth based on 'evidence' is certainly one way of championing a position, but is one which is aimed at silencing alternative opinions, rather than opening them up.

In this chapter I explore what I understand to be the inevitably conflictual process of engagement which arises between people trying to get things done together and which turns on the paradox of cooperation and competition. It is part of the complex responsive processes of human relating. In other words, most people are trying to contribute to the broader undertaking of which they are part and to see their organization succeed and thrive; they are part of one organization with their colleagues to which their success is bound. At the same time they are interested in what they are doing at work, they want to succeed personally, and they strive for recognition and status.

Agreement on how to help the organization prosper will always be a matter of contestation, and contestation with the self, involving the exploration of different conceptions of the good, and a discussion of ends as well as means. Drawing on Elias, Mead, Mannheim and other sociologists who have developed insights into conflict, I discuss the functional importance of conflict. Additionally, I draw on some psychoanalytic literature to see what that offers to the discussion.

On the idea of managing conflict

In organizational theory, Rahim (2001) provides one of the most comprehensive overviews of conflict in organizations which covers a large body of literature, and traces the history of the idea in philosophy, sociology and organizational theory. He notes the way that attitudes towards conflict have evolved from understanding it as a dysfunctional aspect of organizational life which could be removed through a scientific approach to work design (Taylor, 1911), or adherence to impersonal bureaucratic values and rules (Weber, 1929/1947), through human relations approaches which attempted to resolve conflict through organizational and cultural design (Mayo, 1933), to what he deems more 'modern' understandings of conflict as a necessary and important aspect of organizational regeneration, provided that it is kept within certain bounds.

Rahim provides a useful service with his literature review, finding in his survey 10 classifications of conflict (affective conflict, substantive conflict, conflict of interest, conflict of values, goal conflict, realistic versus non-realistic conflict, institutional versus non-institutionalized conflict, retributive conflict, misattributed conflict, and displaced conflict). Just as there are 10 categories of conflict, so there are five ways to deal with it: integrating, obliging, dominating, avoiding and compromising (2001: 33).

I am using Rahim as an example, but in managerial literature he is one amongst many writers who try to subsume conflict within a management discourse: for example, some scholars writing in the same tradition promise that it is possible to become a conflict-competent leader to produce win-win situations (Runde and Flanagan, 2013), or that managers can proactively design conflict management systems (Constantino and Merchant, 1996). In choosing to focus on management literature I have not, of course, done justice to the rich thread of research in social psychology (for example, Deutsch, 1973; Schelling, 1960) which developed out of Kurt Lewin's field theory, or to the large literature on conflict resolution and mediation. What interests me about orthodox management literature on conflict are its assumptions, which we will explore, and how these are covered over.

Rahim has developed two research tools to assist with the identification of the categories of conflict that may exist in organizations: one classifies the types of conflict prevalent in a particular company and the second measures the effectiveness of the five ways of dealing with it. This is undertaken with a view to managing conflict towards greater organizational effectiveness: managers need to match styles with categories, to know what to do when conflict occurs, how to enhance it or reduce it, and when to do so in a manner which enhances organizational performance. Managing conflict is offered as an alternative to simply eliminating it, since Rahim is writing in what he would term a 'modern' paradigm or harnessing an appropriate degree of conflict for organizational development:

> What we need for contemporary organizations is conflict management, not conflict resolution. Conflict management does not necessarily imply avoidance, reduction, or termination of conflict. It involves designing effective strategies to minimize the dysfunctions of conflict and enhancing the constructive functions of conflict in order to enhance learning and effectiveness of an organization.
>
> *(Rahim, 2001: 76)*

Rahim recommends a linear and sequential approach for the effective management of conflict. First, one analyses the problem through a diagnosis using one of the tools to develop identified above so that the problem can be measured. Next, one intervenes in the processes to encourage organizational learning and transformation, or to change organizational structure. For Rahim there is a clear role for what he understands as transformational leadership in the changing of organizational process. Each situation offers the possibility of encouraging staff to learn more about the five ways of dealing with conflict and to use them when they are appropriate. The structural approach involves changing the structure of a department to fit with the requirements of its environment. The idea of both approaches is to try and move conflicts away from those involving affect, towards what he terms substantive conflicts, which centre on disagreements about tasks.

In a chapter acknowledging ethical questions in conflict resolution, Rahim argues that conflict management requires wise leaders, ethically sensitive employees and a broad stakeholder base for considering conflictual questions. Using Kohlberg's (1969) *schema* for understanding moral development, Rahim argues that senior managers need to be of high moral development, in the third or 'post-conventional' stage of moral development, and those deemed to be less so need to be trained so that they can rise through the moral hierarchy. Drawing on Aristotle he recommends four methods for dealing with conflicts ethically: logistic, problematic, dialectical and agonistic. As one proceeds through the methods so fewer and fewer rules apply and more and more voices are added to the discussion about what to do.

So, logistic methods involve instrumental reasoning in a defined area of the business; meanwhile, problematic conflict resolution involves basic agreement on ends, but mild disagreement about means. A dialectical approach involves two parties agreeing to argue rationally along which includes problematizing their own positions. Finally, by the agonistic approach Rahim understands that:

> Any device is permitted if it leads to victory; might makes right; what is good is what works; and so on. Agonistic discourse includes the use of informal logical fallacies such as the appeal to force, the illegitimate appeal to authority, irrational appeals to fear, playing upon a person's emotional relations to a group, and so forth.
>
> Akin to agonistic discourse are the 'political tactics' typically used in factional struggles, such as unfairly blaming others for an unsuccessful policy or program; selectively releasing information to create a false impression to maximize the interests of one's faction; using control over scarce resources to create obligations to oneself or one's faction; flattering the already powerful to gain his or her protection; and priming a minority of a committee in order to get a quick consensus from an apparently free, but actually constrained, discussion …
>
> *(Rahim, 2001: 186–87)*

For this reason he feels that agonistic conflict resolution can never be the norm in organizations if they are healthy. That is to say, he regards the last method to involve a level of infighting and political intrigue too extreme for a healthy organization to function.

In concluding his work, Rahim makes a distinction between substantive and affective conflict. He argues for a proportionate amount of substantive conflict, as long as it is well managed, to keep an organization generative and effective. He understands competition as a subset of conflict. Affective conflict, on the other hand, he considers dysfunctional. The role of the manager, then, is to move the organization from dysfunctional conflict to functional conflict using the five styles of conflict management previously outlined. They do so by analysing the type and extent of conflict through questionnaires, then designing an appropriate response.

Critical reflections on the idea of managing conflict

Rahim's understanding of conflict, in keeping with a great deal of orthodox management theory, turns on the idea of the manager as detached, dispassionate observer and one with no stake in the game. This is a perspective which he encourages those caught up in conflict to adopt, since for him conflict becomes dysfunctional when it involves affect, a point I want to return to below. Although he is not so naïve as to suppose that all conflicts can be solved through diagnosis and the application of his suite of tools, nonetheless, he does assume that managers are in a position to tune the degree of conflict so that it is not too much, not too little, but just right. As usual with this way of thinking, the author assumes that managers are in a position to predict and control, to act on complex areas of human experience to effect an outcome which they have decided in advance.

I am not arguing that there is nothing to be done about conflict in organizations and that managers have no role in dealing with it. What I am calling into question is the degree of over-claiming of managerial influence and that a smooth-functioning, optimally conflictual organization is the norm. I also think that Rahim leaves managers short of what they most need to know. Organizations provoke very strong emotions in people, which do not disappear just because professional orthodoxy makes it difficult to express them or talk about them. The best that Rahim can do is to say that they are unhelpful and intractable.

Readers can make up their own minds about the extent to which Rahim lives in an idealized world when he argues that politically engaged, no-holds-barred agonistic conflict can never be a healthy norm in organizational life. By contrast, it is interesting to consider Robert Jackall's seminal study into the ethics of North American corporate life, in which he states that:

> First, some of the fundamental requirements of managerial work clash with the normal ethics governing interpersonal behaviour, let alone friendship in our society ... at bottom a great deal of managerial work consists of ongoing struggles for dominance and status. Real administrative effectiveness flows, in fact from the prestige that one establishes with other managers. Prestige in managerial hierarchies depends not only on position as determined by the crucial indices of rank, grade, title and salary, and the external accoutrements that symbolize power. Even more fundamentally, it consists of the socially recognized ability to work one's will, to get one's way, to have the say-so when one chooses in both the petty and large choices of organizational life.
>
> *(Jackall, 2010: 208)*

There is a similar account of the daily experience of politics, cooperation and competition to be found in Watson and Harris's ethnographic study of British organizations:

> Most managers did not, however, expect to stay above or out of organizational politics and career competitiveness. Career rivalry and the unpleasantness which goes with it, whilst typically regretted, were again spoken of as 'something which goes with the territory'.
>
> *(Watson and Harris, 1999: 84)*

Increasing numbers of critical and process management scholars have written about the importance of both politics and strong feelings in organizational life (Sims, 2005;

Howard-Grenville et al., 2013). Reading Rahim's account and setting it alongside Jackall's, and Watson and Harris's, where Jackall argues that 'big organizations often seem to be vast systems of organized irresponsibility – even, perhaps especially, to those within them' (Jackall, 2010: 208), it would appear that for the latter three scholars, factionalism, politics and ethical ambiguity are the norm rather than the exception.

Here we have a good contrast between a more idealized form of organizational research, which focuses on what managers ought to be doing, and two studies of what managers actually are doing to survive and thrive in their organizations. Where Rahim is working with identifiable and measurable categories, tools and techniques, idealizations, both Jackall's, and Watson and Harris's managers live and work in a world of ideology, ambiguity, contingency and complexity. In many ways, Rahim's account stops at the point that organizational life becomes most vital: it has nothing to say about the lived experience of many people working in highly conflicted contexts where cooperation and competition are inevitable.

On agonism and taking up a position

I also want to take issue with Rahim's understanding of agonism, a term which crops up again and again in political science. For example, political philosopher Chantal Mouffe (2005) has noticed a trend in broader political debate of appealing to reason and rationality, particularly in politics of the 'third way' (i.e., 'not left, not right, but what works'). She sees in this a technocratic attempt to cover over contestation and thinks the appeal to reason potentially makes discussion more fraught: if it is 'us' who are being rational, setting aside our emotions and following the evidence, then everyone who disagrees with us is automatically irrational, driven by their emotions and whimsy.

Claiming that reason is on one's side can, ironically, have the opposite outcome of a less reasoned and more polarized discussion. From Mouffe's perspective, political vitality and pluralism arises because of the vigorous back and forth movement of engaged opinion. There is no floating above contentious areas of life which matter to us. What is required, she argues, is agonistic debate, a word she understands differently to Rahim; that is, she argues that agonistic discussion is a form of engagement which does not tip over into antagonism, but which equally does not assume a disengaged rationalism. We fall into conflict with others because what we are arguing for or against matters to us: we cannot just put our commitments aside. This was a point I made much earlier in the book in Chapter 1, when I described the way that I fell into arguing with my colleague on the board.

It is important to note that, in their different interpretations of agonistic engagement Rahim and Mouffe also tell us something about their attitudes to politics. So it seems to me that Rahim, despite his discussion of ethics, is constrained in his thinking about what kind of politics is possible in contemporary organizations. From a managerialist perspective, which privileges the idea of control, it may seem as though contestation is potentially too disruptive. Only arguments about how to solve differences about defined projects seem permissible. This seems to me to be a very reduced understanding of political life in organizations and merits further exploration.

In what kinds of circumstances is political struggle necessary? According to the sociologist Karl Mannheim (1936/1972), who was Norbert Elias's supervisor for his *Habilitazion*, contestation is inevitable in any area of social life which has not yet been adequately organized. In situations where there is broad agreement about how to proceed, then it is possible to develop routines and rules. However, in areas of social life which are marked by disagreement, resulting in competition and struggle, then there is no obvious way to proceed until the matter has been settled. It will only be settled through contestation and the exploration of differences.

Mannheim argues that this presents a problem for orthodox science and, I would argue, orthodox management which aspires to being scientific, in the sense that the problems in view do not consist of static entities which operate according to predictable rules, but with 'tendencies and strivings in a constant state of flux. A further difficulty is that the constellation of the interacting forces changes continuously' (Mannheim, 1936/1972: 103).

It is hard to know how to codify and respond to a social situation which is constantly changing, particularly when, according to Mannheim, there is nowhere to stand outside the struggle. Participation in the flux and change can only be from a particular point of view and from a particular position in the social hierarchy. In much management theory, and certainly in Rahim's treatise on conflict, this partial point of view is obscured since the manager is assumed to be objective and dispassionate. Nonetheless, and despite this, he accords to managers the wisdom of being above the struggle and grants them the capacity to analyse it and decide how to work it through to a rational conclusion. What is excluded from this assessment is that the manager's position in this perspective is already caught up in the ideology of improvement and control, which is inherent in managerialism. It already implies a particular position.

Mannheim also draws attention to the intellectual assumptions in this way of engaging with contestation in social life. The tendency of administrators, or 'functionaries' as Mannheim calls them, is to come at political problems looking for solutions which exist in pre-formulated rules and laws. They have little understanding that existing laws and rules arose in the first place as a result of previous political struggles, and might have been decided otherwise. Their response to disorder is to try and subsume it within the existing order, and to view it as merely an extension of it. He argues that:

> Every bureaucracy, therefore, in accord with the peculiar emphasis on its own position, tends to generalize its own experience and to overlook the fact that the realm of administration and smoothly functioning order represents only a part of the total political reality. Bureaucratic thought does not deny the possibility of a science of politics, but regards it as identical with the science of administration.

(ibid: 106)

Bureaucracy proceeds just as Rahim recommends, and conflict has to be brought within managerial control and stabilized so that it is not too much, not too little, but just right. Will, interest, emotion and a particular point of view can all be subordinated unproblematically to reason. Mannheim refers to this perspective as intellectualism: an intellectualist perspective assumes that they can be disentangled and the former subjected to the latter. It separates theory from action and privileges the former and is a way of understanding the social world as a search for pure theory.[1]

To an extent, this would explain the preoccupation in a great deal of orthodox management literature with categorization, tools and techniques which are developed to apply to a particular area of organizational life, rather than assuming, as one might, that a particular problem and a means of solving it are inextricably linked. Mannheim argues that 'a schematically ordered summary' informed by thinking derived from the natural sciences, is occasionally useful but nonetheless 'tears apart the organic interconnection' between theory and practice in order to arrive at an ordered system.

It is just this point which I have been trying to emphasize throughout this book concerning the indivisibility of theory and practice: the way we work implies a theory, just as theory suggests a way of working. Indeed, by drawing on the pragmatists I have been suggesting that practice precedes theory, an idea I explore again in the next chapter, that the hand often precedes the brain.

What Mannheim tries to demonstrate in his work is that there is no meta-position above and beyond the contested situation in hand:

> It could be shown in all cases that not only do fundamental orientations, evaluations and the content of ideas differ, but that the manner of stating a problem, the sort of approach made, and even the categories in which experiences are subsumed, collected and ordered vary according to the social position of the observer.
>
> *(ibid: 130)*

The reader may notice the similarities in this argument to the ones we explored in Hegel's speculative logic in Chapter 2 of this book: Mannheim, like Hegel, takes issue with Kant's a priori universal categories of thought. The way to proceed, then, is by trying to understand the spectrum of difference and trying to synthesize it. By synthesis, Mannheim does not mean homogenizing differences or trying to come up with some kind of average. Nor is it possible to do so through disengagement with what is unfolding, but instead through active participation with it. Mannheim recommends that one tries to understand both oneself and one's adversaries 'in the matrix of the social process' (ibid: 153).

What is important is not the suppression of difference, but the exploration of difference, including one's own perspective, since the revealing of a point of view and its opposite can lead to the toning down of polarities. A temporary and partial synthesis can only be achieved by understanding the historical origins of the particular points of view expressed by the parties present, and an engagement with the particular situation in which these perspectives are being expressed:

> There is no more favourable opportunity for gaining insight into the parti-
> cular structure of the realm of politics than by grappling with one's oppo-
> nents about the most vital and immediate issues because on such occasions
> contradictory forces and points of view existing in a given period find
> expression.
>
> *(ibid: 164)*

It seems to me that Mannheim is setting out a much richer, subtler and more helpful theory of politics in organizations than does the dominant school of organizational theory. He argues that politics cannot be avoided because it is inevitable wherever areas of social life are not routinized and settled. This point reinforces the argument I was making about innovation in the last chapter when I claimed that what counts as innovation is always reflective of a particular figuration of power and inevitably involves politics. It is not difficult to imagine that this will include whole swathes of activity in many contemporary organizations, not just projects aimed at innovation.

Being more scientific about politics, he argues, involves not trying to close it down, but making the perspectives of each of the protagonists more explicit to each other, including one's own perspective. In other words, managers who try to engage skilfully in politics need to be rigorously self-critical if they are to take into account their own prejudices. And prejudices, pre-reflected orientations arising from our own particular histories and position in the social hierarchy, are not necessarily impediments to finding a way forward, but may be illuminating as another factor in the mix. Mannheim argues that participation in the political process with a view to making its origins and dynamics more explicit is the most helpful way of finding a way through.

Paradoxical individuals, oppositions in groups, tension between groups

In the section which follows I will investigate in more detail why conflict is a necessary and emergent phenomenon which arises in us as individuals as we try to reconcile paradoxical aspects of our social selves, it emerges between us and other individuals as we mutually adjust to each other in groups, and it develops between groups struggling over resources and status. In other words, I am arguing that conflict is both ubiquitous and a necessary consequence of living amidst thoroughly social individuals who are negotiating their power differences. Without it there could be no social evolution.

I also want to point to the importance of acknowledging and working with the emotional content of conflict on the grounds that, without so doing, it resurfaces in other ways and can make the work more intractable.

Conflict within individuals

Starting with conflicts that arise in us as individuals, I have explained previously that Mead (1934) argues that the development of human physiology has enabled us to call out in ourselves, as we communicate with others with significant symbols, a similar reaction to the one we are calling out in others. Mind, or our conversation of gestures with ourselves, the internal conversation which is thinking, allows us to make continuous adjustments to problems which arise between us and our environment, and between different aspects of ourselves:

> For it is their possession of minds or powers of thinking which enables human individuals to turn back critically, as it were, upon the organized social structure of the society to which they belong (and from their relations to which their minds are in the first instance derived) and to reorganize or reconstruct or modify that social structure to a greater or lesser degree, as the exigencies of social evolution from time to time require.
>
> *(Mead, 1934: 308)*

We try to adapt the world better to enable our progress through it, and equally and at the same time, we have to make adaptations to our sense of self. These are two sides of the same coin. In our very make-up, Mead argues, we have asocial and pro-social aspects (both of which are socially derived), which are in conflict. On the one hand, he argues, we are oriented towards cooperation because of our inter-dependence with all other individual selves and our identification with the wider society, and which is the basis of all our ethical ideals. But on the other hand and at the same time we have asocial feelings of superiority, independence and individuality towards other individual selves, which is the basis for ethical problems in society.

Mead does not make a simplistic distinction that the social aspect of the self is good and the asocial bad: the latter is the most precious part of us, he argues, and it makes us who we are. However, the degree of conflict experienced by the individual is directly related to the extent to which he or she can integrate their behaviour towards others in situations where they might be members of very different, and perhaps antagonistic social groupings. The difficulty facing all of us is how to bring the asocial aspects of the self over into the social, to make the necessary adjustments to the self and to the environment that I was referring to above. According to Mead we might think of conflict as a permanent part of the human condition:

> Thus, within such a society, conflicts arise between different aspects and phases of the same individual self (conflicts leading to split personality when they are extreme or violent enough to be psychopathological) as well as between different individual selves. And both these types of individual conflict are settled or terminated by reconstructions of the social situations, and

modifications of the given framework of social relationships, wherein they
arise or occur in the general human life process.

(ibid: 307–8)

Social life, in Mead's terms the life process, is a series of ruptures and accom-
modations, within us and between us. We are obliged continuously to adapt to
others, and in the process of doing so we develop as people as we make the
necessary adaptations to ourselves. It is in this way that social life evolves as we
learn to accommodate ourselves to others.

Conflict and emotions

What are we to make of orthodox management theory's squeamishness about
affect? Some initiatives have been taken by scholars in the critical, pragmatic and
process tradition to open up affect as a legitimate area of management research and
interest (Cascón-Pereira and Hallier, 2012; Coupland et al., 2008; Marshall and
Simpson, 2005; Samra-Fredericks, 2004; Denzin, 1983) to explain the importance
of feelings in the organizational context, but it still remains a minority pursuit. In
this chapter I am arguing that because it is impossible not to be affected emotionally
by one's involvement in work, then paying attention to what we and others are
feeling is crucial in order better to understand and to deal with the contradictions
of working life.

Going back to sociologists concerned with conflict from the early twentieth century
drawn on by Rahim, it is clear that for George Simmel and Lewis Coser, who
developed Simmel's work, affect was an important factor for understanding the
complexity and quality of conflict. Simmel was a contemporary and friend of Max
Weber, and was interested in everyday social interactions, and how the social arises
from dualisms and oppositions. In this sense he is helpful to our argument that
relationships between people are dialectical and develop paradoxically. His ideas
are a long way from the notion that conflict needs to be managed, or that 'constructive conflict' can be channelled in ways which are helpful for organizations to
improve performance.

Rather, like Mead, he argues that both tendencies, cooperation and competition,
arise at the same time and are two sides of the same coin. Conflict for Simmel was
one of the elementary forms of socialization. He argues that within the unity of a
personality are the contradictions that make it up, so there can be no surprise that
social unities can also be shot through with divergencies: this is a similar argument
to the one made by Mead explored above. In fact, he argues, a group which is
entirely harmonious would display 'no essential life process and no stable structure'
(Simmel, 1904a: 491). Unity and divergence suggest each other and are both
necessary:

> As the cosmos requires '*Liebe and Hass*,' attraction and repulsion, in order to
> have a form, society likewise requires some quantitative relation of harmony

and disharmony, association and dissociation, liking and disliking, in order to attain to a definite formation.

(ibid)

It is not that one is additive and the other is destructive, i.e. that one simply deducts from the other, but that both play a constitutive role in the production of the overall warp and weft of society. Nor is Simmel being naïve about conflict: I do not understand him to be trying to turn all negatives to positives by claiming this. He is well aware of the profoundly destructive nature of some conflicts, but it is not clear to Simmel that the forces that keep people apart, enmity and antipathy, are any more capable of disappearing from our social make-up than are sympathy, assistance and harmony. In all situations of peace, he argues, there exist the conditions for conflict and, vice versa, all situations of conflict have the potential for peace.

I am guessing that what Simmel has to say about social life resonates for people with practical experience of working in organizations, which provoke strong feelings and rivalries between people trying to get things done together.

Simmel has further thoughts on the quality of conflict between people. So, for example, he points to a number of paradoxes about intimacy and conflict. On the one hand, conflicts between people who know each other well have the potential to escalate because so much is at stake. Ordinarily we would expect there to be differences with strangers, and so proceed with a degree of anticipation of these and some degree of caution. However:

> The more we have, however, as total personalities in common with another, the easier will our whole personality become involved in each separate contact with him. Hence the quite disproportionate intensity with which otherwise quite self-contained persons frequently allow themselves to become moved in their conduct toward their most intimate associates.
>
> *(ibid: 516–17)*

On the other hand, the predisposition for intimate relationships to provoke deep conflicts is a testament to the quality of that relationship: other, more harmonious relationships may be so because they are based on more superficial feelings. Simmel also points out that intimate relationships are also more capable of adapting to conflict: they become intimate because they are so adaptive. Paradoxically, closeness can be forged out of the exploration of difference, but that exploration may also tip the relationship into an intense and conflictual state. Simmel regards compromise and negotiation as the most important forms of civilized behaviour, and which enable us to engage generatively with our rival claims, our similarities and differences. This, he argues, implies an ability to rise above the 'prejudices of immediate desire' (Simmel, 1904b: 805) and has had a long psychological development.

What happens to affect if it is denied or covered over? Lewis Coser (1956) argues that it simply resurfaces in renewed and more intense form:

> If conflict breaks out in a group that has consistently tried to prevent expression of hostile feelings, it will be particularly intense for two reasons: First, because the conflict does not merely aim at resolving the immediate issue which led to its outbreak; all accumulated grievances which were denied expression previously are apt to emerge at this occasion. Second, because the total personality involvement of the group members makes for mobilization of all sentiments in the conduct of the struggle.
>
> *(Coser, 1956: 152)*

Ironically, he suggests that groups with frequent conflicts are less likely to experience them intensely: 'One may venture to say that multiplicity of conflicts stands in inverse relation to their intensity' (ibid). Coser offers no prescriptions for how to handle conflict or manage it away, and suggests that organizations without conflict can become stale and rigid.

It is important to note the differences between what Simmel and Coser are arguing about, affect and conflict on the one hand, and Rahim on the other, whom I am taking as an exemplar of the orthodox discourse on management because it has important implications for managers. Simmel and Coser suggest that it is no more possible to avoid emotion in conflictual situations than it is to sidestep being human. Indeed, it may be the emotion in conflicts that creates trust and intimacy in relationships which makes good teamwork possible.

From a management perspective, fluency with emotions, both productive and difficult, is at the heart of good teamworking and key to a more human organizational working environment, rather than an impediment to it. This can be no surprise given that spending long periods of time with one's colleagues in an organization and trying to get things done together is bound to matter. And when things matter they provoke strong feelings in us. Anger, rivalry, jealousy, passive aggression, love, respect, admiration and elation are all possible emotions felt in the course of the same day between colleagues involved in intense work together.

For example, heartfelt resistance to change is a widespread phenomenon in contemporary organizational life, given the ubiquity of the focus on change in many organizations (see Chapter 5), as Yung (2013) has pointed out in her work on organizational change in the NHS. Yung recounts a number of situations at work where she had to convince colleagues of changes that she herself did not believe in, and where she encountered empassioned resistance from some of her colleagues (as well as resistance within herself).

However, Yung contrasts what she understands to be the more orthodox assumptions about resistance to change, which is usually described in the organizational literature as individual resistance to necessary and beneficial change, with her own highly social understanding of what she encountered. For her, resistance arises, when professionals work against the disruption of their habitual ways of relating in the groups to which they belong, and therefore try to maintain their current identities. And this was the same for her. Group belonging and threats to group cohesion provoke strong reactions in us and our colleagues, a phenomenon which I explore next in greater depth.

Psychoanalytic perspectives

Psychoanalytic and psychological theories of conflict are based on the assumption that strong feelings are both common and inevitable in groups. In Chapter 2 I mentioned Bion (1961), who was one of the first psychiatrists to draw attention to and try to explain unconscious processes which provoke strong emotions in group members. Predominant for Bion were feelings of anxiety which can be elicited particularly around the way groups of people are led. When anxiety in groups increases, so members abandon focus on their task and fall into three basic assumptions, without realizing that this is what they are doing.

The first basic assumption is dependency, where group members search for an omnipotent and charismatic leader who can lead them out of their crisis and resolve their anxieties. However, if the leader proves inadequate then they will attack this person and search for another one. It is not too far of a stretch to see much contemporary discussion of charismatic leaders to be located very much in the domain of dependency, no doubt amplified by business school curricula and the cadre of managers who aspire to leadership positions themselves. There are a number of high profile chief executives, such as Fred Goodwin, who were first knighted for their services to banking, then stripped of their titles for having contributed to the crisis. The degree of public denigration is proportional to the scale of lionization. If what Bion says has validity, then the stakes are high for leaders who put themselves in the position of calling out these feelings of dependency in their followers.

The second basic assumption is pairing, where group members look for two of their members to pair off and create a solution, perhaps a new leader with a utopian vision. This basic assumption engenders passivity in most of the group as they look to two others to resolve their problems for them. The last basic assumption is flight/fight, where members unite to fight against a perceived enemy or flee from them. This third basic assumption covers over attempts to understand the predicament that the group is in by apportioning blame somewhere else.

To extrapolate, in the UK during the period of economic duress since the economic collapse of 2008, a great deal of opprobrium has been heaped by the coalition government and certain tabloid newspapers on people claiming state benefits. This has led to an enormous increase in the numbers of people in the general population who have come to support the government's harsh measures towards people who are already poor. One way of understanding this phenomenon is that the anxiety provoked by the general economic collapse has prevented critical enquiry, leading instead to the demonization of the already marginalized, that is to say people who are much less likely to argue back.

Later on the psychoanalyst Turquet (1974) added another basic assumption: oneness. This basic assumption leads members to want to join passively with some omnipotent force so that they can experience feelings of wholeness, positivity and wellbeing. Anyone who has experienced large organizational meetings which are predicated on idealized and up-beat scenarios of the organization's imagined future will have some insight into what Turquet was trying to describe. The meetings take on the quality of a cult.

Whether or not the reader accepts the validity of psychoanalytic theories of the social, what Bion and Turquet were trying to point to is that unconsciously generated anxiety can sabotage the work that a group of people is trying to do.

Psychoanalysts Kenwyn Smith and David Berg (1987) also assume that the paradoxical conflicts arising from being a member of a group are inherent and cannot be managed away. Conflicts provoke anxiety and strong feelings, which can be disruptive of group life if they cannot be explored. They argue that they are an important part of the emotional life of the group and, like Simmel and Mead, they consider them to be constitutive of social evolution. Conflicts can of course be treated more or less helpfully by group members and failure to address paradoxical conflicts can, according to Smith and Berg, create 'stuckness' in groups, or even bring out the polarities that group members explicitly fear.

Generative paradoxes can also turn vicious, with negating poles cancelling each other out and or driving the group in repetitive loops between one pole of the paradox and another. The kinds of things they have in mind are the paradoxes that to be a member of a group means on the one hand wanting to be included, and yet on the other not wanting to give up one's individuality. Equally, all groups have to focus on completing a task together and at the same time they have to look after the needs of group members. The ability to be involved in the working life of the group also implies the ability to take a more detached view. Many of the paradoxes that interested both Elias and Mead arise again in Smith and Berg's view of group life.

Smith and Berg suggest that groups may follow a number of strategies to avoid dealing with the emotional pain of working with their contradictions. They may try to find a 'middle ground' of compromise, hoping that the contradictions will disappear. Or they may try to settle on one pole of the paradox, which may have the opposite effect of making the contrasting pole stronger. In doing so they may have weakened themselves fundamentally. Or they may yo-yo between one pole of the paradox and the other, dithering between one outcome and its opposite, appearing to anyone on the outside as incapable of making a decision. In all these instances groups are trying to change the inherent nature of group life, Smith and Berg argue, where thriving groups have to be able to endure the opposing tensions that being a member of a group evokes.

As an alternative, Smith and Berg recommend that groups learn to immerse themselves in the polarities of the experience of paradox in order to reconnect with the anxiety and emotions that it may have provoked. This involves discussing the inevitable anxiety which arises in the group because of the seeming impasse into which they have fallen. They argue that it is only by 'working through' the paradoxes, by which they mean 'repetitive, progressive, and elaborate explorations of the resistances that prevent an insight from leading to change' (Smith and Berg, 1987: 223) that groups can begin to experience movement. Only this way, they argue, is it possible to discover new ways of adapting to what is happening. One way of thinking about this is as the search for a new presentation of an old polarity, as with Hegel's idea of dialectic, which nonetheless preserves the old contradiction within it.

Again, I think it is instructive to compare this approach with what I am calling the orthodox school of management, where affect is something to be treated with extreme caution. Smith and Berg are recommending that greater comfort with the inherently conflictual aspects of belonging to the same group can only be achieved through immersion in them. There is no rationalizing uncomfortable processes away. Quite the opposite. The paradox here is that people working in organizations have to immerse themselves more thoroughly in the contradictions that arise from working together in order to gain greater detachment from them. It means developing much greater comfort with our rational irrationality, and how our unconscious selves intrude into our everyday lives.

Although I have drawn attention to internal conflicts and intra-group conflicts, in reality there is no dividing line between them. Equally, inter-group rivalries are inevitable and connected too, and in the next section I will explore some of the dynamics that Elias identifies and show how he links them to the evolution of our sense of self, and society.

Inter-group conflict

One of Norbert Elias's central ideas in *The Civilizing Process* (2000) is that the development of longer and longer chains of interdependence between people has brought about greater social control through self-control. In other words, as we have become more dependent on more others more of the time, so we have to regulate our behaviour more and more precisely. We depend on others just as they depend on us, and we become who we are because of our membership of various groups. But at the same time our anxieties and fears provoked by belonging to groups and the rivalry between them always threaten to undermine our sense of self, as we explored earlier in the work of Yung (2013).

According to Elias, the development of self-governing processes 'within' people can only be understood if we understand how they are linked to the mutually governing processes between people. For Elias, we are governed by strong feelings, for example guilt and shame, which are directly linked to the evolution of rationalization in humans because they are social emotions: they inhibit and condition our relations with others. His theories about the mutually forming process of self and society were based on a detailed study of mediaeval French court society. It is interesting to revisit some of his sources to see how our modern lives in organizations are not so different in many ways from those of our ancestors. One of the sources he drew on, a courtier called La Bruyère, writes as follows:

> Life at court is a serious, melancholy game, which requires of us that we arrange our pieces and our batteries, have a plan, follow it, foil that of our

adversary, sometimes take risks and play on impulse. And after all our measures and meditations we are in check, sometimes checkmate.

(La Bruyère, quoted in Elias, 2000: 397)

Rather than competing with each other for supremacy using force of arms, as had happened in previous times before the development of kingdoms, Elias notes how courtiers developed in their thinking to use strategy and intrigue to get the better of one another. Social advantage was gained by those who could exercise self-control, using reflection and foresight over the whole social domain:

A man who knows the court is a master of his gestures, of his eyes and his expression, he is deep, impenetrable. He dissimulates the bad turn he does, smiles at his enemies, suppresses his ill temper, disguises his passions, disavows his heart, acts against his feelings.

(ibid: 399)

Courtiers were also likely to form alliances with others to gain temporary advantage, and these alliances would shift and change, depending upon their perceptions of their own value in the social network, as well as that of their allies. This ability to effect some degree of separation from one's own feelings and to develop psychologized theories about oneself and about others, which he noted amongst courtiers, marked the evolution of what Elias refers to as the civilizing process. Tensions between individuals vying for ascendancy were also mirrored by rivalries between groups, different social strata within the same society, with the king tilting first this way and then that way in order to play one group off against another. I am guessing that the perceptive reader has already noticed some parallels with contemporary organizational life.

The highly involved and intense game of court life is a paradigm for the way in which we have learnt over the centuries to regulate ourselves and respond to others. We have developed greater detachment about ourselves and our relationships. For Elias, increased drive control and greater social rationality led to spurts in social development and the production of knowledge, although sometimes both of these could have adverse effects. Elias takes an ambivalent view of social development, which he thinks brings as many difficulties as it solves. The civilizing process takes place irrespective of whether developments are useful or pleasant to particular groups:

They arise from the powerful dynamics of interweaving group activities the overall direction of which any single group on its own is hardly able to change. They are not open to conscious or half-conscious manipulation or deliberate conversion into weapons of the social struggle, far less so than, for instance, ideas.

(ibid: 408)

It is important to note that Elias takes a very different view to the taken-for-granted assumption that new knowledge can be produced in a controlled way and is necessarily to the good. Rather, and in his view, the struggle over social pre-eminence sets in train tensions between people in the same social stratum as well as between social strata. Those who are in positions of power and privilege are keen to maintain their status, and those who belong to groups who do not have access to privilege are keen to emulate them.

In setting out his ideas this way, Elias was keen to avoid a reading of his work which simply focused on class relations: instead, he preferred what he considered a more comprehensive formulation of established–outsider relations, which refers to his work of the same name. In *The Established and the Outsiders*, Elias (1994) describes how groups come into conflict with each other without necessarily intending to, and simply because they find themselves contiguous and thus in competition for the same resources. Competition between groups sparks fears and anxieties in human beings which are difficult to deal with and these manifest themselves in organizational life too: we might fear dismissal, or exposure to those in power, or loss of our status and privileges. Keeping our own advantages may only be achieved by blocking the changes of others who aspire to the same thing.

For Elias, competition within and between groups is an inevitable part of social development and necessarily provokes strong feelings in those who are caught up in striving for greater status, or clinging to the privileges they have. The struggles within and between groups take us into the world of politics, which we explored above drawing on the work of Karl Mannheim.

Summary of the paradoxes of self, intra- and inter-group politics and conflict

In this chapter I started out with a review of an exemplar of what I have been terming an orthodox managerial understanding of conflict in organizations, which treats it as a necessary but containable phenomenon in organizational life. This is so as long as emotions can be kept out of the picture and managers can be provided with the requisite tools and techniques to deal with it. Many managerial accounts of organizational life present a very ordered world, where managers are proposing and disposing, as well as encouraging an optimum degree of conflict to assure innovation. I questioned whether this is really the case by drawing on two studies, one based in corporations in the United States and one in the UK, which gave very graphic accounts of the power struggles which are by no means the exception in today's organizations. Both these latter accounts resonate with my own experience of working in, and being a consultant to, organizations.

From the perspective of complex responsive processes of relating, managerialism has difficulties in accounting for or dealing with politics, what might be termed agonism, because in political contestation the outcome is uncertain and this runs contrary to the narrative of managerial control. Without an insight into the exact nature of the struggle it would be hard to know what to recommend that managers do about it. The author I used as an example of orthodox thinking, Rahim, suggests that political engagement, when it is understood as politics red in tooth and claw, is somehow unethical and therefore beyond managerial treatment.

Drawing on Mannheim, Mead and Elias I made the case that, far from being an unethical exception, politics is inevitable in those areas of social life which are yet to be settled. The bureaucratic response to contestation is to try and fit it into rules and procedures which have already been decided, at the same time forgetting that these rules are the more settled result of previous struggles over what to do. Even then, procedures have to be reinterpreted and renegotiated in each new situation.

There are two more important insights to take from Mannheim. First, there is no detached point of view in political situations – one can only proceed with the perspective which is formed as a result of one's background and the groups one belongs to. And having a point of view is not necessarily a disadvantage, but when explored more explicitly might produce a helpful understanding of what is to be dealt with. In Elias's terms the test is a paradoxical one of trying to become more detached about one's involvement. Making headway in political situations, which, I am arguing are very common in organizational life, involves taking into account a variety of points of view, including one's own.

The second insight is Mannheim's insistence that there is no separating theory and practice in working out how to proceed in practical situations. Abstract, idea-lized categories, pure theory, may be partially helpful but make an artificial separation between the specific situation that particular people are confronted with at a particular time. Political situations are best explored with full participation because they are constantly in flux, constantly emerging depending on the balance of forces involved in the struggle.

One of the key ideas in complex responsive processes is how contradictions arise in the forming of the self (because of our pro- and asocial tendencies), between selves operating in groups, and between groups. There is a degree of agreement between the scholars I have adduced in this chapter that cooperation and compe-tition are two paradoxical sides of the same coin, and that conflict is inevitable and necessary. It is necessary because without it social life would cease to evolve and organizations would be lifeless. Of course, it can take a variety of different forms, more or less protracted, but the degree of emotional involvement is commensurate with the potential risk of conflict escalating. At the same time, the degree of emotional involvement contributes to the quality of relationships – in other words, when groups develop greater intimacy between their members, then there is greater potential both for good working relations, as well as for major ruptures.

Implications for managers

It seems to me that in investigating the paradox of cooperation and competition I have come round to the opposite point of view than that recommended by what we might term the dominant discourse on managing conflict. Instead of assuming managers can adopt an objective position, deciding what type of conflict they have on their hands and so which tool or technique they might choose to resolve it for the optimum working of the organization, I am assuming that there is no objective position to be found.

Rather, what managers might do instead is to immerse themselves as fully as possible in the complex responsive processes of relating which take place in all social life, noticing their own reactions to and perspectives on the situation as important data in deciding what to do about it. They are caught up in complex social relationships which are forming them, and which they are forming, and these contribute to the regular irregularity of organizational life. Managers would be naïve to anticipate that emotions are absent from everyday organizational life; indeed, it is most likely to provoke strong emotions as people endure the flux and change in the emerging balance of forces.

This calls for a good degree of practical judgment and reflexivity, which we explored in Chapter 3. A good manager is not someone who disdains politics, or is naïve about it, but who is politically savvy. It means being more honest with oneself about what stake one has in the game. This is part and parcel of developing a robust approach to dealing with uncertainty and assuming that it is the negating paradoxical pole of certainty, and cannot be separated from it.

Case study

We're all in this together

I had been working with staff from an international aid agency to review a new service that they set up a year ago. For them, this involved creating a new department, launching a new vision and strategy, and team building within the new entity. There were a number of away-days and launches. Inevitably there were glitches, miscommunications, lacunae. Additionally, the ambitious work plan of creating the new department, with new policies and procedures, had been run over by events. So staff were doing their best and trying to set up something new at the same time as they were responding to business as usual. Everything had taken much longer than anticipated.

The newly created department comprised people who worked in the UK and those who were based overseas. Some of these latter were doing a similar job to the one they were doing previously, but were now considered to be in a different department. Some of them were not clear that they had become part of a new department – their everyday reality was much as it was before, although they might be reporting to a different manager. For staff in the UK the changes were more obvious and more talked about. They were engaged in struggles with the old department from which the new entity had been carved concerning who was responsible for what, who was to take responsibility.

As part of the work I was doing to interview managers and new department members, some of them made observations which seem very familiar to me from previous similar situations. The first was to criticize the senior management team who set this process going in the first place. Why didn't they plan this properly – why didn't they foresee some of the difficulties which were going to arise and pre-empt them? The second was to bemoan the lack of clear communication. If only we could have communicated clearly, or even have designed a better system of communication, then some of these problems would not have arisen. The third was to draw attention to the feelings of demoralization experienced by some: they complained that they had not been sufficiently consulted, or they may have been made anxious by the turbulence of change, or they may have lost out in terms of power and autonomy in the new department. Some people were moved out of the new department, and were now only loosely connected to it, and were feeling excluded.

We came together for an away-day to reflect on what had happened and to discuss the three complaints.

It was the third area of complaint which provoked the greatest disagreement amongst the group when I suggested that the new department, by including some and excluding others, will have changed power relationships. Some who were previously included are now outside the new grouping, and others, who were previously in lower status jobs or perhaps came from outside the organization, have been promoted. In any reorganization, I suggest, there are always winners and losers. When there is an attempt to create a new grouping, a new 'we', there will inevitably be people who struggle to recognize themselves as being a member of the new group. Some will be feeling passed over, or will have felt that their contribution is no longer recognized to the degree it was previously.

This observation nonplussed some people including, although not exclusively, some of those who have gained in the reorganization. They argued that they feel alarmed by what I have said. For them the organization they work for is one organization, a unity. Everyone should feel empowered: it is unhelpful to propose that some people may have been disempowered or excluded. These are our values, they said: empowerment and inclusion for everybody. Others point out that if people in the room could not find a way of talking about what had happened, feelings of disempowerment resulting from the reorganization, feelings of not being recognized and valued, then they would never be able fully to come to terms with what had happened.

One person said that this kind of thing, the inability to sit with discomfort, happens a lot in the organization and maybe it offered a new opportunity for talking about things in a way that is usually avoided. Perhaps, in order to come to terms with what has been going on, we needed to persist in talking about things even if it made everyone feel uncomfortable to see where that may lead. Maybe it was too limited to think that only by paying attention to 'the good', and denying the painful aspects of being together, good things will necessarily flow.

And so, that was the way we began to proceed, to dwell as long as we could with some of the difficulties which had arisen as a result of some of the profound changes which took place.

What I recognize in this event is how the painful experience of being together in difficult circumstances nearly prevented the group of managers reflecting on the situation they found themselves in, just as Bion described it might.

Note

1 Mannheim's argument is supported by the work of the neurosurgeon Antonio Damasio (2001), who extrapolates from his clinical work that it is impossible to separate out the intertwining of emotion and cognition.

References

Bion, W. (1961) *Experiences in Groups*, London: Tavistock.
Cascón-Pereira, R. and Hallier, J. (2012) Getting that Certain Feeling: The Role of Emotions in the Meaning, Construction and Enactment of Doctor Managers' Identities, *British Journal of Management*, 23(1): 130–44.
Constantino, C. and Merchant, C. (1996) *Designing Conflict Management Systems: A Guide to Creating Productive and Healthy Organizations*, San Francisco: Jossey-Bass.
Coser, L. (1956) *The Functions of Social Conflict*, New York: The Free Press.
Coupland, D., Brown, A., Daniels, K. and Humphreys, M. (2008) Saying It with Feeling: Analysing Speakable Emotions, *Human Relations*, 61(3): 327–53.
Damasio, A. (2001) *The Feeling of What Happens: Body, Emotion and the Making of Consciousness*, New York: Vintage.
Denzin, N. K. (1983) A Note on Emotionality, Self and Interaction, *American Journal of Sociology*, 89(2): 402–9.
Deustch, M. (1973) *The Resolution of Conflict: Constructive and Destructive Processes*, New Haven, CT: Yale University Press.
Elias, N. (1994) *The Established and the Outsiders*, London: Sage.
——(2000) *The Civilizing Process*, Oxford: Blackwell Publishers.
Howard-Grenville, J., Metzger, M. and Meyer, A. (2013) Rekindling the Flame: Processes of Identity Resurrection, *Academy of Management Journal*, 56(1): 113–36.
Jackall, R. (2010) *Moral Mazes: The World of Corporate Managers*, Oxford: Oxford University Press.
Kohlberg, L. (1969) Stage and Sequence: The Cognitive-Developmental Approach to Socialization, in Goslin, D. A. (ed.) *Handbook of Socialization: Theory and Research*, Chicago: Rand-McNally, 347–480.
Mannheim, K. (1936/1972) *Ideology and Utopia*, London: Routledge and Kegan Paul.
Marshall, N. and Simpson, B. (2005) Socially Constructing Emotion and Learning in Organisations: A Pragmatist Perspective, in Gherardi, S. and Nicolini, D. (eds.) *The Passion for Learning and Knowledge. Proceedings of the 6th Annual Conference on Learning and Knowledge*, Trento: University of Trento e-books.
Mayo, E. (1933) *The Human Problems of an Industrial Civilization*, New York: Macmillan.
Mead, G. H. (1934) *Mind, Self and Society from the Standpoint of a Social Behaviourist*, Chicago: University of Chicago Press.
Mouffe, C. (2005) *On the Political*, London: Routledge.

Rahim, M. A. (2001) *Managing Conflict in Organizations*, Westport, CT: Quorum Books.
Runde, C. and Flanagan, T. (2013) *Becoming a Conflict Competent Leader: How You and Your Organization Can Manage Conflict Effectively*, San Francisco: Jossey-Bass.
Samra-Fredericks, D. (2004) Managerial Elites Making Rhetorical and Linguistic 'Moves' for a Moving (Emotional) Display, *Human Relations*, 57(9): 1103–43.
Schelling, T. C. (1960) *The Strategy of Conflict*, Cambridge, MA: Harvard University Press.
Simmel, G. (1904a) The Sociology of Conflict I, *American Journal of Sociology*, Jan: 490–525.
——(1904b) The Sociology of Conflict III, *American Journal of Sociology*, May: 798–811.
Sims, D. (2005) You Bastard: A Narrative Exploration of the Experience of Indignation within Organizations, *Organization Studies*, 26(11): 1625–40.
Smith, K. and Berg, D. (1987) *Paradoxes of Group Life: Understanding Conflict, Paralysis and Movement in Group Dynamics*, San Francisco: Jossey-Bass.
Taylor, F. W. (1911) *The Principles of Scientific Management*, New York: Harper & Row.
Turquet, P. M. (1974) Leadership: The Individual and the Group, in Gibbard, G. S. et al. (eds.) *The Large Group: Therapy and Dynamics*, San Francisco and London: Jossey-Bass.
Watson, T. and Harris, P. (1999) *The Emergent Manager*, London: Sage.
Weber, M. (1929/1947) *The Theory of Social and Economic Organization*, trans. Henderson, A. M. and Persons, T., New York: Oxford University Press.
Yung, F. (2013) A Middle Manager's Response to Strategic Directives on Integrated Care in an NHS Organization: Resistance and Prejudice, unpublished PhD thesis, University of Hertfordshire.

7

AMBIGUITY, CONTRADICTION AND PARADOX IN THE NATURAL SCIENCES

Creative entanglement between the knower and the known

> The opposite of a true statement is a false statement. But the opposite of a profound truth may be another profound truth.
>
> Attributed to Nils Bohr

In Chapter 1, I rehearsed some of the arguments exploring the scientific basis for management, and what it means to be scientific about the social. I set out some of the thinking of those management scholars who argue that it is, and that it should develop more and more evidence of 'what works'. The aspiration that management could be considered a scientific discipline is also a longing for certainty, or at least, of being more certain that one course of action is more likely to be effective in organizational terms than another. I mentioned that in general, natural science disciplines abhor a contradiction, since formally they would consider it weak thinking. In public at least, natural scientists have low tolerance of uncertainty, contradictions and paradoxes.

However, in this chapter I will explore the work of some scholars of different natural science disciplines, many of them practising scientists themselves, who are interested in the uncertain, the ambiguous and the paradoxical in scientific concepts and practice. The reason for doing this is to demonstrate the ways in which natural scientific method is itself problematized by historians of science, some of its practitioners and theorists alike, and to destabilize the idea that there can be a single and naïve view of scientific method which portrays science as being everywhere the same and all of a piece. In general the literature I draw on in this chapter tries to take a view on the metaphysical debate about whether nature and laws about nature are discovered or created by paying attention to how science is practised.

Some of the scholars I adduce refer to their perspective as a pragmatic theory of science, or in some cases an agentic theory (people, and perhaps even objects, act or proscribe action, and so demonstrate agency), and argue that science is a practice alongside other practices. Science is a particularly disciplined response to specific problems which arise at particular periods in human development, and is socially and historically situated. These scholars make the case that scientific insight emerges from the contingent, messy reality of social life, and does so because scientists make productive use of the very uncertainty, contradiction and indeterminacy where problem and solution are co-present.

The reason this is important for my argument in this book as a whole, is that I am trying to persuade the reader similarly that this is also true in our experience of the social, particularly if we are concerned to manage people and develop organizations. Rather than relying solely on the helpful but inadequate tools and techniques of management, which aim to simplify and reduce, creativity and innovation arise from the ambiguous, the contradictory and the paradoxical. The complexity of organizational life can never by contained by formal tools and approaches, and will constantly burst through the methods designed to contain it. In pragmatic terms the best we can produce is what helps us to take the next step together, by which time we may be facing a completely different set of problems.

Of course, the argument I am making is hotly contested within the natural sciences and contingent disciplines such as science and technology studies.

On being scientific

In writing this chapter I am certainly not going to take a relativistic position towards science and claim that the truth of scientific theories depends upon people's point of view: I am content with Norbert Elias's formulation (1978) that science is a discipline which is capable of producing knowledge relatively independent of the groups of scientists producing it. In other words, a theory developed on the basis of careful experimentation can be replicated to produce similar results by other scientists following the same procedure. It has resonance in the material world. That is what makes it scientific.

However, scientific theories tell us little about the background story, the way they were discovered, perhaps through chance, contingency and life histories of the scientists who were involved in developing them, who, according to the historian of science and former geneticist Steven Shapin (2010) 'are people with bodies situated in time, space, culture and society, struggling for credibility and authority'. Ignoring the contextual nature of science as a discipline lends credence to the seductive platonic idea that science is the discovery of the timeless and the immutable, and which is free from contradiction. Instead, I want to pay attention to the often contradictory and ambiguous nature of what scientists are dealing with, and the way they are dealing with it, to see if we can generalize to the social domain, in particular in management theory.

The link that I am making to management and organizational theory is that management scholars are also caught up in discussions about the usefulness or otherwise of the specific, the contextual and the contingent, or whether management

theory can produce general laws independent of the context in which it is practised. Managers are also called upon to make productive use of ambiguity and
contradiction which they experience daily, in order to form theories about what is
going on in their organizations. Both scientists and managers experience conflicts
arising from being part of a social group, having more or less power to influence
things, and having to argue their case.[1]

Whether science is or is not about producing timeless truths about the world
'out there', one of the effects of this appeal to the metaphysical in public discourse
is that the sometimes simplistic reference to evidence or to the scientific method is
a means of covering over contestation, or is intended to create certainty where this
is impossible. Invoking science can sometimes be a way of obscuring other
important issues and relevant discussions, and thus is useful in preserving the *status
quo*, or legitimizing a particular power figuration.

Engaging critically with what we mean by being scientific is crucial for the way
that we talk about a whole variety of problems that we face in general, be they
environmental, economic or social, which have both scientific and political aspects.
Scientists create workable, testable models of how we might understand reality, but
these models carry with them their own assumptions and deficiencies, and are
intended to help begin the debate rather than bring it to an end. There is no scientific theory so robust and so clear that it is obvious what it means for the way we
should act here and now.

There is an equally lively discussion about the extent to which theories
describing the natural world are helpful in understanding the social. As we
discovered in Chapter 1, for purists there is only one scientific method, and this has
led in current times, for example, to the proliferation of randomized control trials
(RCTs), a method regarded as the 'gold standard' in the development and testing
of medicines, for the evaluation of social development (Banerjee and Duflo,
2012).

Rather than trusting expert judgment, the importation of natural science methods into the social puts trust in numbers, as Porter (1995) has argued. This is a
thread of discussion, aspiring to the purity and precision of mathematics and natural
science for social enquiry, dating back to Plato and amplified during the Enlightenment by, amongst others, the philosopher Marie-Jean-Antoine-Nicolas de Caritat,
Marquis de Condorcet (1795/1955). Condorcet is considered the first sociologist
and was keen to develop social science as a precise and unambiguous discipline
more akin to mathematics, and he did so with emancipatory intent. He was keen
to banish ambiguity by producing a language of the sciences in order to liberate
ordinary citizens:

> We shall show that this language, ever improving and broadening its scope
> all the while, would be the means of giving every subject embraced by
> human intelligence, a precision and a rigour that would make knowledge of
> the truth easy and error almost impossible.

(Condorcet, 1795/1955: 198–99)

As is often the case when science is adduced in schemes of human improvement, as with Taylorism in management (Khurana, 2007) it is often done with high moral purpose to rise above the arbitrariness and contingency of everyday life. Condorcet's project understands human development in evolutionary terms: he considers that the human race is developing towards perfectibility through 10 different stages. The last stage lies in the future and was a utopian dream that the deployment of reason would eventually bring about the end of inequality, and the promotion of public happiness based on the 'general laws directing the phenomena of the universe'. In this sense, Condorcet's dream that reason can solve all social problems begins to sound unreasonable. However, echoes of what Condorcet aspires to are still alive in debates over the role of science and social science today.

The sometimes uncritical importation of methods from the natural sciences and the ubiquity of quantitative methods in contemporary social research have provoked an equally vigorous response from some social scientists such as Flyvbjerg (2001), who have argued that the natural sciences can have nothing to say about the social. I developed this discussion in Chapters 1 and 2 as well as in my last book (Mowles, 2011), so will leave it aside for now, except to say that I think Flyvbjerg takes too extreme a view.

Instead, I want to draw attention to how taking uncertainty, ambiguity and paradox seriously is something that is common to a variety of disciplines which pursue enquiry systematically, whether in the natural or social science domain. These questions are of central relevance to the study of management and organizing and contribute to the vigorous debate in the domain of management scholarship about what it means to produce evidence-based management and whether the observer can ever be independent of what is being observed, a matter we will explore further in this chapter.

Contradiction and creativity

In Chapter 2 I mentioned the physician and psychiatrist Albert Rothenburg (1979), whose book *The Emerging Goddess* is a study of creativity amongst artists and scientists. His method was to interview 57 eminent scientists and artists over several years to explore with them how they worked and how they accounted for their creativity. He contextualizes their reflections within broader theorizing about the creative process drawing on other scholarship, including psychological and psychoanalytic theories, autobiographical accounts, and the correspondence of famous artists and scientists writing about their own creativity.

Rothenburg notices many similarities between the creative processes of artists and scientists, although their products are very different. Both involve a creative engagement between the artist/scientist and his or her environment: he argues that all theories about nature bear the imprint of the human mind. This dialectical account of the development of knowledge, the entanglement of the knower and the known, is similar to the pragmatic philosophical project which we have explored throughout this book.

Additionally, he takes an interest in ambiguity, contradiction and opposition in the development of artistic and scientific knowledge, as well as arguing for the importance of chance and the creative interruptions of the unconscious. Ambiguity, he argues, is a necessary but insufficient condition for being creative, since ambiguity alone may be diffuse and chaotic. Rather, what Rothenberg notices is the scientist's ability in times of uncertainty to bring together opposites, moving from the known to the unknown, often in flashes of inspiration. He argues that scientists are capable of working painfully and methodically through their experiments in stepwise fashion, but are also capable of ground-breaking insights which depend upon the tension of the bringing together irreconcilable opposites into the same frame.

He gives a variety of examples of scientific insight arising from bringing the known together with the unknown, or contradictory opposites. He quotes at length an essay written by Einstein and discovered posthumously, describing how he had been provoked into writing his general theory of relativity. What troubled Einstein was the two opposing theoretical interpretations by Maxwell and Lorenz of the conductivity of magnets in Faraday's experiments. On the one hand, Maxwell argued that if a magnet moved in a stationary conducting circuit, electricity is generated. On the other hand, Lorentz hypothesized that if the magnet was at rest and the conductive field moved, then no electricity would be generated.

These countervailing and opposing views created a profound tension in Einstein. 'The thought that one is dealing with two fundamentally different cases was, for me, unbearable' he wrote (quoted in Rothenburg, 1979: 112). The mental anguish provoked a moment of insight where both theories were held together and transcended, a moment of *Aufhebung* in Hegel's terms: both theories could be true at the same time dependent upon the reference point of the observer. His enquiry into electromagnetic induction led him to postulate the (special) relativity principle. This led Einstein to extend the insight to Newton's theory of gravity, arguing similarly that a gravitational field also only has a relative existence: 'Thus, for an observer in free fall from the roof of a house there exists, during his fall, no gravitational field' (ibid). In other words if someone falling off a roof releases objects which remain close to him they will remain, relative to him, in a state of rest.

Einstein's insight was subsequently proven by Arthur Eddington and Andrew Claude de la Cherois Crommelin on 29 May 1919, during a solar eclipse. The astronomers took photographs which proved that light was bent by the sun's gravitational field, a fact which was normally obscured by the sun's radiance. All manner of scientific developments were made possible by this insight, including nuclear power and new lines of enquiry in physics and astronomy.

Central to Rothenburg's argument about scientific and artistic creativity is the idea that the creator is willing to take risks with contradictions and opposites, rather than denying them. Working with contradictions is a way of bringing specificity and a particular kind of order to complex reality, which begins to separate out a particular problem area from its wider environment:

> The creative process is a matter of continual separating and bringing together, bringing together and separating in many dimensions – affective, conceptual, volitional, physical – at once. There is differentiation, diffusion, dedifferentiation, connecting and unifying at every step of the way. All these functions produce entities that are independent and free from the initial chaos.
>
> *(Rothenburg, 1979: 369)*

What I notice about Rothenburg's argument is his insistence that scientific discovery and creativity is not a Cartesian paradigm, with a detached rational observer calmly contemplating a world 'outside'. Scientists, he argues, become involved in problems because they matter to them and, because they matter, they engage conscious and unconscious thought, affect and intuition. This is a long way from my academic colleague, whom I mentioned in Chapter 1, who argued that a good scientist leaves his or her values, and persona, at the door. The scientist's involvement for Rothenburg leads to an articulation of the scientist's own ideas – he uses the word articulate in both of its meanings, to state out loud and to mean a joint, as between two bones. A joint is both a connector and a separator and the creative scientist is constantly connecting and separating him/herself and elements in the external world in unusual and opposing combinations. According to Rothenburg, the creative scientist drives towards the new:

> He [*sic*] defies the laws of ordinary logic and is willing to conceive the apparently illogical or inconceivable. He is willing to conceive and to entertain the simultaneous validity of a postulate or body of knowledge that is as far from the known and accepted as possible, the antithetical or opposite postulate or body of knowledge.
>
> *(ibid: 378)*

Rothenburg understands scientific creativity as a paradox bringing together humans and their environment, the known and the unknown, our separateness and uniqueness at the same time as our connectedness to nature and to each other.

The creativity of ambiguity and paradox in mathematics

In Chapter 1, I mentioned that paradox is explored in mathematics, literature and philosophy, and said that I would be pursuing philosophical paradoxes. Nonetheless, it is helpful to understand how paradoxes inform the way that mathematics as a discipline develops. In his book *How Mathematicians Think* (2007), the mathematician William Byers points to the way that ambiguity, contradiction and paradox help inform the way that mathematical ideas develop and evolve over time. He argues that this is because mathematics is a creative process, which tries to articulate something about the human condition and is therefore rich, varied and contradictory like the reality it seeks to describe.

Ambiguity, Byers argues, is a single situation or idea which is perceived in two self-consistent but mutually incompatible frames of reference. He gives examples from the mundane, i.e. using decimals to express fractions ($1/3 = 0.33333 \ldots$) to the complex, such as using the Taniyama–Shimura conjecture, which attempts to reconcile elliptic curves and modular forms, to solve Fermat's last theorem. To describe paradox, Byers pushes the definition of ambiguity to the point where the self-consistent but mutually incompatible frames of reference create an 'absurd truth': many of his examples of paradox turn on the Cantor's development of the idea of infinity, and approximation, such as Zeno's paradox, where approximations approach, but never quite fully capture the 'truth'.

For example, Zeno's paradox attempts to undermine common-sense notions of plurality and motion by drawing on a *reductio ad absurdum*, which Byers argues is very close in spirit to the mathematical proof by contradiction. The paradox states that in a race between Achilles and the tortoise, Achilles can never catch it up if the tortoise starts 50 metres ahead. By the time Achilles has reached the tortoise's original position, so it will have moved ahead; by the time Achilles reaches the second position, so the tortoise will have moved again, ad infinitum so that the two will never be neck and neck. However, we also know that Achilles can beat the tortoise and can calculate exactly when he will pass it. What Byers is claiming is that the Greeks' desire to banish paradox in thought led them to develop ways of problem-solving which proved very powerful in mathematics, and carried over into other disciplines. In other words, the problem is reduced to an infinite series of frozen moments which loses the dynamic process of what is actually happening.

Hernes (2014) draws on both Bergson (2007) and Whitehead (1929) (the latter a mathematician as well as a philosopher) to argue that the spirit of Zeno has continued in much organizational theory, when the processual and emergent is reduced to a series of static moments. This leads to organizational theorists understanding organizational change to be a 'problem' to be 'solved'. He argues instead for the centrality of time, understood as continuous, in understanding organizational change, where the past is always 'contained' in the present and anticipates the future.

Using the very paradoxical processes on which he draws, Byers argues that pure formalism can never capture the creative processes that drive mathematical development, which are, he says, never fully subjective, nor completely objective, but are an objectification of the subjective, a formulation which is very close to Elias's idea of becoming more detached about our involvement, which I described in previous chapters.

He makes the claim that not only do mathematicians make creative use of ambiguity and paradox, but that mathematics itself is both ambiguous and paradoxical, moving back and forth between clarity and structure on the one hand, and fluidity and openness on the other. It is both a product of the human mind, yet it also helps us to describe patterns in nature which are independent of any one human mind. In answer to the conundrum as to whether mathematics is invented or discovered, Byers answers 'both': it is a form of intelligence in action, both a product and a process at the same time.

Byers draws on a famous paper by Wigner (1960) entitled 'The Unreasonable Effectiveness of Mathematics in the Natural Sciences', in which he argues that it is the ingenious definitions of mathematics which have helped scientists to articulate some profound truths about reality. This is fine as far as it goes, Byers argues, but what is it about mathematical concepts that makes them so useful? His response is to argue that profundity, or what mathematicians refer to as 'depth' in mathematical reasoning, arises from the interplay of clarity on the one hand, and ambiguity and paradox on the other:

> Ambiguity and paradox are aspects of mathematical thought that differentiate the 'trivial' from the 'deep'. The 'trivial' arises from the elimination of the ambiguous. The 'deep' involves a complex multi-dimensionality such as those evoked by the successful resolution of situations of ambiguity and paradox. Even the word 'resolution' is misleading in this context because it usually implies the reduction of the ambiguous to the logical and the linear. What really happens is that the ambiguity gives birth to a larger context, a unified framework that contains the various potentialities that were inherent in the original situation.
>
> *(Byers, 2007: 381)*

In Byers's framing of mathematical creativity we can see a parallel in the dialectical process that Hegel referred to as *Aufhebung*, the negation of the negation within a new frame which contains the original contradiction. Mathematical profundity is exemplified for Byers in its inexhaustibility: formal solutions do not completely close off other possibilities. A similar point is made at length by Douglas Hofstadter (1979) in his book *Gödel, Escher and Bach: An Eternal Golden Braid*, when he discusses the importance of Gödel's 'Incompleteness' theorem. Gödel's paper was written in response to the work of Bertrand Russell and Alfred North Whitehead who, in *Principia Mathematica*, had set out to banish ambiguity and contradiction in mathematics. As I mentioned in Chapter 1, Gödel demonstrated that there would always be some propositions that could not be proven either true or false using the rules and axioms of that mathematical branch itself. According to Hofstadter, Gödel exemplified paradox in a mathematical proof.

Similarly, in a book which draws on what she calls 'productive ambiguity' in the sciences, Emily Grosholz (2007) gives a variety of examples from different scientific disciplines, including mathematics, where language and notation are irreducibly ambiguous, and are productive precisely because they are so. In one of the chapters she compares and contrasts the development of Galileo's thinking about projectile motion with the scientific ideals of the logical positivist philosopher Rudolf Carnap (1928/1967), who wanted to free language from its ambiguities, much as Condorcet did as I outlined above.

Carnap's intellectual project builds on the work of Bertrand Russell and Alfred North Whitehead in the twentieth century and was intended to produce scientific language, which was in constructional definition 'pure' and free of unnoticed conceptual elements: 'it must be neither ambiguous nor empty ... it must not designate more than one, but it must designate at least one, object' (quoted in Grosholz, 2007: 18). Carnap's ideal language of science and mathematics is a symbolic language of 'logistics' (symbolic logic), where there is an exact correspondence between the symbol and the object referred to. In this way all ambiguity is eliminated so that there is only one kind of thing we are attempting to describe.

In contrast, Grosholz demonstrates how Galileo used a variety of ways to develop his thinking over a number of pages in his notebooks to explain projectile motion, furnishing proportions, geometric figures, numbers and natural language. She notices how he exploits the ambiguities that arise between the different ways of presenting and representing the problem, inviting the reader to compare and contrast one diagram with another, and draws attention in discursive text to his argument, to carry his illustration further. Grosholz draws on the distinction between Galileo's practical method, which approaches the same problem from a variety of different perspectives, and Carnap's idealism to mount a challenge to the latter's logical positivist project and its search for an ideal and reductive language. She argues that it is the very ambiguity which Carnap abhors that gives rise to Galileo's mathematical creativity.

In this and other examples in the book Grosholz sets out her alternative understanding, which depends upon taking note of the way that scientists represent their problems and solutions as well as following, in pragmatic fashion, the way they went about trying to develop their arguments, as she has done with Galileo. She makes the point that formal languages such as logic play an important part in mathematics, but that formalization is not the only way of representing. Later on in the book she argues:

> The point of this chapter, and of the whole book, is to show that mathematicians typically reason about individuals as well as abstractions, refer successfully to specific things; link heterogeneous items and exploit and construct ambiguity, in problem contexts that cannot escape geometry, modalities and historicity. Because they do this successfully all the time, it is no wonder that logic all by itself cannot express mathematics.
>
> (Grosholz, 2007: 284)

What I draw from both Byers's and Grosholz's argument is that creativity and richness in mathematical thought is connected with preserving the generative capacity of ambiguous or contradictory ideas often within a novel framework, rather than eliminating it. This is similar to the argument I am making about management where I am encouraging leaders and managers to work with the paradoxes that they encounter in everyday organizational life rather than assuming that they can eliminate them or control them. Approaching problems in all their multiplicity can lead to a depth of understanding which is missing from more simplistic methods which reduce complex reality.

Dialectic, paradox and contradiction in physics – implications for research methods

In her book *Meeting the Universe Halfway*, the theoretical physicist Karen Barad (2007) draws on quantum theory and the philosophy of the Nobel prize-winning physicist Nils Bohr, to develop her thinking about the paradoxical relationship between the knower and the known and the sense we can make of the world through our engagement with it. The reason I am interested in her argument is because it is exactly this question that I feel I have been exploring in much of this book. In orthodox management scholarship it is assumed that leaders or managers are separate from the social phenomena they are concerned with and can act in a detached way upon them. I am contesting this assumption, assuming instead that managers are part of the very phenomenon they wish to influence.

Barad also argues that Bohr's philosophical reflections on his work in physics provide opportunities for linking the natural and social worlds in the sense that we are part of the natural world we seek to understand. She accepts that both Bohr's views (he was regarded as too philosophical for a physicist!) and her own interpretation of them are contested, but I will explore them nonetheless because both perspectives are interesting and helpful in the context of our discussion of uncertainty, contradiction and paradox.

In order to explain Bohr's philosophy she discusses and represents in great detail two now famous manifestations of quantum physics: the slit experiment conducted by a variety of scientists since the original claim by Thomas Young in 1806, that light demonstrates the properties of both waves and particles and the principle of uncertainty/complementarity debated by Bohr and Werner Heisenberg.

Briefly to explain the slit experiment and what it reveals about the behaviour of matter, when particles of light are fired towards a light receptor through a barrier which has a single slit cut into it they appear to go in a straight line and strike the receptor directly in line with the firing mechanism. When a second slit is opened up in the barrier next to the first, then the particles appear to interfere with each other and demonstrate diffraction patterns of light and dark lines on the receptor, much like the patterning produced by waves becoming superimposed over each other.

From a classical physics perspective, particles are entities which occupy a given amount of space at a particular time. Waves, on the other hand, are disturbances which propagate in a medium such as water or air and can overlap at the same point in space. If this happens then their amplitude can be combined or they can cancel each other out. We may all have noticed the way that wave patterns interfere with each other when we throw two stones into a pond.

So if the experiment is conducted with one slit, then a physicist would conclude the light behaves like a continuous stream of sequential particles. When conducted with two slits, then light particles (or other experiments have demonstrated the same phenomenon given certain physical conditions with other types of matter, whether it be electrons, neutrons or atoms) behave very differently. This wave/particle contradiction is important because:

This situation is paradoxical to the classical realist mind-set because the true ontological nature of light is in question: either light is a wave, or it is a particle; it cannot be both.

(Barad, 2007: 198)

Barad directly addresses the point usually made about the quantum paradox, that insights gleaned from microscopic entities have little relevance to considering nature at the grander scale and disputes the interpretation that they have little relevance for the world we live in. She points out that when the wave nature of light or matter is insignificant, i.e. when the wave length is small in relation to other important dimensions, then classical physics provides a useful shortcut for calculations. She regards classical formalisms as an often helpful approximation to the more elaborate calculations of quantum physics which operate at all scales and are a much more comprehensive account of what we observe in nature.

She concludes that: 'As far as we know, the universe is not broken up into two separate domains (i.e., the microscopic and the macroscopic) identified with different length scales with different sets of physical laws for each' (ibid: 85). Quantum effects are small if the mass of the object is large. However, Barad argues that quantum physics does not complement Newtonian physics, but supersedes it (ibid: 110).

By analogy with management, we might also argue that the ubiquitous management tools and techniques are sometimes helpful shortcuts if we are new to a particular domain and have little experience of them. However, and in my view, there is great danger is assuming that grids and frameworks based on generalizations and abstracts can have any more than general relevance for the particular problems that a specific organization may be facing. This will be true, in MacIntyre's words from previous chapters, 'characteristically and for the most part'.

The impossibility of separating the knower from the known

Additionally, Barad treats Heisenberg's uncertainty principle, an idea he explored in a famous paper he wrote in 1927 which involved a *gedanken*, or thought experiment. The paper considers the hypothetical detection of an electron by a photon using a gamma ray or high-energy spectrum microscope. Heisenberg reflects upon the way that the photon would disturb the electron in trying to measure it in a discontinuous way (owing to the Planck constant). Heisenberg concludes from this that there is an epistemic principle of quantum physics, that there is a limit to what we can know about the momentum or the position of an electron because of the incalculability of the technique of measurement.

Bohr was dissatisfied with this explanation and argued that it was not an epistemic difficulty, but an ontological one; that is to say, what we take reality to be. Whilst Heisenberg argued that it was impossible for a physicist to *know* simultaneously the momentum and position of the same particle using quantum calculations, Bohr argued instead that particles do not *have* determinate values of position and momentum simultaneously. In other words, and according to Bohr, in order to measure a particle's position, then one set of apparatus and measurements is required and, in order to calculate momentum, then an entirely different configuration of equipment and measurements is required. The two sets of apparatus are mutually exclusive: in being precise with one measurement the experimenter is electing to be imprecise about the other. In an addendum to his paper, Heisenberg later accepted this qualification of his work:

> In this connection Bohr has brought to my attention that I have overlooked essential points in the several discussions in this paper. Above all, the uncertainty in our observation does not arise exclusively from the occurrence of discontinuities, but is tied directly to the demand that we ascribe equal validity to the quite different experiments which show up in the corpuscular theory on the one hand, and in the wave theory on the other (i.e. that we acknowledge complementarity, that is, the necessity of considering mutually exclusive experimental conditions).
>
> *(Heisenberg, quoted in Wheeler and Zurek, 1983: 83)*

This movement in Heisenberg's position has been largely forgotten, even by some physicists, Barad insists, in favour of what is now popularly thought of as the uncertainty principle. Both Bohr and Heisenberg are contributors to what is broadly known as the Copenhagen interpretation of quantum physics, although, as Barad points out, this comprises a variety of contributors and positions superimposed one on the other: there is no one comprehensive, coherent and determinate position on the variety of theories which make up quantum physics.

Barad goes on to draw some quite profound philosophical conclusions from this insight, drawing on Bohr's work and his theories about the natural world. For Bohr, quantum physics problematizes the strict determinism of Newtonian physics, which states that if it were possible to measure the initial conditions of any particle, i.e. the position and momentum and the complete set of forces operating on it, then its entire trajectory, past and future, is determined. A Newtonian world view also assumes observer independence passively gazing on reality, the Cartesian separation of knower from the known, subject from object. In contrast, she argues, Bohr called into question both of these assumptions:

> that the world is composed of individual objects with individually determinate boundaries and properties whose well defined values can be represented by universal concepts that have determinate meanings independent of the experimental practice, and ... that measurements ... can be properly assigned to the premeasurement properties of objects as separate from the agencies of observation.
>
> *(Barad, 2007: 107)*

What I take Barad to mean by this is that the world and everything in it is hopelessly entangled: the way we proceed to measure and understand the world has an impact on the measurements and knowledge we derive. Rather than assuming that the world is made up of discrete entities consisting of properties which can be captured and accurately represented by the human mind, knowledge arises from the combination of nature and our engagement with nature, of which we are part (Rorty, 1979).

For Bohr, there was no separating nature from the arrangements to measure nature, which he expressed in his own words in his book *Atomic Theory and the Description of Nature* (1934/2011) thus:

> the very recognition of the indivisibility of physical processes, symbolized by the quantum of action, has justified the old doubt as to the range of our ordinary forms of perception when applied to atomic phenomena. Since, in the observation of these phenomena, we cannot neglect the interaction between the object and the instrument of observation, the question of the possibilities of observation again comes to the foreground.
>
> *(Bohr, 1934/2011: 93)*

Despite criticisms that Bohr is an 'anti-realist' in his philosophical stance, i.e. that he is somehow denying the materiality of nature or objective standards in science, Barad claims that Bohr is claiming no such thing. To choose one configuration of apparatus to measure the momentum of a particle gives replicable results, and to choose a different apparatus to measure its position gives other replicable results, leaving the other quantities indeterminate.

These measurements are objective in the sense that they are calculable and reproducible by other scientists. Bohr's point is that it is the specific nature of the material arrangements that is responsible for producing some values to the exclusion of others. These arrangements evolve through a history of what she terms socio-material practices, which I take to mean the development of methods involving objects and human reflection on objects, which determine the development of any social practice, including of course, science.

In keeping with the title of her book, *Meeting the Universe Halfway*, Barad is claiming, based on Bohr's thinking, that it is human practices which make the world intelligible to us. We engage with the world with the view of producing accurate descriptions of it of which we are part (part of the world and part of the descriptions) – this is very different from the idea that there is some idealized, human-independent reality which we can accurately and flawlessly represent. We form, and are formed by the natural world we seek to discover. Our consciousness, our methods, the tools we bring to bear and the objects we attempt to study are all part of one mutually constitutive phenomenon, which is non-separable and emerges in the intra-action.

Barad borrows another concept from physics which I do not have time thoroughly to explore here to describe this phenomenon, that of entanglement. We and the world we live in are entangled. This is what Barad calls her agential realist position: the world becomes real to us through our intra-action with it:

> Our (intra)actions matter – each one reconfigures the world in its becom-
> ing – and yet they never leave us; they are sedimented in our becoming,
> they become us. And yet even in our becoming there is no 'I' separate from
> the intra-active becoming of the world. Causality is an entangled affair ...
>
> *(Barad, 2007: 394)*

What Barad calls entanglement, I have argued in this book, is the paradox of
forming and being formed, our subjective experience of the world which is
objectively formed. To understand the world we need to pay attention to both the
world and our experience of it, an argument made long ago by William James
(1909/1996) and John Dewey (1925/1997). Dewey's argument was that there has
developed an artificial separation between objects in nature and our experience of
them: both of these phenomena are important to study if we want fully to com-
prehend the world. What I draw from this is that systematic thinking in management is required in the ways that Barad and Dewey are signalling: that managers
and leaders pay attention to their own experience and to the objectivizing social
conditions into which they are obliged to act with others, which form them and
which they are forming, both at the same time.

The dialectic of subject and object

Andrew Pickering (1993, 1995), a physicist as well as a sociologist of science,
also uses the word entanglement to describe what he considers as the 'dialectic
of resistance and accommodation' between scientists and the objects of their
experiment, which unfold in time. In an extended reflection upon Nobel laureate
Donald Glaser's attempts to invent a bubble chamber to identify and measure
exotic particle tracks, a precursor to the work at CERN and the Large Hadron
Collider, Pickering notes how Glaser's intentions were amended by the failures he encountered in trying to develop equipment which worked, whilst his
modifications of the equipment were framed by his intentions. Neither the failures
nor the successes could have been foreseen in advance. Science emerges in
real time through what Pickering refers to as the 'mangle of practice' through the
interactions of human beings and objects, which are both thought to exercise
agency. Another way of putting this negatively, is that we should look
beyond only the human realm to understand the nature of constraint on human
activity:

> Instead, material agency emerges by means of an inherently impure dynamics.
> The resistances that are central to the mangle are always situated within a
> space of human purposes, goals, and plans; the resistances that Glaser
> encountered in his practice only counted as such because he had some par-
> ticular ends in view. Resistances, in this sense, are liminal: they exist on the
> boundaries, at the point of intersection, of the realms of human and non-
> human agency. They are irrevocably impure human/material hybrids, and

this quality immediately entangles the emergence of material agency with human agency (without, in any sense, reducing the former to the latter).

(Pickering, 1993: 577)

Like Barad, Pickering also addresses the question of the way in which the material world impinges upon human agency. We are constrained by the plasticity or otherwise of the tools we develop, by the objective qualities of materials, which we shape and fashion to our purpose. The idea of 'materiality' has provoked a lively discussion in science and technology studies and in sociology of science. But unlike Callon and Latour (1981, 1992), Pickering does not ascribe perfect symmetry of agency to humans and material objects in the sense that human intentions are future-oriented and are amended by the obstacles they encounter; they are subject to emergent redefinition in practice. Nonetheless, it seems to me that what Pickering is trying to get at is the paradoxical nature of scientific endeavour, which forms and is formed by engagement in practice with a material world which 'resists' human intention, and in doing so, modifies it.

Barad's understanding of Bohrian physics, depending as it does on the importance of the inseparability of a generative paradox of self and others and self and the world, as well as Pickering's attempt better to understand the emergent nature of scientific practice, seems to me to be very close to the pragmatism of Mead and Dewey, and the process sociology of Elias, which we explore elsewhere in this book. At the heart of this is a paradox of practice, or entanglement in Barad and Pickering's terms. For Dewey (1925/1997) the object and the experience of the object were inseparable.

Similarly the contemporary philosopher Mary Midgley (2001) has noted how the tradition of classical scientific thinking has been influenced by metaphysical arguments about finding immutable structures which underlie what we take reality to be. This she calls the atomic model based on the thinking of Democritus. In her book *Science and Poetry* she takes a number of contemporary biologists to task for the ways in which they reduce the social to the biological:

> When we are trying to understand the shifting chaos of human affairs, the idea of simplifying them in this way is hugely attractive to people who have grown up thinking of the atomic pattern as the archetype of all scientific method, which is the way that all scientists thought in the nineteenth century. Since then the physicists, the original owners of the pattern – have seen reason to drop this seductive vision and to recognize that the world is actually more complex. Many biologists, however, still cling to the atomic model and hope to extend its empire so as to bring order into the muddied rainforest of human society.
>
> *(Midgley, 2001: 102)*

She is critical of what she understands as a need to define a ground under the shifting flux of social life, an Archimedean point with which to shift the world. She resists the tendency, which we have been exploring in this book following Elias, Dewey, MacIntyre et al., to found social science on misplaced models uncritically borrowed from the natural sciences.

I am pointing to what I understand to be some consistent themes concerning the practice of science, which provokes thinking about what it might mean to be scientific about the social. The promise of the dominant discourse in organizational theory and management is that a given set of tools, or methods, will give consistent results across a variety of different domains and very different contexts. In this sense it is methods-driven, privileging the method at the expense of the context of the particular problem.

An alternative understanding might emphasize the importance of the context, the circumstances and the particular group of players who are dealing with specific emergent problems as the most important starting point for thinking about organizational development, and then turn to existing methods to see which might help. The application of particular methods will change managerial intentions, and will be changed by them, both at the same time. Each of the contexts will have its own resistance and inflexibility, its own particularities, which will demand a particular response from managers.

The paradox of empathy – from the perspective of a primatologist and brain scientist

In Chapter 1, I explained briefly Mead's view about the social formation of consciousness and self-consciousness. We are able to take the attitude of particular and general others to ourselves: in other words we have an idea about how the world looks from another person's perspective, as well as how people in general might think about what we are doing. The reason why this insight is so important to the general thrust of this book is that it describes a thoroughly social self involved with other social selves. This is a long way removed from the idea of discrete and closed individuals cognizing the world and forming mental models about reality which they can apprehend and consciously change. The idea of the social self has perspective-taking and empathy at its heart, but also the paradox that social processes are individualizing.

In reflecting upon the origins of empathy, the Dutch primatologist Frans de Waal (2009) argues that it is not unique to humans, but is shared with a number of higher mammals, such as bonobos and elephants. He prefers the German word *Entfühlung*, or feeling into, to describe the way in which we helplessly mirror the emotional states of others, unless we are somehow intellectually or emotionally impaired. It is, he argues the way that bodies talk to other bodies. The psychologist Simon Baron-Cohen (1995) describes the inability to do this as 'mindblindness', where conditions such as autism prevent the sufferer from having insight into the emotional world of others.

Empathy for de Waal is more than merely emotional contagion, the phenomenon where troupes of monkeys may become collectively agitated by each other's distress, which is a less sophisticated version of what really interests him. As an example, when a group of baboons crossed a river leaving younger group members behind on the bank, their mothers were clearly keenly aware of their offspring's distress calls, but this did not make them turn back to collect them. They could not take the additional step of seeing the situation from the point of view of their children. Rather than simply mirroring others' distress, de Waal considers higher empathy to be the ability to put oneself in the place of another and to take their perspective.

According to de Waal, perspective-taking co-emerges with the ability of primates to recognize themselves as separate selves, a process that occurs in human beings as young children: over time they develop a sense of an 'I' and a 'me', the latter being the view that others might take of them. He argues that what he terms advanced empathy demands the capacity to experience similar emotional states to those we encounter, but also to realize that there is a self/other boundary. Without the paradox of similarity and difference we would be constantly caught up, and potentially swept away by the emotions of others. Empathy is the ability to experience the distress of others and, as a consequence, offer what he calls targeted helping, assistance which is aimed at ameliorating the other's particular circumstances.

De Waal has tested out his hypothesis by trying to examine the extent to which elephants, dolphins and bonobos are able to recognize themselves in mirrors. For example, on an elephant in the Bronx Zoo de Waal and his collaborators painted a mark above an elephant's eye, and a sham mark above the other. The elephant repeatedly touched its trunk to the visible mark and never to the sham one. De Waal concludes from this that the elephant is able to associate the mark as belonging to itself. Other experiments show elephants 'self-contingency testing' or checking to see that the animal they see in the mirror behaves in the same way as they do themselves. De Waal also shows the way in which animals can share information by pointing, or by encouraging humans to fetch objects for them. He makes a direct link between self-recognition and empathy, arguing that this is a capacity we share with other mammals: he resists the idea that there are sharp dividing lines between human beings as a species and other animals.

What de Waal is pointing to, then, is the paradox of the self and other: we are only able to take up the perspective of others by having a strong sense of self, and we have a strong sense of self because of the otherness of others. As Hegel suggested, we realize ourselves through the other. I explored some of these ideas extensively in Chapters 2 and 3.

Similarly, the brain scientist VS Ramachandran (2011) is also interested in the way that human sociality is dependent upon taking a perspectival viewpoint, a capacity he attributes to the presence of mirror neurons in the brain, a phenomenon which is not limited only to humans. These are the areas of the brain that the neuroscientist Rizzolatti and colleagues observed 'lighting up' in a monkey's brain when the subject of the experiment observed another monkey reaching for food in 1999. The stimulus of activity in another organism calls out a bodily response in the observer, which also involves brain activity.

In a similar vein to de Waal, Ramachandran argues that the body experiences the paradox of being able to respond physically to the physical movements of others, at the same time as realizing that it is another body. He attributes to mirror neurons the following functions. They enable us to anticipate other people's physical intentions, or to have a theory of mind. Additionally, he argues, a higher function of mirror neurons may be that they enable us to appreciate another person's conceptual perspective. As a corollary of this we are able to see ourselves as others might see us, to become self-conscious.

Ramachandran speculates further that mirror neurons assist in the brain's ability to abstract from one dimension to another, and thus lead to our ability, for example, to handle metaphors, which is the capacity to compare similarities between things despite their obvious differences. This kind of abstraction he terms 'cross-modal abstraction'. He also argues that these areas of the human brain allow us to imitate, a skill which permits us to transmit knowledge through example. He reflects further on what has come to be understood as two episodes of enormous human cultural expansion which happened 50,000 years ago and 2,500 years ago, and wonders whether this was due to a genetic change in the brain which has ironically freed us from genetics. He wonders whether the twin capacities of being able to anticipate and imitate have led to the huge flourishing of human culture.

Ramachandran puts forward his own theory of autism, which suggests that the condition arises as a consequence of the misfiring or depletion of mirror neurons. As mentioned previously, there are a spectrum of symptoms associated with the general term autism, but in the main people on the autistic spectrum have difficulties anticipating and interpreting other people's intentions and actions as well as their emotional states. They have difficulties becoming fully social beings. If they are functioning at a higher level on the autistic spectrum, people suffering autism may have difficulties with language, particularly in its more metaphorical usage, but they may also mix up 'I' and 'you'.

This links to de Waal's co-emergence hypothesis that a strong sense of other is also linked to a strong sense of self. Ramachandran wonders whether impairment of the functioning of mirror neurons in people on the autistic spectrum contributes to their difficulty with interpreting skilled actions, understanding action metaphors and even certain aspects of what is known as embodied cognition. By embodied cognition he is pointing to the ways in which experiment shows that action and perception are more closely entwined than we assume. Summing up the functioning of mirror neurons from their presence, and speculating about their absence, he writes:

> Autism reminds us that the uniquely human sense of self is not an 'airy nothing' without 'habitation and a name'. Despite its vehement tendency to assert its privacy and independence, the self actually emerges from a reciprocity of interactions with others and with the body it is embedded in. When it withdraws from society and retreats from its own body it barely exists; at least not in the sense of a mature self that defines our existence as

human beings. Indeed, autism could be regarded fundamentally as a disorder of self-consciousness, and if so, research on the disorder may help us understand the nature of consciousness itself.

(Ramachandran, 2011: 152)

Although one might want to take issue with Ramachandran's idea that the self is 'embedded' in anything, rather than arising from a body's interactions with itself and with other selves, what I understand him to be pointing to is the paradox of self and other, the 'I' in the 'we'; recognizing others is only possible from a strong sense of self, which arises from recognizing the otherness of others. This paradoxical idea is one of the major insights of de Waal's work too.

In earlier chapters I have drawn attention to the importance of the I/we dialectic in Hegel's, Mead's and Honneth's work on consciousness, self-consciousness and mutual recognition. It is on this basis that I have taken a highly social perspective of the way managers manage. In other words, I have been encouraging managers to understand experience.

Summing up the importance of uncertainty, ambiguity and paradox in the natural sciences and making links to management

Since the Enlightenment and certainly since Kant, the methods of the natural sciences, or rather a generalized and idealized understanding of them predicated mostly on classical physics, have come to inform the aspiration of producing secure knowledge about the world. There is a very strong invitation to social science disciplines, and not least organizational research, to emulate natural science methods more or less directly by, for example, adopting quantification and/or experimental methods as the only sure way of creating knowledge and evidence about the social. The appeal is to cut through the messiness and flux of everyday life to discover some essential truths about reality 'out there', to discover unshifting ground.

Some schools of thought within organizational research also aspire to having the predictive certainty and logical clarity of mathematics. Taking a pragmatic view of the philosophy of the social sciences, Patrick Baert (2005) argues that even perspectives such as critical realism (Bhaskar, 1975), which set out to assert both the scientific and critical potential of social research, are still searching for some kind of essence of scientific enquiry so that they can link the methods taken up in both natural and social sciences.

This chapter has not set out to find common ground between the natural and social sciences except in the sense of demonstrating that the former too make productive use of paradox, ambiguity and contradiction. I share the view of historian of science Steven Shapin (2010: 5) that mathematicians, physicists, biologists and brain scientists, amongst others, make full use of their cognitive resources, situated in a particular time and place, practising with their heads and their hands, and that sometimes head follows hand. In other words, it is the imaginative engagement of scientists with their object of study, which involves hunches, wrestling with knowing and not knowing, false starts and the use of formal and informal methods for making progress. Moreover, it often relies upon a tolerance and appreciation of the generative potential of uncertainty, contradiction and paradox.

We have seen in this chapter how engagement with paradox and ambiguity informs mathematical method, allowing mathematicians to approach the same problem from a variety of different perspectives and exploit the nuances and ambiguities between them. It produces a movement of creativity.[2] What Byers refers to as deep insight does not necessarily involve resolving paradoxes in logical and linear ways, but reconfiguring them in a wider context so that the original contradiction persists but may be represented in a way which creates more possibilities.

I pointed out that this has many similarities with Hegel's idea of dialectic, where the movement of one pole of a paradox and its opposite produces a new state, which still contains the original contradiction. For both Byers and Emily Grosholz, mathematics develops as a consequence of melding the formal and the informal, linearity and guesswork: formal logical methods are necessary but insufficient for the creative development of mathematics, they argue.

Both Karen Barad and Andrew Pickering take up the idea that it is the paradoxical engagement between the knower and the known, what Barad calls causal entanglement, that produces research outcomes. Scientists and researchers are acting, and when they act and the way they do so contribute to the area of enquiry which drives them. They contribute to greater understanding of the world and at the same time they themselves are transformed by the experience. Barad argues that the physicist is of course interested in objective results, i.e. ones which can be replicated by other scientists, but the results derive from the scientist's actions in the world: scientific method passes through what Pickering refers to as the mangle of practice, and what Shapin and Barnes (1976) refer to as hand leading head. It is the particular constellation of humans, objects and practices which form, and are formed by scientific endeavour.

Primatologist de Waal and brain scientist VS Ramachandran both make extensive use of paradox to develop concepts to explain the development of consciousness and empathy. Perspective taking and consciousness of self both arise at the same time, they both argue. Ramachandran argues that the self emerges from a 'reciprocity', what I am calling paradox, between the individual and his/her body, and between the body and other bodies. These are assumptions which also permeate particularly pragmatist philosophy in the writings of Dewey and Mead, which we have explored in this book.

Paradox, ambiguity and contradiction seem to me to be central to the scientific undertaking, whether as the engine of creativity, the core of method or as a means of developing theory. For those who understand science to be a particularly systematic activity amongst other human activities, this will probably come as no surprise. There is no reason for organizational researchers and managers to assume that their messy, sometimes fractious, everyday reality and their approach to try and understand it is somehow lesser than the working world of natural scientists.

In all domains of life we struggle with the stable instability of the living world. The manager's task is to make the best sense possible of the complex responsive processes of relating, making the full use of the resources available to him or her. These include the mess, the ambiguity, contradictions and paradoxes which arise from trying to get things done with other people.

Notes

1 When chemist Daniel Shechtman first articulated his theory of quasi-crystals in the early 1980s (crystals that have a regular structure but one which is never repeated), both the head of his laboratory and the double Nobel prize-winning scientist Linus Pauling told him he must be wrong (the latter doing so publicly at a scientific conference). When other scientists also came across other examples of what Schechtman described, he was finally vindicated, and was later awarded the Nobel prize in 2011.
2 The cognitive psychologist Mihaly Csikszentmihalyi (1997) developed his theory of creative flow based on the idea that creative people have 10 contrasting and dialectical personality traits. Given his background in cognitive psychology, it is no surprise that Csikszentmihalyi's hypothesis is highly individualized.

References

Baert, P. (2005) *Philosophy of the Social Sciences*, Cambridge: Polity.
Banerjee, A. and Duflo, E. (2012) *Poor Economics: Barefoot Hedge-Fund Managers, DIY Doctors and the Surprising Truth about Life on Less Than $1 a Day*, London: Penguin.
Barad, K. (2007) *Meeting the Universe Halfway: Quantum Physics and the Entanglement of Matter and Meaning*, Durham: Duke University Press.
Baron-Cohen, S. (1995) *Mindblindness*, Cambridge, MA: MIT Press.
Bergson, H. (2007) *The Creative Mind*, New York: Dover Publications.
Bhaskar, R. (1975) *A Realist Theory of Science*, Brighton: Harvester.
Bohr, N. (1934/2011) *Atomic Theory and the Description of Nature*, Cambridge: Cambridge University Press.
Bourdieu, P. (1982) *Leçon sur la Leçon*, Paris: Editions de Minuit.
Byers, W. (2007) *How Mathematicians Think: Using Ambiguity, Contradiction and Paradox to Create Mathematics*, Princeton, NJ: Princeton University Press.
Callon, M. and Latour, B. (1981) Unscrewing the Big Leviathan, or How Do Actors Macrostructure Reality?, in Knorr-Cetina, K. and Cicourel, A. (eds.) *Advances in Social Theory and Methodology: Toward an Integration of Micro- and Macro-Sociologies*, Boston: Routledge & Kegan Paul.
——(1992) Don't Throw the Baby Out with the Bath School! A Reply to Collins and Yearley, in Pickering, A. (ed.) *Science as Practice and Culture*, Chicago: University of Chicago Press.
Carnap, R. (1928) *Der Logische Aufbau der Welt*, Hamburg: Meiner. English translation by Rolf, B. and George, A. (1967) *The Logical Structure of the World and Pseudoproblems in Philosophy*, Berkeley: University of California Press.
Condorcet, Marie, J. A. M. (1795/1955) *Sketch for a Historical Picture of the Progress of the Human Mind*, trans. Barraclough, J., London: Weidenfeld and Nicolson.
Csikszentmihalyi, M. (1997) *Creativity: Flow and the Discovery of Invention*, New York: Harper Perennial.
Dawkins, R. (1976) *The Selfish Gene*, Oxford: Oxford University Press.

de Waal, F. (2009) *The Age of Empathy: Nature's Lessons for a Kinder Society*, London: Souvenir Press.

Dewey, J. (1925/1997) *Experience and Nature*, New York: Open Court Publishing.

Elias, N. (1978) *What Is Sociology?*, New York: Columbia University Press.

Flyvbjerg, B. (2001) *Making Social Science Matter: Why Social Enquiry Fails and How It Can Succeed Again*, Cambridge: Cambridge University Press.

Goodwin, B. (1994) *How the Leopard Changed Its Spots: The Evolution of Complexity*, London: Scribner.

Grosholz, E. (2007) *Representation and Productive Ambiguity in Mathematics and Sciences*, Oxford: Oxford University Press.

Heisenberg, W. (1927) The Physical Content of Quantum Kinematics and Mechanics, *Zeitschrift für Phsyik*, 43: 172–98.

Hernes, T. (2014) *A Process Theory of Organization*, Oxford: Oxford University Press.

Hofstadter, D. (1979) *Gödel, Escher and Bach: An Eternal Golden Braid*, London: Penguin Books.

James, W. (1909/1996) *A Pluralistic Universe*, Lincoln: University of Nebraska Press.

Khurana, R. (2007) *From Higher Aims to Hired Hands: The Social Transformation of American Business Schools and the Unfulfilled Promise of Management as a Profession*, Princeton: Princeton University Press.

Learmonth, M. and Harding, N. (2006) Evidence-Based Management: The Very Idea, *Public Administration*, 84(2): 245–66.

Midgley, M. (2001) *Science and Poetry*, London: Routledge.

Mowles, C. (2011) *Rethinking Management: Radical Insights from the Complexity Sciences*, London: Gower.

Pfeffer, J. and Sutton, R. (2006) *Hard Facts, Dangerous Half-Truths, and Total Nonsense: Profiting from Evidence-Based Management*, Boston, MA: Harvard Business School Press.

Pickering, A. (1993) The Mangle of Practice: Agency and Emergence in the Sociology of Science, *American Journal of Sociology*, 99(3): 559–89.

——(1995) *The Mangle of Practice: Time, Agency and Science*, Chicago: University of Chicago Press.

Porter, T. M. (1995) *Trust in Numbers: The Pursuit of Objectivity in Science and Public Life*, Princeton, NJ: Princeton University Press.

Ramachandran, V. S. (2011) *The Tell-Tale Brain: Unlocking the Mystery of Human Nature*, London: Heinemann.

Reay, T., Whitney, B. and Kohn, K. (2009) What's the Evidence on Evidence-Based Management?, *Academy of Management Perspectives*, 23(4): 5–18.

Rorty, R. (1979) *Philosophy and the Mirror of Nature*, Princeton, NJ: Princeton University Press.

Rose, H. and Rose, S. (2012) *Genes, Cells and Brains: The Promethean Promises of the New Biology*, London: Verso Books.

Rothenburg. A. (1979) *The Emerging Goddess: The Creative Process in Art, Science and Other Fields*, Chicago: University of Chicago Press.

Rousseau, D. (2006) Is There Such a Thing as 'Evidence Based Management'?, *Academy of Management Review*, 31(2): 256–69.

Shapin, S. (2010) *Never Pure: Historical Studies of Science as if It Was Produced by People with Bodies, Situated in Time, Space, Culture, and Society, and Struggling for Credibility and Authority*, Baltimore: Johns Hopkins University Press.

Shapin, S. and Barnes, B. (1976) Head and Hand: Rhetorical Resources in British Pedagogical Writing 1770–1850, *Oxford Review of Education*, 2: 231–54.

Wheeler, J. A. and Zurek, W. H. (eds.) (1983) *Quantum Theory and Measurement*, Princeton, NJ: Princeton University Press.

Whitehead, A. N. (1929) *Process and Reality*, New York: The Free Press.

Wigner, E. (1960) The Unreasonable Effectiveness of Mathematics in the Natural Sciences, *Communications in Pure and Applied Mathematics*, 13(1): 1–14.

Wilson, E. O. (2012) *The Social Conquest of Earth*, New York: Liveright Publishing.

8

UNCERTAINTY, CONTRADICTION AND PARADOX

So what can managers do?

In the course of this book I have written extensively about uncertainty, contradiction and paradox, and the reader may come away with the impression that somehow I am making an argument against managing. This is sometimes the reaction I get after a presentation to groups of managers about organizational complexity: if I point to the limits of management as a discipline of prediction and control, some managers think that what I am saying is equivalent to arguing that managers do not matter and that they cannot make a difference.

Perhaps it is time to state unequivocally that there is nothing wrong with trying to plan, to lead, to make sense, to order, to make things cohere, to try to control conflict. Perhaps all I am drawing attention to is the way that complex reality constantly breaks out of our attempts to control and define it. In other words, when managers become convinced that they have to control meaning, to impose one culture on the organization, to fix sense-making, then they have overreached themselves and are likely to stifle spontaneity and creativity in organizations and create the kinds of problems that I have pointed to in this book, by calling out the opposite of what they intend.

For example, the notion that you can control people's beliefs so that they 'align' with some idealized notion of organizational values often impels managers to manufacture all kinds of managerial instruments that they and their staff are then obliged to maintain. It is likely to call out gaming behaviour on the part of members of staff, both dividing and uniting, making the whole exercise a hollow one. They can become hedged around with metrics, league tables, cultural 'barometers' and all the other managerial appurtenances putting 'trust in numbers', as Porter (1995) has argued. In recent decades we have seen what Power (1997, 2007) refers to as an audit explosion as one reaction to organizational uncertainty. Alternatively, attempts to manipulate and control can lead to the creation of organizational cults which are totalitarian in the way that they operate.

In a way, the whole of this book, and many like it in the critical and process traditions of organizational theorizing, are *para-doxical*, that is to say against the *doxa*, what is taken for good sense or common sense about management (Ten Bos, 2007) by perhaps the majority of managers and academics. In doing so, it strives to create more nuance, more possibilities for thinking, which I will admit are not always welcome in organizations which are rushing forward towards excellence. This is not an argument against every organization aspiring to be the best it can be, however.

I have sketched out two broad approaches to managing organizations, one based more or less on the idea that managers and leaders are capable of predicting and controlling, the other assuming that there is a limit to such managerial powers. Approaching organizational life from these two perspectives leads to very different consequences for managers: what they do and what they think they can achieve with others.

In this chapter I am going to assume that the first position, the idea of management as a discipline of prediction and control, is familiar to the reader. We have explored some of the arguments in the chapters by drawing on orthodox management literature. In doing so I can see how the Cartesian split between an autonomous self and a world 'out there' has an instinctive appeal because it creates a comforting illusion of control. I suppose this accounts for the anxiety in groups of managers I meet when I suggest that they may only have limited control over what unfolds.

I hope it is worth rehearsing my ideas on the importance of paradox in organizational life, not as a means of simply restating them, but as a way of reflecting on them further as a prelude to continuing the discussion about what leaders and managers might do about them.

Understanding the dualism as a paradox

Let us assume that there is no splitting our rational and emotional selves, but rather our emotions allow us to act reasonably, particularly in social situations which require an empathetic understanding of what others are thinking and feeling. In order to act reasonably in social situations we need a theory of mind, that is to say, an insight into what is going on for other people, in order to anticipate their actions. Otherwise we would not know how to behave in the company of others.

We are subjects to other people, who are our objects, but we are also objects to ourselves because we can take their perspective on us. If we take the view that we are socially formed, able to call out in ourselves what we anticipate calling out in others, realizing ourselves through the recognition of others, then it would then be impossible for us to leave our values and our commitments at the door. We are caught up in the game of social life because it matters to us: we are absorbed in it because being part of the game is constitutive of our sense of self, our identity. And, paradoxically, we have values about having values (Frankfurt, 2004).

Whilst logic is an extremely useful method for framing problems, it is insufficient for understanding the dimensions of complex social reality with which we are faced where we interact with thinking, feeling, imaginative human beings. We are capable of eliminating contradictions with logic, but as the ancient Greeks observed our minds are also capable of conceiving of one thing and then its opposite – the mind can overreach itself. Paradox is a helpful way of construing complexity, but it comes with the downside that there are no solutions that do not call out further paradoxes (Chapter 2).

Next, rather than assuming that we are discrete individuals cognizing the world 'out there', taking paradox seriously involves exploring those theories developed in particular by the pragmatists and process sociologists (Elias, Bourdieu) that we are forming the world at the same time as it is forming us. We are born into a world of activity and meaning which is already 'in' us, and we are entangled with it (Mead, 1934: Chapter 1; Barad, 2007: Chapter 7).

A moment's reflection on our own circumstances will bring to mind how our habits and categories of thought, our ways of being in the world, are framed and guided by the particular society and time we are born into, the language that we learn and the cultural habits, the *habitus*, we accept as natural. At the same time by re-enacting this culture, by reflecting on what we are doing and thinking about how we are thinking and acting, we recreate it in slightly different ways. We take up general themes in particular circumstances creating the potential both for repetition and renewal both at the same time.

Instead of assuming that we think, then act, on the basis of accurate representations of the world in the shape of models, perhaps our engagement with 'brute reality' through action provokes thinking, another form of action, which in turn informs further activity. Our taken-for-granted ways of acting in the world only become conscious to us, according to the pragmatists, when we encounter an obstacle which momentarily makes our habits and prejudices clearer to us. Prejudice and habit is paradoxically both helpful and unhelpful, as the English essayist William Hazlitt observed:

> The best way to prevent our running into the wildest excesses of prejudice and the most dangerous aberrations from reason, is, not to represent the two things as having a great gulf between them, which it is impossible to pass without a violent effort, but to show that we are constantly (even when we think ourselves most secure) treading on the brink of a precipice; that custom, passion, imagination, insinuate themselves into and influence almost every judgment we pass or sentiment we indulge, and are a necessary help (as well as hindrance) to the human understanding; and that to attempt to refer every question to abstract truth and precise definition, without allowing for the frailty of prejudice, which is the unavoidable consequence of the frailty and imperfection of reason, would be to unravel the whole web and texture of human understanding and society.
>
> *(Hazlitt, 1839: 93)*

This is a sentiment later echoed by John Dewey a century later, that our habits and prejudices are helpful shortcuts to getting things done in the world. At the same time, and paradoxically, they can prevent us from seeing what we need to see to overcome our practical difficulties: they stop us noticing. The entanglement which Hazlitt, the pragmatists, Barad (2007) and Pickering (1993) write about obliges us to think differently about what it means to be scientific about the social if we assume that there is no standing outside ourselves from an objective position. We are part of the social relations we seek to study and we have a stake in the game.

Abstract models about social life will only take us so far because they are abstract and lack the precision, the fine-grained detail for us to know how to take them up in our own particular circumstances. They may only be true in general and for the most part, and we can never predict when they will apply and when not. Collecting evidence is problematic because there is no agreed way of doing so that is above contestation.

Paradox in some key areas of contemporary management discussion

The discussion of entrepreneurial leadership in Chapter 3 poses a split between leaders and managers, and puts a particular obligation on leaders to act in an entrepreneurial way, encouraging their staff to do the same. Taking a longer-term perspective, we might understand this as an old idea showing up in a new context, since it borrows extensively from the transformational/transactional dualism created at the end of the 1970s/early 1980s. To a degree the idea has continuity over time and is perpetuated, simply repackaged in new contexts. But there is no inevitability that it need simply continue if we can bring together the paradoxical perspective of the airman and the swimmer, understanding time as both diachronic and synchronic.

Noticing how we are caught up in longer-term processes which are instantiated in the moment requires reflexivity to pay attention to how this particular social object is taken up by everyone in this context, and which presents opportunities which can be seized or missed. Dewey (1958, 2008) in particular brought out the paradoxical implications of reflecting on one's involvement in social life in this way. We can only become more certain by investigating uncertainty; when we have cause to doubt this can lead to a line of definite questioning; and we can be more objective about social life if we include our subjective experience.

There is much to recommend reflection and reflexivity to managers to prevent rushing in to taken-for-granted organizational practices which are neither automatic nor inevitable. It allows for the exploration of the ethical implications of what we may have taken for granted and offers a chance to act differently. However, reflexivity also has paradoxical properties: it does not automatically lead to the good but can also disrupt, provoking feelings of shame, guilt and anxiety. It can also produce trivial insights.

In Chapter 4 we began to think of culture as emerging from what we all do together rather than assuming that culture is something an organization 'has', which the leader is split off from, can analyse and reorder. The appeal to culture is also an appeal to conformity and obedience, and is often policed by standards and measurements of behaviour. This is because it is impossible to change people's beliefs directly, although this is what leaders may be trying to do when they appeal to shared culture by invoking symbols, figureheads or, in the national context, flags. In doing so, however, they often provoke strong feelings in people which can have paradoxical consequences. They will include and exclude and create insider and outsider communities: they will unite some and divide others.

Additionally, Elias argues (1997), strong feelings provoked by cultural symbols are capable of producing a self-amplifying dynamic, which defies the control of even the most powerful leaders and groups. There is a strong invitation in some organizational literature to create a 'cult-like' culture in organizations, which Tourish (2013) demonstrates can have disastrous consequences.

Thinking of culture as what we do, or the *habitus*, implies no position outside of culture: we form it, and it forms us both at the same time. This would mean that in organizational life it is impossible to balance cooperation and competition, align values and converge differences, at least, not without creating totalitarian conditions. Rather, what we do together would provoke the inevitable contradictions between self and other, pro- and asocial behaviour, abstract ideas taken up in a local context:

> Our codes of conduct are as riddled with contradictions and as full of disproportions as are our forms of social life, as is the structure of our society.
>
> *(Elias, 2000: 443)*

A number of authors have borrowed from Aristotle to term the skill of wrestling with these contradictions, like particularizing general standards, *phronesis*, or practical judgment. Exercising good practical judgment requires both political and moral sensitivities, assuming that working with any group of people involves different conceptions of the good and fluctuating relationships of power. What gets in the way of people acting creatively, morally and *phronetically*, Gadamer (1993) argues, is the imposition of abstract standards derived from rationality alone, where the paradox of abstract and contextual is lost in favour of the former. The rational development of culture based on abstract standards paradoxically creates organizational irrationalities. Benchmarking, standardizing, disciplining, can have unintended consequences of driving out the very creativity with which staff deploy the work with the paradox of the abstract and the particular, the local and the global.

The innovation discourse, which we explored in Chapter 5, builds on an argument of dissatisfaction, splitting the inadequate present from an ideal future. With a sense of urgency organizational employees can be encouraged, cajoled or inspired to innovate more and more and thus enhance each economy's competitiveness endlessly into the future. Innovation can be led, planned, predicted and controlled, and it is implied that it is always good. An alternative understanding of innovation raises the paradox of stability and change, questions how distinguishable they are, and asks who it is that decides. Whether an innovation is considered 'good' or not implies an ideological position.

Taking an alternative view questions the assumption of predicting the future if we are as unpredictable to ourselves as others are to us, and if we are subject to fate and unintended consequences. If we accept the argument set out above, that employees constantly innovate to take up generalized prescriptions in particular circumstances, then when are they innovating and when are they not? A longer-term, processual view of innovation would understand it to be a discourse arising from certain historical conditions and reflective of particular power relationships between different groups in society. Social innovations too result from the struggle between groups for advantage and sometimes produce consequences which nobody wants, as we have recently experienced in Western economies.

We could offer a similar critique of an orthodox conception of conflict to the one we rehearsed on culture above. Management theory based on assumptions of prediction and control imply a detachment and a splitting of the concerned manager from the conflict he/she seeks to resolve. If we were to assume instead that there is no view from nowhere (Nagel, 1986), and that the manager has a stake in the conflict too, then conflict cannot be avoided, but has to be entered into. If we turn to Mead, we may learn that conflicting tendencies arise in us as individuals, since engagement with others calls out our pro- and asocial tendencies. He does not make the case that the former is good and the latter bad; rather, he suggests that our asocial tendencies make us the individuals we are and we are left with the constant dilemmas surrounding how to work with our individuality in social contexts.

There are tensions too within a group and between groups. A number of ethnographic studies of contemporary organizational life point to the fact that it often comprises what Karl Mannheim referred to as 'tendencies and strivings in a constant state of flux' (1936/1972: 103). From a manager's perspective, areas of social life which are not settled are intensely political situations best explored with full participation, because they are constantly in flux, constantly emerging depending on the balance of forces involved in the struggle. Rather than denying and dismissing the political manoeuvring, which arises inevitably from our membership of particular groups with a particular view of the world, the question is how managers might bring all the perspectives into the open, including their own.

Refusing to relinquish paradox, allowing the process of thinking to move to its opposite, makes the world more problematic and complex because there can be no assumption of detachment and control, nor of harnessing contradictions for the good of the organization. The move to resolve contradictions in organizational life can simply provoke more contradictions.

So what are managers to do?

One strong thread of argument throughout has been the necessity of thinking systematically about managing, but I have also pointed out the limitations of doing so based on logic and rationality alone. I have made the case that there is a great deal about organizational life which escapes an appeal to a narrow understanding of what it means to be scientific about the social because of the paradoxes in human activity and thinking, the number of factors which come into play. In the parallel field of education, Gary Thomas (2010, 2012) makes some similar arguments about the irreducibility of practice in the classroom and the limitations of assuming that there is one best scientific method to capture 'what works'. At one point in his 2012 paper he summarizes his argument thus:

- Systematic enquiry in different domains rarely follows the same methodological avenues, nor even does it adhere to the same precepts.
- Not all science is about generalization; it is certainly about explanation, but explanation does not always require generalization from the few to the many.
- The cumulation of know-how knowledge differs from the cumulation of know-that knowledge.
- Education's cumulation is by the cultivation and sharing of practical understandings, not an accumulation of facts (2012: 40).
- The methods used in a scientific endeavor must *emerge from* questions; they should not be prescribed in advance.

I find this a helpful summary of some of the arguments in this book which treats management, like teaching, as a practical discipline which takes place between people in a particular place at a particular time. The practical disciplines need their own particular forms of research and enquiry.

However, undertaking one's role unthinkingly, not asking too many questions, getting on with the job, doing what most other organizations are doing, also contribute to organizational life. They make it more stable and produce social regularities, what GH Mead (1938) referred to as social objects; the generalized tendencies of large numbers of people to act in similar ways. As I hope I have made clear throughout the book, drawing in particular on the pragmatists, we cannot doubt everything all of the time otherwise we would never get anything done. Doubt arises in particular when we are confronted with practical problems which impede our progress. There remains, then, the dilemma about what to do with doubt.

One of the main themes of this book has been the importance of thinking, reflection, reflexivity and critique in unfreezing what may be frozen, particularly the unhelpful categories of thought which are consistently brought to bear on contemporary organizational life. I mentioned Hannah Arendt in Chapter 3. In a later article on thinking, a development of her position in *Eichmann in Jerusalem*, she argues that thinking is not, and should not be, just the preserve of the intelligent: there are lots of examples, she argues, of highly intelligent people who are unable to think. If society were dependent merely on the highly intelligent, or on professional thinkers such as philosophers, then society would be in even more of a parlous state.

This insight has particular poignancy for Hannah Arendt herself since her first supervisor and subsequent mentor, the philosopher Martin Heidegger, a professional thinker, had Nazi sympathies. Clearly, there is nothing about being a professional thinker that necessarily leads to justifiable conclusions about the world. But thinking is a crucial part of what makes us human and enables us to make moral and aesthetic judgments. Questioning and thinking do not necessarily lead anywhere, Arendt argues, but unravel what we are thinking about. Whilst she warns us against simply turning things upside down so that the reverse of the current situation is true, she nonetheless maintains that:

> When everyone else is swept away unthinkingly by what everyone else believes in, those who think are drawn out of hiding, because their refusal to join in is conspicuous and thereby becomes a form of action. The purging element in thinking, Socrates' midwifery, that brings out the implications of unexamined opinions and destroys them – values, doctrines, theories and even opinions, is political by implication. For this destruction has an effect on another human faculty, the faculty of judgement which one may call, with some justification, the most political of man's abilities. It is the faculty to judge particulars without subsuming them under those general rules which can be taught and learned until they grow into habits which can be replaced by other habits and rules.
>
> *(Arendt, 1971: 445)*

So for Arendt, thinking and judging draw on two different human faculties but are interrelated and inseparable, as are thinking and acting: thinking deals with 'invisibles', things which are absent. Meanwhile judgment, inextricably linked to thinking, is demanded in particular circumstances of particular things allowing us to say, 'this is beautiful' or 'this is wrong'. Just as thinking allows us to be conscious of our difference, and leads to conscience as a by-product, so judging manifests itself in the world as action as a manifestation of thinking, which in turn leads to more thinking. Arendt's hope is that this uniquely human capacity will help to prevent catastrophe 'particularly when the chips are down' by becoming a habit. It will help us constantly to call into question and make judgments about what we are doing so that we are never in the position of Eichmann, claiming that we were just doing our job.

I would like to stay with Arendt's sentiments but to enlarge upon them to reflect further about what the activity of thinking might mean for groups of managers and staff presented with everyday organizational dilemmas, contradictions and paradoxes. The difficulty with Arendt's position, as an admirer of Kant, is that it puts enormous responsibility on the individual. Of course, Arendt is aware of the paradox of the individual and the social and one of the central themes in her work is the importance of political activity as a way of bringing power into the public domain. Nonetheless, her challenge merits further exploration in organizational contexts to seek better ways of dealing with uncertainty and contradiction.

On the art of reflecting together

What follows is my attempt to make sense of the way we work with managers who attend the Doctor of Management programme at Hertfordshire Business

School in the UK, to offer some parallels and suggestions for working with paradox. As I described in the introduction, on the Doctor of Management programme
we meet face-to-face in a variety of fora during four-day quarterly residentials. The
students, who are all senior managers or leaders, or senior consultants, from all
sectors of the economy are invited to talk about their work, to write, to reflect,
and then to discuss further. For these four periods during the year we are a temporary organization which gives rise to its own uncertainties, contradictions and
paradoxes. There are relationships of power between faculty members and students,
and within the student group itself between those, say, who are deeper into the
programme and those who have joined more recently. Joining and being part of
the group raises all the paradoxical dynamics which we have described throughout
this book: students would like to be a member of the research community but
maintain their individuality at the same time; they may feel silenced by the high
level of discussion they are joining; the intense desire to belong may provoke
feelings of exclusion.

We encourage them to develop their reflexive ability to become more detached
about their involvement in the group, and about their practice in the respective
workplaces. Despite everything that we send students in advance of their joining in
the way of brochures or information, despite what management literature they may
have read, and despite the two interviews that we give them before they come,
nothing can prepare them for the experience of being in the group until they
become part of it.

On three occasions during a residential we meet in the tradition of the Institute
of Group Analysis (Foulkes 1948/1983, 1990), which means that for three sessions
of an hour and a half we meet without an agenda and discuss whatever members of
the research community want to discuss. The meeting stops when the time is up,
rather than when we have reached a predefined end point: there is nowhere to get
to because we are meeting with no end in view. These sessions can be very anxiety-
provoking, particularly for those coming from organizations which have meetings
that are highly agenda-driven, or perhaps even where there is an expectation that
you set an objective for the meeting before you even start. The point of these
particular meetings is to pay attention to what is important for us, now, in this
moment, and the dilemmas that arise for us in the task that we are all engaged in.

I am by no means suggesting that organizations can run themselves the way we
run a particular research programme which has a very specific purpose. But what is
it we think we are doing, and how might this be helpful to managers?

The programme is deliberately offering an alternative to rushing around not
thinking, but seeks to find ways of reflecting in common. Discussion and reflection
is primary, rather than problem identification and resolution. Of course, the doctoral students do have to identify an organizational 'problem', otherwise they will
not come up with a research question, but just as important is why it is a question
and why it matters to them.

This draws on a very old tradition of practice dating back to the ancient Greeks.
One of the conditions that Aristotle sets for deliberation and dialogue to take place,

according to Eikeland (2008), is sufficient time, time freed from the immediate need to act. There is no suggestion that actions or solutions may not emerge as a by-product, but this is not the primary purpose of deliberation. Rather, it turns on a better understanding of what we are dealing with and who we are in dealing with it: so understanding what we are doing together is inextricably linked to self-understanding. Deliberation and dialogue involve exploring the similarities and differences emerging between the group members. In this sense it provokes a critical discussion and encourages different perspectives:

> We deliberate about things where there are many ways of proceeding, where different means might produce similar results, where outcomes are uncertain even though they for the most part follow general rules, and where what and how we contribute (or not), makes a real difference. In relation to questions like these, then, we also deliberate continuously wherever what we interact with are other thinking minds and logos-users able to listen and understand.
>
> *(Eikeland, 2008: 88)*

Deliberation is less interested in things which we cannot affect, abstractions or large scale phenomena over which we have little control, but is rooted in the concerns of what confronts us now, as a community of mature people. Because other people are involved, active participation in a group like this inevitably raises questions of ethics and power, since we end up exploring our interdependencies and our obligations to each other.

In this sense, and as I argued in Chapter 4, we cannot get 'outside' of practice, since practical ways of knowing do not lie outside what we are doing, they arise from it. As Eikeland argues, we are struggling to produce knowledge *from* practice, rather than knowledge *for* practice, although the former inevitably leads to the latter. Better understanding requires deep involvement, participation and practical observation of what is going on, rather than detachment, disengagement and non-interference in the phenomena we are interested in. It requires immersion in similarities and differences, and the inevitable conflicting perspectives that will arise as a consequence.

The other thing which interests me about Eikeland's interpretation of Aristotle is the focus he places on the relationship between master and apprentice. Of course, this has particular significance in the supervisor–doctoral student relationship, but the parallel in the workplace might be the relationship between novice and old-timer, or manager and managed. It is a relationship of power, but one which has the potential for greater equality. What is important in the relationship according to Eikeland (ibid: 432) is that it is about learning, which arises out of interdependence and working with difference:

> They explore together what they might do here and now, what they have done, what it means to do what they do, in spite of any other differences in levels or in fields and kinds of substantial competence, or in any other

accidental attributes ... Masters are there for the benefit of apprentices, apprentices there to become masters.

(ibid: 431)

The learning relationship involves bringing what is understood in common into view, starting the development from what already is, rather than brushing it all aside in favour of some grand and idealized abstract plan. Transferring this insight to strategizing in organizations might suggest focusing much more on the here and now, what we are struggling with in our daily work, asking why it is important to us, rather than imagining an idealized end point and working logically back from there.

On the Doctor of Management programme we work with the intention of creating opportunities to think together and out loud. In contrast, Eikeland (ibid: 467) reminds us of the similarities between Aristotle's understanding of totalitarianism and Foucault's (1991) description of the development of the apparatuses of scrutiny and control in the modern state. The first thing tyrants do, according to Aristotle, is to ban open meetings where people can come together and engage in dialogical exchange. They split and atomize citizens, create an artificial need for a leader, and keep them under constant surveillance. For some staff, working in contemporary organizations must sometimes feel like this. They are pushed from pillar to post without the time to think – in fact, thinking and talking are sometimes regarded as a 'luxury' and an enemy of 'delivery'.

I hope I have not idealized what we are trying to do at the University of Hertfordshire. There is no technique we are using which is called deliberation or dialogue, which is a special method of creating the right conditions for dealing with uncertainty. Although we are practised, we are practised enough to know we are feeling our way. Although we are experienced, we are still surprised by things that happen, including what meeting together calls out in ourselves. We provoke strong emotions in each other, we fall out, then make up; some students succeed and others fail. There is no mystery to what we are doing other than paying attention to the quality of conversational life in the group when we set aside the time to explore the complex responsive processes of relating.

References

Arendt, H. (1971) Thinking and Moral Considerations, *Social Research*, 38(3): 417–46.

Barad, K. (2007) *Meeting the Universe Halfway: Quantum Physics and the Entanglement of Matter and Meaning*, Durham: Duke University Press.

Dewey, J. (1958) *Experience and Nature*, New York: Dover Publications.

——(2008) *The Quest for Certainty: The Later Works 1925–1953, Vol 4, 1929*, Carbondale: Southern Illinois University Press.

Eikeland, O. (2008) *The Ways of Aristotle: Aristotelian Phronesis, Aristotelian Philosophy of Dialogue and Action Research*, Bern: Peter Lang.

Elias, N. (1997) *The Germans: Power Struggles and the Development of Habitus in the Nineteenth and Twentieth Centuries*, Cambridge: Polity Press.

——(2000) *The Civilizing Process*, Oxford: Oxford University Press.

Foucault, M. (1991) *Discipline and Punish: The Birth of the Prison*, London: Penguin.

Foulkes, S. H. (1948/1983) *Introduction to Group Analytic Psychotherapy*, London: Karnac.

——(1990) *Selected Papers: Psychoanalysis and Group Analysis*, London: Karnac Books.

Frankfurt, H. (2004) *I Taking Ourselves Seriously, II Getting It Right*, The Tanner Lectures on Human Values Delivered at Stanford University (April 14–16 2004).

Gadamer, H.-G. (1993) *Reason in the Age of Science*, Cambridge, MA: MIT Press.

Hazlitt, W. (1839) *Sketches and Essays*, London: William Templeton.

Mannheim, K. (1936/1972) *Ideology and Utopia*, London: Routledge & Kegan Paul.

Mead, G. H. (1934) *Mind, Self and Society from the Standpoint of a Social Behaviourist*, Chicago: University of Chicago Press.

——(1938) *The Philosophy of the Act*, Chicago: University of Chicago Press.

Nagel, T. (1986) *The View from Nowhere*, Oxford: Oxford University Press.

Pickering, A. (1993) The Mangle of Practice: Agency and Emergence in the Sociology of Science, *American Journal of Sociology*, 99(3): 559–89.

Porter, T. M. (1995) *Trust in Numbers: The Pursuit of Objectivity in Science and Public Life*, Princeton, NJ: Princeton University Press.

Power, M. (1997) *The Audit Society: Rituals of Verification*, Oxford: Oxford University Press.

——(2007) *Organized Uncertainty: Designing a World of Risk Management*, Oxford: Oxford University Press.

Ten Bos, R. (2007) The Vitality of Stupidity, *Social Epistemology*, 21(2): 139–50.

Thomas, G. (2010) Doing Case Study: Abduction Not Induction, Phronesis Not Theory, *Qualitative Inquiry*, 16(7): 575–82.

——(2012) Changing Our Landscape of Inquiry for a New Science of Education, *Harvard Educational Review*, 82(1): 26–51.

Tourish, D. (2013) *The Dark Side of Transformational Leadership: A Critical Perspective*, London: Routledge.

INDEX